The Notorious Astrological Physician of London

The

Notorious Astrological
Physician of London

WORKS AND DAYS OF
Simon Forman

Barbara Howard Traister

The University of Chicago Press
Chicago & London

Barbara Howard Traister is professor of English at Lehigh University. She is the author of *Heavenly Necromancers: The Magician in Early Renaissance Drama*.

The University of Chicago Press, Chicago 60637
The University of Chicago Press, Ltd., London
© 2001 by The University of Chicago
All rights reserved. Published 2001
Printed in the United States of America

09 08 07 06 05 04 03 02 01 1 2 3 4 5

ISBN: 0–226–81140–9 (cloth)

Library of Congress Cataloging-in-Publication Data

Traister, Barbara Howard.
    The notorious astrological physician of London : works and days of
Simon Forman / Barbara Howard Traister.
        p.   cm.
    Includes bibliographical references and index.
    ISBN 0-226-81140-9 (cloth : alk. paper)
    1. Forman, Simon, 1552–1611.   2. Physicians—England—Biography.
I. Title.
    R489.F585 T73   2001
    610'.92—dc21   00-009585

⊗ The paper used in this publication meets the minimum requirements of the
American National Standard for Information Sciences—Permanence of
Paper for Printed Library Materials, ANSI Z39.48–1992.

AS ALWAYS, FOR DAN, REBECCA, AND AARON

CONTENTS

❧ ILLUSTRATIONS ❧

FIGURES

TABLES

❦ INTRODUCTION ❦

Simon Forman, as revealed in his own manuscripts, differs markedly both from the character portrayed in A. L. Rowse's 1974 study and from the "Forman" whose name has appeared sporadically in historical and literary texts since the early seventeenth century. Study of his manuscripts changes our perspective on Forman. His papers reveal much about the period and culture in which he lived, not only the eccentric and exotic personal details that may have made Forman "notorious" in his own time and ours, but also— and at least as notably—the mundane details of sixteenth-century life (which modern readers often find exotic).

In fact, this study is less of Simon Forman the man than of the cache of manuscripts that bears Forman's name. These texts treat medicine, astrology, alchemy, the theater, genealogy, giants, creation, Forman's biography, gardening, and a host of incidental subjects. They are quite frequently fragments, texts begun but never finished; with few exceptions, even the completed texts are unpublished and largely unknown. In many cases their stories are tantalizingly incomplete: Forman often asks an astrological question, for example, and then does not record the answer he read in the stars; or he speaks briefly of traveling abroad without explaining where he went and why; or he makes repeated reference to books that were confiscated from him and returned decades later without explaining why they were taken or why they were returned. In some cases, the jigsaw puzzles presented in the manuscripts can be completed; in others, pieces remain missing.

One of my purposes in this study is to introduce the contents of Forman's manuscript papers to scholars of various disciplines in the hope that they may prove individually useful. To that end, I quote frequently and at length, since other access to the manuscripts is possible only by visiting British libraries and deciphering Forman's handwriting.

Whom did Forman expect to read his papers? In an age newly aware of the possibilities of moveable type, Forman chose to print only one six-page pamphlet. A few of his medical and occult essays, carefully prepared with ruled margins and rubricated initials, appear ready to be given to a reader or a printer. But nothing indicates that he intended them for the press. Some were copied and handed about among a circle of astrological devotees, and thus found an audience, but the manuscripts prepared with the most care— the ones with margins and rubrications—often have Forman's own notes scrawled carelessly in those margins as though he kept them for himself rather than circulating them.

The medical casebooks, of course, were intended for Forman's own use, as he several times explained (see chapter 3), but his explanation does not account for certain coded passages (usually sexual or political in nature) or his use of the Greek alphabet to mask certain phrases. Had he been their only expected reader, such precautions would have been unnecessary. His autobiographical materials have no obvious audience, leading one scholar to comment that Forman's motivation for writing his autobiography was "apparently, simple self-amusement."[1] But Forman, a busy, driven man who lacked any discernible shred of humor, is unlikely to have done anything merely for amusement, and the question of his intended audience looms large as we examine his manuscripts.

Writing was clearly an obsession with Forman. He turned himself into text, recording what his body did and what his brain absorbed, both from encounters with the texts of other men and from his own experience. More obviously than most texts, Forman's bear the imprint of their creator. He inserted himself—most particularly his name—into virtually every manuscript that he composed or copied. He was certain, at the beginning, middle, or end (and sometimes in all three spots), to identify himself as author, as translator, or even as scribe ("scriptor sed non factor"). His 1593 essay on plague typifies his practice: the title page reads "A Discourse of the plague written by Simon Forman gent. 1593. and verie necessary for all men to reade and truely to remember." At the end of the text, his name appears again: "Amen / 1593 / per Simonem Forman."[2] Even when copying another's text, Forman often inserted his own personal anecdotes or examples into the work.

This habit of insertion, of adding to texts already written, gives some of Forman's manuscripts a particular physical appearance. Those used for daily records, the best examples of which are his medical and astrological casebooks where he recorded each day's patients, are closely written on both sides of the leaf with only the rare blank spaces or pages. But manuscripts that he prepared as instructional books, whether of medicine, astrology, or alchemy, usually contain a number of blank leaves and partially written pages (in an age when paper was expensive and rarely wasted). In chapter 2, I explain at some length how Forman took a manuscript he acquired while a student, rebound it with interleaved blank pages, and annotated it over a number of years. This is a model, I think, for the way he used his own manuscripts, whether those he copied or those he composed himself. He expected that as new information or new ideas came to him he would insert that material at the appropriate place in the already existing manuscript. Thus he left blank spaces for such additions in nearly every instructional manuscript he wrote.

One of the best examples of this practice can be found in the versions of his text "The astrologicale Judgmentes of Phisick and other Questions." The Ashmole manuscript collection contains at least three versions of this text, in three different hands.[3] The version in Forman's own hand contains examples from his practice that illustrate his instructions for casting medical horoscopes and has a good many blank leaves interspersed among sections of text. The version of this text copied by Richard Napier (MS. Ash. 403) has Forman's instructions, almost no examples, and a good deal of blank paper. Napier might have copied the text at an early stage, before Forman had inserted many examples, or he might have omitted Forman's examples, intending instead to insert examples from his own practice to illustrate the instructional text. The third and most complete version is copied by Napier's nephew, Sir Richard Napier, who first shared his uncle's practice and then took it over at his uncle's death. His copy includes more examples—all with dates and names, which indicate that they are from Forman's practice—than those found in Forman's own manuscript dated 1606, although Sir Richard's copy also includes the examples given in that text. This suggests that Forman had made even more additions to the 1606 text in a version I have not seen and that Sir Richard copied that later version. Sir Richard's copy has almost no blank paper. Copying Forman's manuscript after Forman's death, Sir Richard knew that no more insertions would be made. There was thus no need to leave room in the copy he was making.

Forman added marginal comments to manuscripts he owned, inserted anecdotal material in manuscripts he copied, and regularly added material to his own works. Thanks to his penchant for signing and dating his material, this habit of addition can be seen in many of his manuscripts in the Ashmole collection; the versions of "The astrologicale Judgmentes" provide just one example of his common practice. One of the reasons for Forman's lack of interest in taking his manuscript books to press, then, may have been that he regarded them as "works in progress."[4]

Having mentioned Sir Richard Napier, I should perhaps give a brief synopsis of the chain of events (in which Sir Richard plays a part) by which Forman's manuscripts journeyed from his Lambeth study to the confines of the Bodleian Library. There is no account of Forman's death in September 1611, aside from William Lilly's dramatic narration of his collapse in a boat in the middle of the Thames (see chapter 1). Richard Napier, Forman's friend and medical associate who lived in Buckinghamshire, apparently traveled to London shortly after he heard of Forman's death. Cases in Napier's records halt abruptly on September 15, 1611, and resume again on October 1. A note in a hand other than Napier's writes in the 1611 casebook: "R. N. came home to Linford Sept. 30 Monday 2:56 P.M. 1611." In Napier's hand is an entry that reads: "I brought Clement Forman from London to Lister Sept 28 1611 & Clement Forman came to Linford to my house Septemb 30 Monday 3 P.M. 1611."[5] Napier had gone to London after Forman's death for a number of days and, when he returned to Linford, brought with him Forman's five-year-old son Clement.

Shortly afterward, some or all of Forman's books followed. Napier writes two notes in the same casebook about the books' dramatic arrival. "Oct. 10. It did ryne mightily & made a great flood & the cariers horse fell into the brook & wet all my bookes yet I thank god they toke no grat harme." A slightly different version follows a few leaves later: "John Rutland brought a chest of mr formans bookes for the use of Clement his sone & he & the horse & chest fell all into the brooke about risbly manor hard by us & the mar[e] sorely wet but God be thanked well handled. Oct. 10."[6] Napier's first response was worry about "his" books, but in the second, more deliberate telling the books are identified as "mr formans . . . for the use of Clement."

I find no other mention of these books for sixteen years until Napier writes the following on May 9, 1627: "Clement Forman came to me to tell me that he had gotten a lawyer that wuld take him for 3 y[ears] but asked a great deal of mony & that he & his mother wuld sell the bookes to make mony of them." Less than a month later, on June 6, Napier records that "Will Gadstem returned from London & brought me an acquittens of the lon paid of Clement R. Forman invested of me for his mathematicall books & all things of his that I had of his in my possession."[7] The entry is enigmatic. Had Napier sent back all the books except Forman's own manuscripts—which we know he retained—so that Clement could sell them, and the acquittance is the receipt for those books? Or—more likely, I think—when Clement decided to sell the books, did Napier himself purchase them, making the acquittance the receipt for the money he had paid? In any case, Napier kept or bought Forman's manuscript books, which form the basis for most of this study. When Napier died, his library and his practice passed to his namesake and nephew, Sir Richard Napier. Within a few months of Sir Richard's death in 1676, his oldest son, Thomas Napier, contacted Elias Ashmole, well known as a book collector interested in astrology and the occult arts, to offer Ashmole his father's library, including the manuscripts of both Forman and Richard Napier.[8]

Ashmole happily accepted and, in February 1677, records sending two batches of twelve folio volumes each "of Astrological Figures of Doctor Forman's" for binding.[9] Once they reached his library, Ashmole read and worked with Forman's manuscripts. For example, he writes of gathering "the seed of Fraxinella [dittany] . . . according to Dr. Forman's rule, which was the reason I ventured upon it"; he repaired a damaged Forman manuscript on the plague; and he prepared a digest of the materials that exist in MS. Ash. 244, which he labeled "Forman abbreviated."[10] When Ashmole gave his massive collections to Oxford University, Forman and Napier's manuscripts were among those included. Forman's manuscripts were read and used by the Napiers and Ashmole in ways that would have been deeply satisfying to Forman, who clearly longed to pass on his knowledge to those who would value it.

In his desire to record in order that he might learn, emulate, and teach, Forman inadvertently managed to be original. His are the earliest surviving chronological case records of an English medical practitioner. His autobiography is among the first English examples of that genre. His theater journal (although very truncated) is the earliest extant record by a member of the London theater audience of the productions that he attended. As he tried hard to find a comfortable niche in his society, to fit in, Forman became an innovator in spite of himself.

In his medical and astrological practice, Forman came into intimate contact with many people and heard many secrets. His medical records offer an unusual view of the daily life and troubles of London citizens of his period. In much the same way he recorded details about his patients and clients,

Forman wrote about himself. The combination of detachment and frankness with which he wrote about his own behavior (displaying emotion chiefly in his accounts of his antagonistic encounters with "the doctors") may be an outgrowth of his practice, in which discussing and recording intimate details about mind and body were necessary for proper diagnosis and treatment.[11]

Despite the flood of details he poured out on paper, Forman was not a writer who naively recorded whatever came into view. Many of his texts, especially those in which he portrayed himself, show a high degree of "fashioning." Unlike the figures from sixteenth-century England studied by Stephen Greenblatt in *Renaissance Self-Fashioning*,[12] however, Forman made little effort to reveal publicly the self he had created in his manuscripts. I speculate in chapter 6, which examines his nonscientific essays, about why he was content to leave that written work, of which he was clearly proud and which did not deal with "secret" occult knowledge, largely unknown.

Ironically, his choice to have his work remain in manuscript, available to only a few select readers, meant that his own version of his story was largely unavailable to compete for attention with the representations of him and his practice that flowed from presses in the wake of the Overbury murder trials. In some ways, Forman's situation resembles that of his contemporary, John Dee. Frozen in the mid-seventeenth century by Meric Casaubon's publication of his conversations with angels,[13] Dee's reputation remained that of a quack and a dupe until I. R. F. Calder and Frances Yates began his rehabilitation in the middle of the twentieth century by taking seriously his Neoplatonic occultism. Since then, a number of scholars have rediscovered Dee as a scientist, a mathematician, an inventor, and as the collector of one of Elizabethan England's finest libraries.

More recently, Frances Howard, the noblewoman who allegedly ordered Overbury poisoned and who was said to have been one of Forman's clients, has received a fresh look from David Lindley. He points out that her character has been constructed by historians from hindsight: because she poisoned Overbury, she must have been a scheming and unpleasant female from her earliest days.[14]

While I do not necessarily wish to "rehabilitate" Simon Forman or deny his many flaws and peccadilloes, I think it fascinating to piece together the story that his papers offer and to put that story beside those told of the "demonic" and "quack" Forman by writers who, in the wake of the Overbury trial, focused almost exclusively on his occult activities and his sexual behavior.

Unlike Dee and Frances Howard, however, Forman was not a court figure; he rubbed shoulders only incidentally, and then in a professional capacity, with the politically powerful and the highborn. A good deal of the fascination of his manuscripts comes from their genesis in the everyday world of urban London where the stench of a privy, the paralyzed limbs of a child, the lost bitch wearing a velvet collar, the amulet warding off ill health and bad fortune, and the thief apprehended in bed with two wenches all offer tantalizing glimpses of a world we have left behind but that is somehow also familiar.

This study has taken a long time to complete, partly because I have had to learn a great deal—about Renaissance medicine, about paleography, about giants, about the occult—in order to begin to do Forman's texts justice. Even so, I have merely scratched the surface of what Forman's papers can reveal. Dr. Lauren Kassell will soon publish a book (from Oxford University Press) examining and contextualizing Forman's medical and occult practice in greater depth than I have been able to do here. Her work was available to me too late to be fully integrated into my study, but I am grateful to her for information and advice. In the course of my work with Forman's manuscripts, I have piled up many debts. I would like to express gratitude first to the foundations and institutions which have generously supported my study of Forman: the National Endowment for the Humanities for a summer stipend and a travel to collections grant; ACLS for a grant-in-aid; the Rockefeller Foundation for a year's support at the College of Physicians of Philadelphia where my self-education in early modern medical history got its start; the Folger Shakespeare Library for a short-term fellowship; and Lehigh University for a series of faculty research grants.

I wish to express my appreciation to the libraries at which I conducted the research for this project. King's MS. 16 is quoted by kind permission of the Provost and Scholars of King's College, Cambridge. Quotations from the Sloane manuscripts are by permission of the British Library. Quotations from the Ashmole manuscripts are by permission of the Bodleian Library, University of Oxford.

My heartfelt thanks also go to the librarians and staff of Duke Humfrey's Library, Bodleian Library, Oxford University, who patiently answered my questions, shared my puzzlement with Forman's hand, and were unfailingly attentive to my many requests; to Peter Murray Jones of King's College Library, Cambridge, who made special arrangements to allow me access to King's MS. 16 when the library was closed and who read and commented on a chapter of my text; to Thomas Horrocks and Jean Carr, formerly of the Library of the College of Physicians of Philadelphia, for their help during my year in residence there; to Georgianna Zeigler of the Folger Shakespeare Library, for help, encouragement, and friendship; to John Pollack of the Annenberg Rare Book and Manuscript Library, Van Pelt Library, University of Pennsylvania, for assistance over many years.

Many individuals have helped and encouraged at various points during my work on this volume: Jan Fergus, Frank Hook, Charles Rosenberg, Christine Ruggere, and Alan Kraut were important in getting it under way; James Green, Deborah Harkness, Lauren Kassell, Carol Laub, Michael MacDonald, Kathleen Mosher, Gail Kern Paster, and Meredith Skura offered help with specific problems. R. Mark Benbow, David Hawkes, and Phyllis Rackin were extraordinarily generous with their time and energy, reading and commenting on early drafts. Rebecca Traister searched for and found the portrait of Simon Forman reproduced in this volume. William Sherman and Arthur Marotti gave valuable suggestions and critiques. Arthur Kinney encouraged me to keep going. Kathleen Mosher and Stephannie Gearhardt assisted with the index. Anthony Bleach and Daniel Traister read with keen eyes for my errors. Alas, I fear even they could not catch them all.

My family has lived with Simon Forman for a long time; indeed, ours is perhaps the only family in America where his name is a household word. My father is no longer alive to see this book in print, but to him and to my mother I offer gratitude for their support and especially for periods of child care. To Jean Howard, James Baker, Elwood Howard, Gilbert Twitchell, Jane and Nigel Noble, thanks for being there over the years. For their patience, good humor, personal sacrifices in the cause of Simon Forman, and assumption of vital household tasks I am extremely grateful to my children, Rebecca and Aaron. To my husband, Daniel, who is "nothing if not critical," I owe more than I can possibly express. He, after all, is the family wordsmith.

The Notorious Astrological Physician of London

ℌ Self-Conscious Life

lyke a man in a maske
which subtilly dothe shifte him self
to diuers shapes and formes
and at the laste forgetes the firste
before aboute he tornes.

—Forman, "The Argument betwen fforman
and death in his Sicknes" (1585)

SIMON FORMAN'S REPUTATION WAS VOLATILE, changed and distorted by events
that occurred following his death. Trapped in the lines of writers more famous
than himself, Forman's self-identification as "the astrological physician of
Lambeth" was obliterated by his contemporaries who rewrote him as "bawd,"
"quack," "poisoner," and "devil." Ben Jonson was one of the earliest makers
of Forman's reputation. In *Epicoene* (1609), Jonson called Forman a vendor
of love potions.[1] In *The Devil Is an Ass*, published in 1616, the year of the
Overbury trials, Jonson writes of "Oracle Forman" to whom ladies flock for
advice on love.[2] Some critics speculate that Forman was the model for Subtle,
the deceptive occultist in *The Alchemist* (1610).[3]

In historical records, Forman fared little better. The College of Physicians repeatedly summoned Forman to fine or imprison him for practicing
physic without a license. Its records characterize him as a "bold and impudent
imposter" and "a pretended Astrologer" who practiced "notorious cheats . . .
for deceiving the people."[4] Popularly believed to have provided the poison
used to murder Sir Thomas Overbury, Forman was discussed during the
state trial of Anne Turner, who was convicted and executed for her part in
Overbury's death. Although Forman was not accused at the trial of supplying
the specific poison—he had been dead for two years before the fatal enema
was administered—Chief Justice Edmund Coke ordered Forman's widow to
bring certain papers, books, and objects from his study into court. On the
basis of the occult materials she produced, Forman was accused of providing
Turner and Lady Frances Howard with love potions to secure the love of
specific men, and of giving Howard materials to make her unwanted first
husband impotent. In his summary of the case against Turner, Coke referred

to "Devil Forman."[5] In the many seventeenth-century retellings of the Overbury affair, Forman usually retains a prominent place, sometimes as devil Forman and sometimes as a con man who preyed on the ladies of the court.

Generations later, in nineteenth-century New England, Nathaniel Hawthorne picked up the suggestion of Forman's diabolism. In *The Scarlet Letter*, Hawthorne sought to blacken his villain Chillingsworth by associating him with Simon Forman:

> There was an aged handicraftsman . . . who had been a citizen of London at the period of Sir Thomas Overbury's murder; . . . he testified to having seen the physician [Chillingsworth], under some other name, . . . in company with Doctor Forman, the famous old conjuror, who was implicated in the affair of Overbury.[6]

In nineteenth-century England, an anonymous three-volume novel titled *Forman* and filled with accounts of demonic dealings was published by an admirer of Sir Walter Scott.[7] A few years later the antiquarian James Orchard Halliwell, attracted to the cache of Forman manuscripts at Oxford University, proposed to edit and publish Forman's autobiography and private diary for the Camden Society. But when he examined the papers closely, he discovered that they included not only the fascinating customs and interesting biographical notes that had first caught his attention but also a detailed account of Forman's active and wide-ranging sex life. Halliwell quickly curtailed his publication plans and printed just 105 copies "for private circulation only," having taken the further precaution of removing all sexual references from the text he did print.[8]

Twentieth-century scholars have done little better by Forman. Thorndike's magisterial eight-volume *A History of Magic and Experimental Science* allots one sentence to Forman in a paragraph that discusses quacks and empirics: "Simon Forman, physician and astrologer, in his diary from 1552 to 1602, has recorded his questionable practices, dabblings in alchemy and magic, and the troubles into which these got him."[9] A book-length study by A. L. Rowse calls particular attention to the sexual material that Halliwell had omitted. His book *Simon Forman: Sex and Society in Shakespeare's Age* emphasizes Forman's sexual exploits and the important patients whom he treated and largely ignores Forman's extensive records of his medical practice as well as his prolific medical, astrological, and alchemical writings.

In one of the more recent books to mention Forman, a 1981 study of the medical practice of Forman's friend and medical "scoller," Richard

Napier, Michael MacDonald takes his cue from Rowse. Crediting Forman with arousing Napier's interest in astrology, MacDonald continues:

> Forman possessed a mesmerizing personality and the sexual appetite of a goat, and he made himself the most popular astrologer of his time. His chaotic moods and exuberant immorality were precisely opposed to Napier's somber chastity, but soon Forman was instructing his new friend in every branch of the astrologer's art: finding lost and stolen goods, predicting marriages and diagnosing pregnancy, treating all the maladies of mind and body.[10]

After all these partial and negative opinions of Forman, it would be satisfying to expose the falsehoods or half-truths. But because Forman's own records are often contradictory and incomplete, they prevent readers from making conclusive judgments. Indeed, among all those who have made free with the details of Forman's life and reputation, who have embroidered and exaggerated and created a portrait larger than life, none is more culpable than Simon Forman himself.

☞ The Manuscripts

Forman's personal story and observations about his society are scattered through a number of manuscripts, which must be pieced together before any coherent picture emerges. Forman was obsessed with his autobiography, his family's riches-to-rags story. In one account, Forman explained that, prior to the English Reformation, his grandfather Richard Forman had been the secular governor of Wilton Abbey near Salisbury, which at the time of the English Reformation, was seized by Henry VIII and given to the Herbert family:

> This William Forman [Simon's father] . . . was sole eyer and executor to his father, and because ther were many accounts and reconinges dependinge betwen the said Richard Forman his father and William [Herbert] Erell of Pembrocke, about the abbey landes and goodes and aboute diuers other matters because [Simon's grandfather] was steward afterward to the old Erelle, [Simon's father] procured a lawiare and a preste to make vp all reckonings betwen them. . . . The said priste and lawiar having the vse and full possession with egresse and regresse of to and from the studdye, countinghouse, bockes, writings, and all deed of landes that were in the said countinge house of the said Richard deceased, stoole awaie alle the deeds and evidences of his landes. And the saide William mistrustinge not, was decyued of all.[11]

Forman believed that his family had been deprived unjustly of land that was rightfully theirs. Unlike his father, he was always "mistrustful," fearing to be cheated. Forman devoted his life to scrambling up the social ladder and claiming a place in the world. His manuscripts contain his claims to prestigious ancestry and to extraordinary medical and occult skill, but these claims were sometimes colored by his imagination and his dreams. Only by looking at his papers as a group can we hope to discover a reasonably coherent narrative.

One printed pamphlet, forty-odd volumes of Forman's manuscript papers in the Ashmole Collection at Oxford University, a few manuscripts in the Sloane collection at the British Library, and Forman's extensive annotations in a medical manuscript he once owned, which is now at King's College Library, Cambridge University, comprise the extant corpus of his work. All make clear Forman's obsession first and foremost with his own life story. His personal experiences intrude upon whatever he is attempting to write about, even when those subjects seem far removed from autobiographical concerns.

Forman produced two substantial autobiographical texts, each of which was reprinted by both Halliwell and Rowse. "This is the Bocke of the life and generation of Simon," written in 1600 (which I refer to as his autobiography), recounted Forman's life from his birth in 1552 through his stay at Oxford University as a poor scholar from 1573 to 1574. This deliberately anecdotal account narrated high spots from Forman's early life and emphasized his emotional responses to the situations in which he was placed.[12] After he left the master to whom he had been apprenticed for six and a half years, for example, Forman briefly returned to school. However,

> his mother wold give him meate and drink no longer nor any maintenance whereupon he was dryven to make many hard shiftes and he was soe gredy on his bocke, that yf his master wold not have beaten him yf he could not saye his lesson well he wold haue wepte and suobbed more then yf he had byne beaten.[13]

He composed this narrative in the third person and carefully divided it into subtitled sections; for instance, "Howe Simon, after he was gone from his said master, became a scoller again at the fre scole" heads the section from which the above quotation comes. The autobiography was Forman's attempt to turn his life into art, to shape and sympathetically interpret his early years.

In contrast, the second autobiographical text is really a personal diary,[14] a first-person account organized by year, of the events of Forman's life, important not for their anecdotal value or for Forman's presentation of his own character, but rather as a record of milestones and molehills in Forman's experience. Starting with annual horoscopes (the first real event recorded was the death of Forman's father on the day after Forman's eleventh birthday), the entries continued until January 1602. They grew increasingly detailed as the years went on. The early records were probably constructed from memory, but in the 1580s Forman began to make longer entries, perhaps recording events as they happened. During 1589, for example, he entered such minutiae as "The 3 of March I went from Sarum [Salisbury] againe to Newberry. . . . The 5 dai I was trobled with the stone in the yerd [kidney stone in the penis]. The 14 dai I was at Quidhampton. The 26 dai I was hurte in the leg with a hatchet."[15] At the end of 1589, he wrote a summary:

> This yere was a wonderful troblesom yere to me. I went from place to place. I was glad to forsake all, and did chang my lodging often. I gote lyttle, I spent & consumed all, till Michelmas then yt began to mend with me. I practised then again nigromancy & magik and phisick, and my enimise prevailed againste me, and I was lik to have run into mani mischiefes.[16]

Forman made no attempt to narrate or interpret in the diary beyond these rather matter-of-fact summaries at the end of nearly every year, apparently written to remind him of dates and events rather than to present his life to a potential reader. Though the diary notes ended abruptly in 1602, a fragment of a diary for 1607, which began on March 13 and ended in early September of the same year,[17] suggests that Forman kept on recording events, but that nearly everything from 1602 until his death in 1611 has been lost. The fragments from 1607 are as circumstantial as the earlier entries, though they place more emphasis on sexual records. Halliwell refused to print the 1607 entries at all; Rowse quoted from them in his text, but he did not reprint them with the other diary entries. In addition to the diary and the autobiography, other notes among Forman's manuscripts focus on the history of his family.[18] They record details about his mother's as well as his father's relatives. The autobiography reveals animosity toward his mother who, he believed, disliked him and would not let him go to school. But other notes—one written in 1604 after her death—show admiration, at least for her stamina: "She had lyved 97 years, and had her eysighte, memory and lymes [limbs] verie well that but fortnight before she deceased she could walke alone two milles, thanks be to God."[19] Aside from this interjection, Forman effaced himself from this family history much as he had done from the autobiography, giving the text a formal tone. Though it offered no mini-narratives, the authorial voice was editorial, analyzing the character of the Formans:

> And ther ar 3 things generally recorded of the Formans from generation to generation yt is to saie they were never covetouse of honor nor of wealth nor of other mens goods, never trecherouse to any nor falls of their word to any, nor never proud, but meke mercifulle and pittifull. They never desier strife but peace and quietnes; they never desier hatred, but frindshipe; they never seeke revendge of any notable injury. They alwaies love justice and maintain the right and ar vtter enemies to injurie and oppression and apte to forgiue. And have bin alwaies good commonwealthes men[20] as yt appeared in old Richard my grandfather in the tyme when the abbeyes were suppressed in Henrie the 8th his daie which refused to haue any of the abbey land when yt was offred him; and in my father and diuers others as after shall appeare more plainly.[21]

This passage demonstrates a recurrent problem in trying to understand Forman's life. He stated here that his grandfather, as a good commonwealth's man, refused abbey lands, but three leaves later, in a passage quoted above, Forman complained that his father was somehow cheated of those very lands. Forman himself seemed oblivious to the jarring effect his inconsistent details had on the narrative he was presenting.

Forman wrote another short autobiographical piece—probably the last of his attempts to write his life—which he titled "The issue of Simon Forman."[22] This carefully prepared manuscript included a page of roundels containing the names of Forman, his wife, and their infant daughter Dority (figure 1). It seems to have been prepared about 1605, in the first flush of parenthood, and to have been emended as late as 1611, the year Forman died. Dority's roundel reads: "Dority—daughter and firste child of Simon Forman and of Jean his wife borne 1605." Squeezed in at the bottom and spilling out of the roundel—obviously a later addition—the text continues: "& died 1606 the first of febari. she died yong. at half a yere old." The birth of his son Clement was also included in Forman's diagram, but placed in a square somewhat to one side, as though it had been added after the original page had been set up.

The text briefly retells Forman's youth. It is by and large a condensation of the much fuller material in the autobiography and diary. One intriguing sentence, however, refers to events in Forman's early adulthood about which he offered no other information:

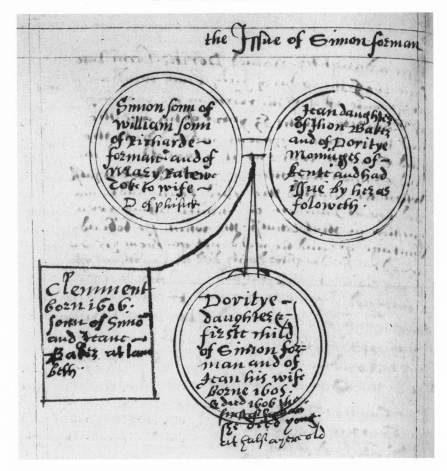

FIGURE 1: The Forman family: Simon, his wife Jean, daughter Dority, and son Clement. MS. Ashmole 802: 226v. Courtesy of the Bodleian Library, University of Oxford.

> He travailed moch in to the Estern countries to seke for arte and knowledge, and was often at Sea, and in his retorne after the portugall voiadge 1589, at michelmas he came to London wher he dwelled at the stone house in philpote lane som 14 yers.[23]

Forman's cryptic reference to much travel in eastern countries raises a number of questions. Which eastern countries? What did he study? Did he get some medical training? Was he seeking instead occult knowledge in astrology and magic? Nothing in Forman's surviving papers provides answers. Nowhere else did he refer to his eastern travels, though William Lilly later reported in his account of Forman's life that he received a medical degree "beyond Seas."[24]

The same passage also provides an example of Forman's creative representation of his life story. Here he claimed to have lived in London, in the stone house in Philpot Lane, for fourteen years, until 1603. Yet several documents elsewhere among his papers indicate that he leased a house in Lambeth briefly as early as 1598 and "gave up London quite"[25] in 1601. His claim to have dwelt in Philpot Lane until 1603 might be dismissed as bad arithmetic or a slip of the pen had Forman not insisted on the same chronology again a few lines later. After telling with pride how Cambridge University granted him his license to practice medicine on June 27, 1603, and how "from that tyme after non for arte durste medle with hym any more," Forman continued, "then he lefte London and went to Lambeth towne a mille of and ther he lyued many yeares to the profit and benefite of many."[26]

Forman deliberately altered the date of his move because he did not want to acknowledge that he had left London in fear of prosecution by the College of Physicians. Placing the move to Lambeth after the receipt of his medical license from Cambridge made Forman's abandonment of London appear to be personal preference rather than flight from repeated imprisonment and fines. Elsewhere too, Forman reshaped his personal story to enhance his self-image.

The date when Forman made his additions to this short manuscript is suggested by its final lines. Having recorded the birth of his son Clement on October 27, 1606, Forman continued:

> He was the gretest child of perseverance wit vnderstanding memory and reason at 2 years old on of them that ever lyved. and soe he perseuered and at 5 years old he was able to read Englishe & full of sprite. all ayer. he was so full of action and wold never stand stille. god blesse him. dyvers tymes like to ben drowned brayned & overronne with horses befor he was 4 yers old.[27]

If Clement was reading English at age five, Forman must have been writing in 1611, making his additions to this manuscript and a letter to Richard Napier on July 23, 1611, the last of his dateable papers.

In addition to these more or less formal accounts of Forman's life, numerous bits and pieces among his papers offer insights into his character and career. The most polished are a series of poems, all religious in tone, which recount aspects of Forman's personal history. Forman's titles suggest something of the contents of these poems: "Forman A Rehersale of his first troble and his thankesgyvinge to God for his deliverie. 1576"; "Forman his Thankesgyuinge and acknowledgmente of the poware of god after his firste & second troble" [1579]; "Psalme per formann of the wickednes of the Tyme"; "Argument betwen fforman and death in his Sicknes"; "Forman 1604 January 19. To be songe at his burialle."[28] Most of these poems recount Forman's struggles with the authorities, conflicts that preoccupied him for much of his adult life. His concern with himself predominates in these poems, and his preparation of a song to be sung at his own funeral suggests an attempt to control and shape his image even after death. The accusations made against him during the Overbury trial would certainly have upset him greatly, for they altered irrevocably the image of respectability he had worked hard to create.

Forman also presented himself in letters to his friend Richard Napier, whom Forman addressed as "Sandy."[29] Napier preserved a number of letters, among them several from Forman. These letters show Forman as a teacher,[30] instructing his "scoller"—the Oxford-educated Napier—in astrological medicine, focusing especially on diagnosis. Forman bought drugs in London for Napier and sent them to Buckinghamshire by carrier. Napier returned the favor by boarding Forman's horse for the winter. At times Forman seems testy and impatient with Napier; other letters are filled with warm regard and friendship for the country rector. Valuable to a biographer for their tone and their help in characterizing the relationship between Forman and Napier, these letters also refer to Forman's troubles with the College of Physicians and to details of his domestic arrangements.

Forman prepared a number of genealogies and illustrated coats of arms for the Forman family (figure 2). Intent on proving his family's importance, Forman traced it back to various periods of history. For example, Conradus, emperor of Rome (ca. 1028, according to Forman), bestowed on a Norman captain in his army "Monsier Ricardus Andisson" the name Forman because the latter "was alwais the formoste man in everie assaulte" and "for that he was for every man more then for him selfe."[31] An alternative founding narrative for the family claimed that the first of the Formans was "a Scot named William forsan errelle of Millom castell in Cumberland . . . in the daies of Henrie kinge of Scotes who changed his name and called him Forman for his valiantnes and forwardnes in the warrs."[32]

Forman tried out identities, doodled with his past, trying to find the most appropriate ancestral line. He was almost as interested in his wife's family,

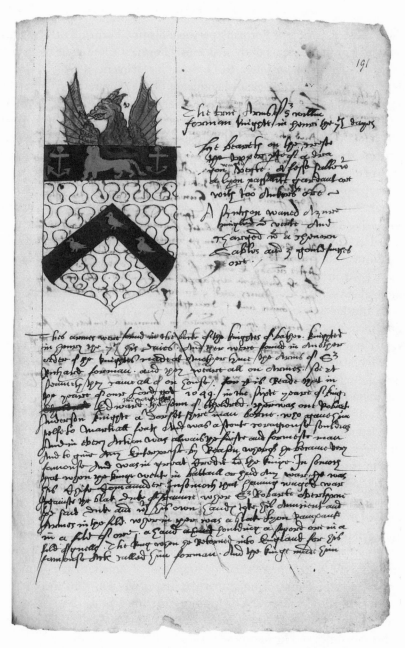

FIGURE 2: One of several coats of arms Forman found or devised for the Formans. MS. Ashmole 802: 191r. Courtesy of the Bodleian Library, University of Oxford.

although he did not have to invent a background for her, for her pedigree was already quite satisfactory. Almost all of Forman's extant genealogies were prepared after Clement's birth, suggesting that he saw his son as a means of perpetuating his family. Although Forman fathered bastard children for whom he was financially and sometimes personally responsible, his focus on family intensified after he had a legitimate heir to bear the Forman name. Concomitantly, he felt a need to invest that name with historical weight and significance and thus searched for an appropriate background, experimenting with one ancestral line after another.

Another kind of manuscript material that yields some biographical detail and a number of hints about Forman's character is his record of his dreams. Like many others in his society, Forman believed that dreams had significance and could be interpreted with relation to events in waking life. Not only did he record the details of dreams—he took an amorous walk with Queen Elizabeth; King James came to visit him; he met an old friend who was dead; he encountered three witches in a church—but also he attempted to understand what the dreams meant. The day after the dream about King James, for example, strangers visited Forman. Clearly, their arrival had been heralded by the dream.[33]

Perhaps the richest vein of biographical information, because it seems most spontaneous and least shaped, runs through the notes of his medical practice and his medical treatises. These materials include narratives. For example, in one of his treatises on the plague, Forman told how his Lambeth neighbors boarded up his house on the very day that his son was born, leaving his family no way to get food and water. The crowd thought, mistakenly, that Forman's maid had plague. Forman not only told the story, he also editorialized about it:

> O howe moche is the mallice of cursed caterpillers of a common wealth. They might haue considered that I bought not the plague with money, neither did I goe abrod to seek yt. But yt was the visitation of the moste higheste. . . . In the last plague I fled not from them they were glad then both of my presentes [presence] and councelle. I did not then shote vp my compassion from any nor my dores as they haue done to me.[34]

The medical casebooks include many random notes about Forman's life. For example, he recorded and commented on the deaths of his bastard son, his nephew, his mother, and his mistress; examined and worried about his own health; recorded details of his sexual activities; and discussed his legal disputes and struggles with the College of Physicians. Various real-estate deals and moves from one house to another received a good deal of attention. His relationships with his servants and his recreational activities—including an interest in theater—were mentioned occasionally. He recorded his magical and alchemical experiments in varying degrees of detail.

Forman revealed his hopes and private ambitions inadvertently in the records of his astrological casts. He cast to know whether he would be a knight, lord, or earl; and again to know "Whether I be the man must set vp the auntient house of the formans again or noe."[35] In 1601, he cast for information about a more specific ambition: should he try to obtain Doctor James's place as physician to the queen?[36] He also revealed magical and alchemical aspirations. In 1598, he cast to know "whether ever I shall haue that power in nigromantic that I desier or bring it to effect,"[37] and in 1599, he asked the stars "what will com of my philosophers ston. wher [whether] yt will proue profitable to me or noe & com to any good effecte."[38] He rarely recorded the stars' answer to these queries, but since he continued in his optimism, their response must have been somewhat encouraging.

Forman's ambitions were unlimited. Despite the unpromising circumstances of his youth, he believed in his own ability to achieve something important. He felt himself gifted by God with occult powers. His nativity horoscopes indicate both his boundless ambition and his subjective manipulation of the stars' messages. In a manuscript headed "Of Nativities in Revolutions. Forman. 1602," he recorded the following horoscope for his own birth date, which combined the fact, fiction, and wish fulfillment that shaped his vision of himself and his potential:

> He shall practice arte with wisemen and with religiouse men and shalbe of greate understange [*sic*] and haue a subtille serchinge wit and be very politick and of great truth in Judgment. and shall haue forsighte and knowledge in many artes and sciences and be apte to learne any thinge, and shall give himself naturally to astronomie physick and chirurgery [surgery] and to distillations. & making of poticary drugs. and new inuentions of arte and geomantia magick cosmografie philosofie diviniti and in all depe and subtile artes but he moste [must] begine at the very foundation of all or ells he shall never attain to the depthe therof. He shalbe alsoe apt to teatch and instructe & shalbe seen in Lawe husbandry [farming] and buildinge & shall haue great delight to doe justice and to maintain the state of a common wealle and shall hate oppression. and shall haue moch strife and troble in youth and hardnes. he shalbe very lucky in marchandis and in bying and selling of ymmouable

goodes and shalbe a grete physision and astronomer. and in his last years he shall find moch treasure by som secreat arte or meanes, and shalbe a horder vp of goold in his old age.[39]

This horoscope suggests the range of Forman's interests and ambitions. While noting those years already behind as "strife and troble in youth," it is primarily an optimistic (and quite inaccurate) prediction for the future.

Forman's vision of himself, presented in the manuscripts enumerated above, has little in common with the picture of "Forman" painted by his contemporaries and later detractors. In chapter 8, I discuss this disjunction among the various representations of Simon Forman, but first I examine Forman's representation of himself. To this end, it may be helpful to divide Forman's life into four periods and summarize briefly the chief events, the information available, and the chief incongruities in the records of each period.

☞ The Biography
Childhood and Youth

Forman's autobiography narrates his early life, from his birth on December 31, 1552, through the end of his sojourn at Oxford in September, 1574. The central event of his childhood—he mentioned it repeatedly in his various accounts—was the death of his father. Ambitious for his obviously intelligent young son, Forman's father had arranged lessons for him when he was nine with a clergyman, William Ryddoute or Ridear, at the priory of St. Giles. After his father's death on January 1, 1564, Forman tried to continue his education. He stayed with an aunt and took lessons for a year, but the family's financial difficulties and his strained relationship with his mother combined to force him to abandon his schooling.

In 1567, Forman apprenticed himself to a Salisbury shopkeeper, Matthew Commins, for a period of ten years, three of which were to be spent at a grammar school. Forman complained in his autobiography that Commins did not honor the schooling part of the agreement and even took away his Latin books.[40] Nevertheless, Forman got along well with his master, although not with his master's wife or maidservant, and even managed to continue his school lessons after a fashion. He roomed at Commins's home with a schoolboy, Henry Gird, whom Forman clearly thought rather stupid and not properly appreciative of his privilege of uninterrupted study. Under the pretense of helping this young man with his lessons, Forman debriefed him every night and tried to learn from him, or through him, whatever he had been taught that day. This method must have been rather frustrating and haphazard, though Forman said because of it "he liste [lost] nothinge of that he had before tyme lerned."[41] Among his various goods, Commins sold drugs and ingredients for compounding medicines, and Forman later explained that his apprenticeship gave him a knowledge of the pharmacopoeia. After nearly six years with Commins, Forman had a terrible fight with Mrs. Commins and asked to be released from his apprenticeship. According to Forman's account, his master agreed with reluctance, and he was again a free man.

After a six-month stint as a schoolmaster in his old school at the priory of St. Giles, Forman and Thomas Ridear, the stepson of his former schoolmaster, set off together for Oxford to become poor scholars. Forman remarked that Ridear's "father in lawe [stepfather] was as moch againe him as Simons mother was againste him."[42]

Forman entered Magdalen College,[43] and Ridear entered Corpus Christi. As a poor scholar, Forman was forced to work, hiring himself out as a servant to wealthy students. In one of the most vivid passages in his autobiography, Forman told of his disillusionment with the two young gentlemen who employed him:

> Nowe ther were too bachelors of arte that were too of his chife benefactors. The one of them was Sir Thornbury. that after was bishope of Limbrike, and he was of Magdalen Colledge. The other was Sir Pinckney, his cossine, of St. Mary Hall. Thes too loved him nying [nothing] welle, and many tymes wold make Simon to goo forth to Loes the keper of Shottofer for his houndes to goe on huntinge from morninge to nighte, and they never studied nor gave themselves to their bockes, but to goe to scolles of defence, to ye dauncieing scolles, to stealle dear and connyes [rabbits], and to hunt the hare, and to woinge of wentches. To goe to Dr. Lawrence of Cowly, for he had too fair daughters, Besse and Martha. . . . ther was their ordinary haunt alwaies, and thether muste Symon rone with the bottell and the bage erly and late.[44]

Perhaps his inability to spend time with his own books due to the demands of his young employers discouraged Forman; perhaps he could not afford to stay at Oxford or simply became disillusioned with university life. The immediate cause of his departure from Oxford may have been twofold. Oxford was threatened by plague, as Forman noted in a diary entry that he later crossed out: "and I lefte all that ever I had ther, bockes and all. my ost & his wife died in the plague."[45] An undeleted diary entry suggests yet another reason for his departure: "the 12 dai of Septemb 1574 I cam from Oxford to Quidhampton to mak an oration before the quene being then at Wilton."[46] Whatever the reason for his departure, Forman left Oxford in September 1574, having been in residence a year and three months. His autobiography ends with his departure from Oxford; from this point on, his life is much more difficult to follow.

Young Adulthood

From 1574 until Forman moved permanently to London in 1592, certain periods of time remain largely unaccounted for. The opportunity to deliver an oration before the queen should have seemed a great opportunity to one as ambitious as Forman. If so, he was uncharacteristically silent about the details of the speech and the occasion.[47] Instead of returning to Oxford, Forman accepted a position as schoolmaster at Wilton, just outside Salisbury.

Once he had left Oxford and found employment as a schoolmaster, Forman was a *literatus*, "someone who had attended one of the universities but who left before taking a degree."[48] This was a common background for teachers in the period. His teaching positions—schoolmaster at Wilton, tutor in a prosperous merchant's family, and usher [assistant master] at the free school in Salisbury Close, among others—rarely lasted longer than six months. Apparently, they paid rather badly: "I kept schole at Urenminster. I had moch adoe with the vicar lived porly and did hunt moch privily."[49] His diary records the positions and their dates with no editorial comment, and Forman did not elsewhere mention his nearly five years as a schoolmaster.

His days in the classroom came to an abrupt halt in June of 1579. Forman, then living in the parsonage at Fisherton Anger, was arrested and imprisoned for sixty weeks, until July 1580. What the charges were Forman never said, but he did report that his books were also seized: "I was robbed and spoiled of all my goodes and bockes first dwelling in Fisherton parsonage and was committed to prison . . . by that cursed villain Gilles Estcourte."[50] The books had not been stolen but confiscated. Years later, in 1587, Forman wrote that "my bockes, which had bin out of my handes long, were brought to Jhon Penruddockes to be seen, wher they lay long after & many wer loste."[51] Finally in 1592, in London, he recovered the books "from Jhon Penruddock at Sarum [Salisbury] which had bin out of my handes since my first troble which was som 14 yers."[52] The trouble about his books suggests that Forman may have been arrested on charges of practicing magic or for some involvement with the occult.

Before this first imprisonment, Forman's notes make no mention of medical practice, and thus it is unlikely that he was arrested for unlicensed practice. He was not yet living in London where strict licensing rules applied, and Salisbury officials would not have been enforcing regulations that applied primarily in London. Were it not for the presence in King's College Library, Cambridge, of a medical manuscript that Forman had owned and annotated since his Oxford days, no evidence would survive of Forman's interest in, much less practice of, medicine before 1579.

Forman's papers also contain no evidence of occult practices until the year of his first arrest, when he mentioned, in his diary, prophecy and attempts to call spirits. Whether it was his books or occult activities in the community that got him into trouble, Forman's long incarceration may have increased his interest in medicine by giving him time to read and copy borrowed medical texts. After his release, he almost immediately began to practice medicine, curing Henry Johnson of consumption a month later and "curing sick and lame folk" in Quidhampton.[53]

Forman wrote about this long first imprisonment in the poems he composed about his "troubles." According to one poem, he was at first fettered in prison but gradually got on better terms with his keepers:

> Then from my fetters was I freed
> And with my kepars well agreed
> That they did favoure to me showe
> And larger scope I had to walke
> And with my frindes somtymes to talke
> When they the truth of thinges did know.[54]

After having been twice called before the judges and twice returned to prison, Forman wrote to "the princes" to hear his case:

> The which was don ymmediatly
> And me again did satisfy
> With letters for my liberty
> And sente my foe vnto the fleete[55]
> . . . .
> The Judges calld me forth to showe
> The Lettars which I had belowe
> Directed from her majestie
> And when the same they all espied

Againste my foe they all forth cried
And set me straighte at Lyberty.[56]

This is all the information Forman provided about his exchange of letters with the queen. He obviously attributed his release from prison to her intervention, but he was once more uncharacteristically silent about this brush with majesty, just as he had been silent about the oration before Elizabeth at Wilton. Forman later claimed that it took nine years after his release from prison before he was completely free of the paperwork and legal charges stemming from this arrest.

Once out of prison, Forman launched into a whirlwind of jobs and travel, presumably to keep body and soul together. He worked as a carpenter and as a thresher, traveled to the Low Countries, went to sea, and then took a new tutoring job that entailed his sometime residence in London. His social life also began to improve. His first sexual experience with a woman took place in 1582 (he was thirty), and a friendship with Ann Young, begun during his apprentice years, deepened into a sexual relationship. Their bastard son Joshua was born in 1585.[57]

Forman's first imprisonment had been only a taste of things to come. He became embroiled in legal battles with the Commins family, specifically with Agnes, probably his former master's wife. Apparently he gave medical treatment to a member of her family and received no payment; suits and countersuits resulted, and Forman was arrested or threatened with arrest several times.

More serious, perhaps, was a thirty-six day imprisonment in 1587, when Forman reported: "I was taken in the church prainge & for my bocke I was sente to prison."[58] An appended note identifies the book as a prayer book. Forman may have been caught with a forbidden Roman Catholic book. He never wrote about his religious beliefs, though he repeatedly expressed his faith in and love of God. In the 1590s he had a lengthy and passionate love affair with a Roman Catholic woman, Avis Allen. Perhaps as the grandson of the former governor of Wilton Abbey, Forman's sympathies were with Roman Catholicism. If so, he learned to embrace the more politic religion. In a note from 1599, he recorded that "I had too offices laid on me, sydman [church warden] and gatherer for the poor,"[59] and Rowse notes that in the Lambeth parish register he is referred to as "Simon Forman, gent."[60] In his plague treatise of 1593, when he listed all God's benefits to an ungrateful

England, he included as one of those benefits being brought from the "bondage of that whore of Rome."[61]

Throughout the somewhat confusing records of Forman's many activities from 1574 to 1591 runs an increasingly strong stream of comments on his achievements in medicine and magic. In 1581, for example, he reported practicing "physic and surgery," and in 1585 he mentioned medicines he had prepared, including aqua vita [alcohol] and distilled waters, as well as individual patients he had treated. His annual summary for 1587 recorded that he had practiced magic. In 1588 he wrote that he had called angels and spirits and practiced necromancy; and in 1589, the year he first rented a room in London, he claimed to have practiced necromancy, magic, and physic and was in trouble because of what he had told a client who came to inquire about the whereabouts of stolen goods.[62]

As his commitment to "physic" and to continued magical experimentation grew, Forman's former interests in teaching and in going to sea diminished. In 1589 and 1590, he spent time in London and tried living in Sussex. Finally in 1592, he settled permanently in London in "the stone house." This seventeen-year period in Forman's young adulthood was full of agitation and restless activity: many brief jobs, short periods of travel, several imprisonments and sea voyages, most of which are mentioned briefly and with few details. Determining the chronology is further complicated by Forman's carelessness with dates, weak arithmetic, and inconsistencies in details.

London and Lambeth, 1592–1603

In contrast to the period of moves, travel, and job changes, Forman's residence in London, where he was quickly busy with a medical and astrological practice, was relatively stable. To be sure, he was in and out of jail, involved in sexual relationships with a number of women, and embroiled in a series of lawsuits; but he identified himself in his manuscripts as "doctor of physick and astrology," stayed in one place, and built a practice. Even being sent to jail for unlicensed practice became a kind of ritual; after a while it was more annoying than frightening because the routine had become so well established.

Forman's stay in London, and later Lambeth, from 1592 until he received his medical license from Cambridge in June 1603, is certainly the most richly documented period of his life. During these years he wrote the extant casebooks, daily records of his professional life, with personal details occasionally added; composed many of his poems and medical treatises; established his strong friendship with Richard Napier; conducted the adulterous relationship with Avis Allen that ended only with her death in 1597; married Jean Baker, age sixteen, in 1599; moved to Lambeth; and prospered financially as a result of his expanding practice.

With prosperity came an increased concern for material possessions. Forman proudly recorded the acquisition of a horse, of additional real estate, of new clothes, jewelry, linens, and of pictures for his wife. No longer worried, as he had been during those difficult years in Salisbury when "I consumed and spent more then I got, & brought my self to beggars state,"[63] Forman wrote in his year's summary for 1600:

> Yt cost me 40£ this yere in apparrell and better, almost 50£ for my wife & for my self. . . . I bought many pictures about our ladi dai [March 25]. This sommer I had my own pictur drawen, and mad my purple gowne, my velvet cap, my velvet cote, my velvet breches, my taffety cloke, my hat & many other thinges, & did let my hear and berd growe. . . . I lent out moch mony on plate jewells this yer and had many trifels gyuen me. I bought my swachele[64] sword this yer & did the hangers with siluer.[65]

At last Forman had come into his own. Despite constant surveillance and occasional prosecution by the College of Physicians, his practice yielded him an excellent living. He had begun to dress and consume as befitted a gentleman. He had a wife, at least one respectable friend, some important patients and—in 1603—he received the one thing he lacked: a license to practice medicine from Cambridge University. No wonder that, after years of failed examinations, scornful words, and fines and imprisonments from the College of Physicians, Forman abandoned his newfound velvet dignity when he wrote of his victory over "the doctors":

> Through out the wordle [world] I had their [Cambridge's] Sealle
> To practice wher I liste
> And backe to Lambeth I retorned
> O then they [the College] were be piste.[66]

Forman's glee was so great that he forgot to alter the chronology of his move (as he had done in other texts) and here admitted that he returned home from Cambridge to Lambeth rather than to London.

With this last barrier to his prosperity and respectability cleared away, Forman, then fifty-one, moved into what should have been untroubled years.

Maturity, 1603–1611

Our understanding of the last period of Forman's life, from the granting of his Cambridge degree until his death, is limited by a disappointing dearth of personal records. No diary entries, except for a few months in 1607, survive. No casebooks for this period are extant, though examples Forman selected when he wrote medical and astrological texts, make clear that such casebooks once existed. When he wrote explanations of medical or astrological procedures, he regularly searched his casebooks for good illustrative examples, and a number of such examples from the last decade of Forman's life were recorded in the texts prepared after 1603.

In a moment of frustration, Forman indicated how he used his books of notes. Writing a list of English locations of precious metals or stone, he recalled a conversation with a man in "the west country" about where excellent lodestones [magnetic stones] could be found in Somersetshire "but he wold not tell me wher because he made much commodity of them and he told me he brought at on time thre score to London & sold them all and they wer very good as he said. I haue noted his name in som of my books of notes but I cannot find yt."[67]

In the preparation of some manuscripts Forman ranged widely through decades of notes to find appropriate examples. In an astrological treatise written in 1609, demonstrating how to determine whether it was better to buy or to lease a house, he cited examples from his own experience reaching back to 1597, when he sold a house for 90 pounds to James Beinton:[68] he had the exact date thanks to his casebook records. He was just as explicit about two more recent real estate opportunities:

> Questo 1608 the 25 of February: Best to buy the land in Barnsey stret that Mr. Britain told me of. Thes wer 5 old houses ruinous & stod in a bad place and pore people dwelled in them scant abell to pay the Rent. therfore I wold none of them.
> Best to by the house & land at Smead in Kent that parson Plasto told me of. Questo 1608 27 October. Buy it not yt is to deare. Yt is an old wide ruinouse country house with no good romes like a barne, fit for a pore country man, but not for a man of any sort, and standes in an open ayer neare the strete or highway in a reasonable dry ground.[69]

These examples make clear that Forman had created records for the last years of his life similar to those that survive from earlier years in the extant casebooks. Perhaps the missing notebooks were among the papers swept up and taken to court by Mrs. Forman for the Overbury trial. She could have taken the records for the reign of James, everything from 1603 on. If so, the papers may have been destroyed by the court or been stored in some court-related collection of records and forgotten.

An apocryphal story about the trial relates how Edmund Coke, the presiding judge, opened one of Forman's books only to spy his own wife's name. Coke quickly closed the volume and refused to admit the books as evidence in the court.[70] If there is any truth in this story, it would give credence to the suggestion that the court had Forman's notebooks destroyed or sequestered in some safe repository.

The previously quoted accounts of two real-estate decisions also suggest something about Forman's values in his later years. One set of houses was a bad investment because its poor tenants had trouble paying rent. The other was a country house fit only for country people and not for a man of substance, like Forman. Both accounts reflect his continued prosperity and growing complacency about his own worldly position and achievements.

One explanation for the difference between the Forman represented in the Ashmole manuscripts and the Forman who was so calumniated by his contemporaries in Stuart England may be that Forman changed considerably in the society that emerged with James's ascension to the throne. Perhaps in his old age, patronized and flattered by giddy young females from the court (like Frances Howard), Forman did furnish aphrodisiacs and anaphrodisiacs and wax figurines designed to harm enemies by magic. These activities were certainly alleged during the court trial of Anne Turner.[71] If Forman practiced this sort of illicit magic, however, he left little evidence in the papers that remain from this period.[72]

Instead Forman wrote, in the scattered notes available, of gardening, real estate, his continuing skirmishes with his old enemy the College of Physicians, and of women with whom he had sexual relations. After the birth of his children, Forman became more concerned with his house and with other real estate. Since no casebooks survive from this period, we cannot know who his patients were or whether the emphasis in his practice changed from medicine to astrology. Rowse states that one-third of Forman's practice was astrological but neglects to mention the basis for or dates of his estimate.[73] My calendaring of consultations recorded in two of the yearly casebooks, 1597 and 1601, indicates that less than 15% of Forman's practice was for nonmedical astrological consultations (see chapter 3). The balance may have shifted in the last decade of Forman's life, but I suspect that it was instead the notoriety he achieved in the Turner trial that solidified Forman's reputation as an astrologer.

Forman's continued friendship with Richard Napier, the pious country divine, suggests that his life and practice had not become publicly unsavory. In fact, references to the interaction between Napier and the Forman family increase around 1608 and 1609. In Forman's abbreviated 1607 diary there is a note for May 12: "Sandie [his nickname for Napier] came"; and again on May 19: "Warran brought a pi from Mr. Sandi."[74] Napier's papers show additional communication and visits:

> Feb. 6 1608 Mr. Forman sick sudenly.
> Feb. 19 8 a.m. 1609 I came to Tisbury. Mr. F was gone to London. Quest [astrological cast] whether he would com to dyn. He came after 12 a little. Mrs. Forman came down. We dined not until 10:30 for Clement was sick of an ague.
> Feb. 23, 1609 I did inquire of Mr. Forman going from his howse when we should meete. . . . I went thither to his house Weddnesday following.
> March 1, 1609 I went to Lambeth from London The second tym to Mr. F.[75]

Surely, Napier would not have visited with the Formans so frequently and so comfortably had Forman's public reputation blackened during these years.

A number of manuscripts that Forman either composed or copied date from this last period; many of them are alchemical or astrological. Forman seemed intent on getting on paper as much of his accumulated knowledge and practice as possible; perhaps he had more leisure than in earlier days.

Despite his Cambridge license, the College of Physicians was unwilling to leave Forman alone. Several notes from the last five years of Forman's life refer to summons from the College. In June 1611, less than three months before his death, Forman cast a figure to know "Whether I shall haue the better this term of the docters or noe. And whether they will procead any farder againste me or noe."[76] Whatever the College's decision, it troubled Forman little after this; he died on September 8, 1611, while rowing across the Thames.

His death, like his life, had its narrative appeal. William Lilly, a seventeenth-century astrologer, gave a rousing account of Forman's last days in his own autobiography. As Lilly told the story, which he claimed to have heard from Forman's wife whom he knew well, Mrs. Forman asked her husband on the Sunday before his death which of them would die first. This was a common question in Forman's astrological practice: who would die first, the husband or the wife? Forman replied that he would die first (not a big surprise considering the thirty-one year difference in their ages). But when Mrs. Forman pressed further, Forman announced that he would die on the following Thursday.

> *Munday* came, all was well. *Tuesday* came, he was not sick. *Wednesday* came and still he was well; with which his impertinent Wife did much twit him in the Teeth. *Thursday* came, and Dinner was ended, he very well, he went down to the Water-side, and took a pair of Oars to go to some Buildings he was in hand with in Puddle-dock; being in the middle of the *Thames* he presently fell down, only saying, *an Impost, an Impost* [abscess], and so died.[77]

Lilly did not explain, of course, who brought news of Forman's self-diagnosis to land from the middle of the river. It was, after all, Lilly's concern to recount and promote astrological marvels, no matter how implausible their details.

Someone cared enough about Forman and his work to prepare, or have prepared, a digest of Forman's writings for young Clement titled "Doctor Forman's booke reserved for the use of Clement his sonne. September 1611."[78] Neither the hand that wrote the heading nor the beautifully even hand that penned the text belonged to Forman, but the materials copied are from his own manuscripts, a collection of useful remedies, simple astrological explanations, and a list of herbs and their uses. Perhaps Napier had the manuscript prepared at the time of Forman's death in order that Clement, then five, might have a remembrance of his father and his work.[79] Notes and letters among Napier's papers of the 1620s indicate that he continued contact with the Forman family.[80]

Forman had foreseen the moment when his writings alone might speak for him. In 1603, at the end of a long poem, "Of Antichrist," he wrote:

> And thoughe I Forman am no priste
> Thus did I write of antichriste
> And of Christes coming to Judgmente
> That youe mighte knowe my wholle entent
> That when my head is laid full lowe
> My writinge may youe all then showe.[81]

However, Forman's two bulwarks against destruction by time, Clement his son and his manuscript books, were quickly forgotten, swallowed up in the flood of rumor and innuendo that surrounded the Overbury murder.

All Forman's attempts to rebuild his family's wealth and reputation were shattered by events that occurred after his death. Simon Forman, doctor of physic and astrology, became Oracle Forman and Devil Forman, known chiefly by the representation he received in the texts of others.

☞ Self-Fashioning

A compelling feature of Forman's record of his life is how deliberately his texts constructed it, especially once Forman settled in London and had the time and perspective to look back and rework his past. As Forman revised and interpreted his own history, he demonstrated his awareness of the power of words to create and shape. He knew how to take rhetorical advantage of past actions. During the great plague of 1592–93, for example, Forman stayed in London among his patients when most other medical practitioners abandoned the city. In part, Forman remained because, having himself con- tracted the plague and been sick for many weeks in the early months of this epidemic, he believed, correctly, that he was unlikely to contract it again. His choice to remain in the city, in both this and the following plague, was thus a fairly safe one. In later writings, however, Forman frequently referred to this decision as an act of self-sacrifice. He used it to define his commitment to his profession and to contrast his own dedication with the selfishness of other doctors and, later, of those neighbors who boarded up his house in 1606 in fear that it contained a plague-stricken maid.

Forman's sense of deprivation, born both from his family's failure to possess the lands he believed they deserved and from his own failure to find support for his educational aspirations, led him to create a self from whatever materials were available. In late sixteenth-century England, having a recognizable identity required a suitable family background. Since Forman did not have one, he created it. He explored genealogies and coats of arms in search of the perfect family to claim. How politically aware his choices were is suggested by his switch to a Scottish line—"Willam Forsan errelle of Millom castle"—once the Stuarts came to the throne.

Forman's aspiration was not to achieve something unique or to change his society; instead he wanted to become as much like successful men as possible, to find a higher place than he was born to within the existing order. Delany finds Forman part of a pattern of early autobiographers:

> The move to London was an especially significant one, and we find that more than half of the secular autobiographers . . . took this step. . . . However, vertical mobility seems to have been an even more effective excitant of the

self-awareness requisite for autobiography. . . . A more adventurous group of autobiographers . . . entered vocations with scope for opportunists, such as soldiering, astrology, international trade, or upper-class parasitism.[82]

Forman desired, and partially achieved, such vertical mobility, which Greenblatt associates with Renaissance self-fashioning.[83]

Despite his considerable intelligence, Forman acted rather like a sponge, soaking up information, valuable and worthless alike, filtering it, and expelling it into his notebooks rearranged and reshaped. He did this with his own life and with most of the other subjects he wrote about. Forman's warrant for all that he did was his belief in God's support. Although his concern was always for his public persona and almost never for moral or ethical issues, Forman believed that he was especially gifted by God with high intelligence and occult powers. Thus he needed to submit to no earthly authority. His God-given abilities put him outside most human jurisdiction, he reasoned, and should have been enough to win him a place within the society whose rules he frequently ignored. In his careful account of his youth, Forman repeatedly stressed his academic intelligence, his hunger for books and, at Oxford, his contempt for the wealthy playboys whom he served. Mentally and ethically he felt himself superior to more privileged members of his culture; therefore he deserved as much, or more, than they.

Carried to extremes, perhaps, Forman's sense of being set apart may have led both to loneliness and to a degree of paranoia. He mentions no close adult friends except for Richard Napier, and though he and his wife carried out social engagements during the last decade of his life, his chief contacts outside his professional life seem to have been with relatives, a few female sexual partners, and servants.[84] Over and over he expresses fear of being cheated, robbed, jailed, fined, gulled, or even murdered.

Poverty and lack of significant family prevented Forman from achieving status in conventional ways. For a man with Forman's interests and ambition, convention dictated an Oxford or Cambridge B.A. followed by a medical degree from a university on the continent, a degree later incorporated at one of the English universities. Forman cut his own route, setting up as a medical and astrological practitioner outside the system, claiming God-given powers as his justification, and fighting off challenge after challenge from the medical establishment he would have been delighted to join.[85]

Forman's enemy was a social structure that was closed against him. In his eyes its most obvious embodiment was the College of Physicians, the "doctors." Many of Forman's autobiographical comments, inspired by his anger against these "enemies," were defensive remarks designed to answer overt or imagined charges against him. He battled the doctors in court; he made notes about their shortcomings and failures; he vaunted his own cures; he challenged the methods of establishment doctors, extolling astrological diagnosis over "pisspot" diagnosis. At the same time, he fought in a more practical way by acquiring a great number of patients and a good deal of wealth.[86] How anxious he was to emulate those physicians he curses, however, is obvious in his description of his newly ordered clothes—as much as possible like the velvet worn by members of the College—and by his obvious joy over his Cambridge license. He could have regarded the license as a convenience, a way to avoid further trouble with the College. But he carefully preserved his parchment from Cambridge among his papers (figure 3)[87] and referred to himself from 1603 on by his new title. This is as close as he ever came to social acceptance.

Forman was always alert for the crack in the door that might allow him entrance to the establishment. This continued hope—evident in his dreams of socially interacting with royalty and his hope of becoming the queen's physician—led him to watch the world with unusual care, to read and observe and write down anything he might usefully incorporate in his own self-construction. His well-known plot summaries of contemporary plays, for example, make clear that Forman viewed plays not as art or history or even as narratives, but rather as a series of exemplary lessons from which he might profit. "Remember," he wrote over and over in these inaccurate digests of plots:

> Remember . . . howe Jack Straw, by his overmoch boldnes, not beinge pollitick nor suspecting anythinge, was soddenly . . . stabbed by Walworth. . . .
> Therfore, in such a case or the like, never admit any party without a bar betwen, for a man cannot be to wise, nor kepe him selfe to safe.[88]

Writing of *The Winter's Tale*, Forman was concerned primarily with the rogue Autolycus and not at all with the great reawakening and reconciliation scene at the play's end. "Beware of trustinge feined beggars or fawninge fellowes" was Forman's closing comment about the romance.[89] This selective appropriation from dramatic plots is an excellent example of the selectivity with which most of Forman's observations were made, a selectivity that must be remembered as we examine areas of early modern experience that Forman's papers address.

His constant defensiveness and his attempts to create for himself a profile that would allow him a place in the power structure cost Forman

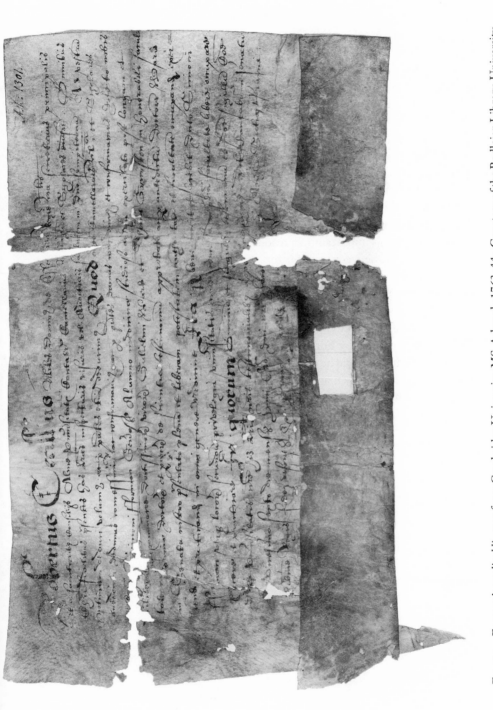

FIGURE 3: Forman's medical license from Cambridge University. MS. Ashmole 1763: 44r. Courtesy of the Bodleian Library, University of Oxford.

dearly. Unlike MacDonald's characterization of Forman's "chaotic moods and exuberant immorality," my own sense of Forman is of a humorless, anxious man trying desperately to become something he was not. There are moments of great satisfaction in Forman's records, to be sure, but these usually occur only at the end of long periods of struggle and anxiety. There is something of the chameleon in Forman's self-portraits. Like the masker whom he images in the epigraph to this chapter, Forman shifted frequently "to diuers shapes and formes / and at the last forgetes the first." Thanks to his curiosity and his drive to learn as much as possible, Forman's records offer insight into corners of Elizabethan London usually shaded from view. But while Forman's papers illuminate one area of his life or society, they create shadows in another.[90]

Moreover, the self-consciousness with which Forman set about revising his own image is important to a reading of his papers. He clearly understood the difference between writing for an audience (perhaps an audience far in the future) and writing for himself; a comparison of the autobiography and the diary provides a clear example. His literary style may have been naive—even inept—but his ability to select or repress particular details was highly developed. Observing Elizabethan culture and society from the perspective offered by Forman's manuscripts, the reader should remember that all Forman saw and heard was filtered through a consciously selective lens that magnified his own achievements and minimized anything and anyone who failed to interest him.

Medical Theories: A Physician Evolves

ALTHOUGH FORMAN'S INTERESTS in medicine and magic remained intertwined from the earliest references during his first long imprisonment until his dying day, for purposes of this study I will try to tease them apart. During Forman's life, it was the study and practice of astrological medicine[1] that brought him legal and social trouble; posthumously, it was his association with magic and "necromancy" that branded him as evil or, alternatively, as a mendacious quack. The medical side of his activity was more public—his practice paid the bills and eventually made him financially comfortable—than his magical activity. Forman treated both necromancy and alchemy as avocations, to be studied and experimented with primarily for his own satisfaction, though occasionally for profit in the service of others. Astrology, on the other hand, was central to every activity in which he engaged, most particularly to his medical and prognostic practice.

Maintaining this admittedly artificial and tenuous separation between his medicine and his magic, I will begin by looking at Forman's study and practice of astrological medicine, turning later to the more overtly occult side of his life. Forman's approach to medicine changed and evolved during the thirty years of his practice, the result partly of his growing experience and partly of the changing demands of his patients. Like most medical practitioners of the period, Forman operated within what C. D. O'Malley has characterized as "a framework of Galenic medicine"; also like them, he elaborated his theory "beyond the established borders, reinterpreted the facts, and here and there deliberately opposed specific and hitherto accepted classical views."[2] The differences between the most highly educated licensed physicians and uneducated empirics were not so much differences of therapeutic approach as differences in sophistication and education. Harold J. Cook explains:

> The physicians were marked off from all other practitioners by their learn-
> ing, or apparent learning, certified by their M.D.'s. But that was the sole
> distinguishing mark of the physician, his only clear claim to medical supe-
> riority. . . . [The physicians] were neither guaranteed . . . success nor so far
> elevated above other practitioners to be exempt from their competition.[3]

Forman approached medicine in the context of Galenic humoral theory, the need to keep the body in balance.[4] Within this basic framework, however, he added or adapted particular therapies, prompted either by his own empirical experience with patients or by new medical texts, including some by Paracelsus, which he procured for his personal library.

To understand these changes, we must turn to the narrative about Forman's medical development that emerges from his papers. The earliest evidence of Forman's interest in medicine is a medical manuscript in the library of King's College, Cambridge, which is inscribed on the flyleaf "Simon Formann" and dated February 2, 1574. He apparently acquired the manuscript while a student at Oxford and continued to annotate it for many years; the last dated entry is May 13, 1600. The manuscript demonstrates both changes in Forman's approach to particular medical problems and his seriousness about the study of his chosen profession.

The original manuscript contains two Latin texts: one, a "compendium of medicinal simples arranged alphabetically by name of disease, possibly written by the Franciscan William Holm around 1415,"[5] and the other, lectures on medical practice composed around 1450 by an Oxford scholar who identified himself "ego Johannes Cokkis." At some point during Forman's ownership of the manuscript, he interleaved it with blank paper folios on which he made copious notes. Mary Edmond's careful work with the manuscript has revealed that a large percentage of the interleaved notes were transcribed, with some editing and a few personal interjections, from a vernacular medical book, *The Breviary of Helthe*, first published in 1547 by Andrew Boorde.[6]

What Forman, in fact, created for himself was a dual English and Latin text, treatments of the same subjects by different authorities. The task of annotating the original manuscript by adding much of Boorde's text was onerous and not merely mechanical, for the terminology used in the two texts was frequently different, and Forman had to search through Boorde for appropriate information to match Cokkis's entries. To further complicate the task, Boorde's text had a double alphabet, the first in the main text, and a second entitled "The Extravagants," which included entries omitted from the first alphabet.

Thus, when Forman wished to annotate Cokkis's entry for "Emoroyde" he turned to Boorde's "H" section to find "Hoemoerhoidea"; similarly, Cokkis's "saliva" is annotated with Boorde's entry for "sputum." For an entry "formica," spelled the same in both Cokkis and Boorde and defined by Boorde as "a little wheall growing out of the skin," Forman not only copied Boorde's definition from *The Breviary of Helthe* but turned as well to "The Extravagantes" where he found additional remedies for the complaint.[7]

The manuscript served as a textbook for Forman (Edmond correctly called it his vade mecum) and contains evidence that he was assembling information and gradually teaching himself his craft. There are even indications that he tried out various remedies on himself. One entry entitled "Of suppuration or matering in the breste/ / /1575" dealt with coughs and congestion and recommended a liquid preparation, three or four drops of which were to be put in the nose with a quill or from a filbert shell. The eyes were to be closed and the nostrils pinched:

> within a quarter of an howar yssueth a grete deall of slimmy moystnes, out
> of thy mouth, wherof a man maye marvayll. I have once sin [seen] 6 oz. cum
> out of a mans mouth at on tim and out of my own mouth 4 oz. of this wise
> cam out, wher I thought I should haue had non at all.[8]

Forman was cautiously experimenting with advice he found in written texts, testing what his "authorities" recommended. This early self-experimentation apparently continued throughout his life. In 1610, writing about "Renewing of age" [rejuvenation], Forman reports that eating an eviscerated, boiled snake will make "a man yong and lustie again." After giving details about how this was effective in the case of Sir Michael Sandes's fool, he continues: "and my selfe did boill 2 snakes in my strong water when I distilled it. and after I drank of that water and yt made me loke fresh and toke away all my gray hairs when I was 56 yers old & many toke me not to be aboue 40 or 42."[9]

His interleaved notes in the Cokkis manuscript, many of which deal with basic humoral theory, demonstrate the autodidactic nature of his task. He noted what humors reigned at what season and how the four humors were vented from the head: blood from the nostrils, choler from the ears, phlegm from the mouth, and melancholy from the eyes. He drew a male figure and labeled the primary veins for bloodletting.[10] He listed signs that sick persons were about to die: if the white of the eye appeared when a sick person was asleep it indicated death. And he quoted from authorities like Galen and the *Isagogue* of Johannitius.

Because most of the material Forman added to the Cokkis manuscript is undated, his exact route to becoming a practicing physician cannot be charted. However, some indications of his progress are present. In this manuscript he elaborately described the most basic medical procedures: taking a pulse, tying off a vein, and letting blood. The minute detail that he provided for the bloodletting of John Waller suggests that this may have been his first (or first successful) phlebotomy.

> 1579—Monday am. beinge the 19 January, begining my year at Christmas, at what time that I did let blod John Waller of Wickham in the right arme on the vaine of the lyuer for certaine diseases. and I toke from him of blod in quantitie of a pint or more. The Order that I vsed in letting him blod. Item. I bound his arem aboue the Elbo with a garter hard. Then did I chafe his arme a good with my hand to make the blood com downe/ & then the vaine did appeare full. Soe I tooke my pen knife bye the tope. And quickly pekt [pecked] hym into the vaine and made a little houlle/ out of the which the blod did yssue. And when he had bled sufficient, I losed the garter & the blod did slowe. Then did I put a lyttle piece bumbast vpon the woond. And staid hit down hard with my fingare. And then did laye lyttle clouts that wer wet in water theron and on that a clout wrapt hard in a bad [band?] together and bound hit fast & swathed hit. And then upt his arme with a towell [made a sling] & so gaue him his charge not to strain him self & sugar is verie good to put on it to staye the blood & wet clouts vpon.[11]

Forman was attempting the procedures that he had been studying. His patient was probably not very sick, and the bleeding "for certaine diseases" may have been merely prophylactic. Waller's bloodletting occurred just a few months before Forman's lengthy jail stay, after which he reported medical cures and a few patient names in his diary. The only dates earlier than the phlebotomy in the King's College manuscript are those in an entry on urine and his self-experiment with congestion, neither of which offers evidence that Forman was yet practicing on real patients.

Other dates appear in Forman's annotations in this manuscript. A lengthy entry on scrofula or the King's evil,[12] drawn from Forman's experience, includes a more detailed explanation of the spectacular case mentioned in the 1580 diary entry as the "fellow of Chillhampton"[13] who had eighty-six worms in his neck:

I had on in cuer for this dizeas 1580 that had 24 holes from on ear bur to another, and a very gret hole in his throte that I could put in my finger aboute his kekhorne [Adam's apple?] and out of that hole in a morninge at on dressinge with an instrumente I toke out 86 worms lyke maggots and as big as maggots such as be in meate or in chease, and his wonds did stinck mightily. and the flesh loked exceeding red & full of blod and they [the holes] were round as yf a man had thruste in his finger in diuers places in his necke & throte. Another tyme I cured on whose father and mother did both die of that dizeas and this fellowe was som 18 yers old or 20 at moste and yt was swollen outwardly moch in his throte and in his cheakes and Jawes soe that he could not open his mouth to take in any licoure or to eate & yt was hard in his throte and not broken [no holes, as in the previous case] and all over his throte & necke outwardly. I opened his mouth with a kaie [key] and did put drinke in his mouth to kepe him a lyve and so I cured him by godes holp.[14]

After more examples, Forman gave his cure:

hote poure into the holes or wondes the oille magistrall spoken of in this bock 129. And yf ther be moch blod in the holes or fleshe, then scarrifie the flesh with an incision knife well and often and make yt bled well that the ranck blod and corruption may com forth and yt will healle the sonner.[15]

At the end of the discussion, Forman concluded, "I haue cured many of them of all sortes I thanke god, and thervpon I Simon Forman haue writen this chapter 1596. novem 28 pm deo gras [thank God] because I had then a gentlewomane in cuer for the same which was as big as halfe an eg." By 1596, Forman had the confidence and experience to supplement the entries of Cokkis and Boorde with his own, adding yet another layer of text to this manuscript.

Two other features of the King's College manuscript suggest that it is a text of the young Forman. First, there are a number of entries on the care of wounds—wounds received in battle, wounds made by arrows, chest wounds. All of these are to be treated with "olevm magisterale," the same oil Forman used to treat scrofula. The manuscript includes directions for making this oil.[16]

Wounds would ordinarily have been treated by a surgeon, not a physician. Since Forman was formally trained in neither profession, he could—and at first did—lay equal claim to both. In 1581, he "dwelte practising phisick & surgery."[17] Occasional notes from the 1580s refer to dressing arms or legs, and the procedures that Forman used in the scrofula case were those of a surgeon. In fact, his first summons to court in London was to appear before the barber surgeons who "calld me in question for my practice" in 1593.[18] In 1592, he had written, "[I] was called in question among the surgeons but I had many cuers in surgery but little phisick."[19]

Forman's few detailed accounts of dressing wounds are dated between 1584 and 1593. One patient had an ulcerated leg, injured by a kick from a horse. With the painstaking detail typical of his pre-London case histories, Forman described his procedure:

> perceiving the vlcer to loke blacke and to be full of grose blod, I with a fine knife did firste scarifi the flesh & lipes ther of and made yt to bled welle, and wipte yt dry. then did I put therin a lyttle precipitate, and a plaster theron, and yt lay 24 howers or better. The second tyme I washed yt with sharpe viniger, and I did caste into yt of my pouder Imperialle and laid a plaster theron for 48 howars. Then did I washe yt againe, and laid a simple plaster or too ther one. and yt was hole without farder a doe.[20]

Though Forman does not record surgical procedures after 1593, he apparently continued to be interested in surgery. In one of his late alphabetical compendia, he included under "Somnes or Slepe" a method "to make on slepe whille he is cut," clearly for use in surgical procedures. The directions follow:

> Take iii sponfulls of the galle of a swine and of the Joice of hemloke. of wine viniger iii sponfulls. mix them all and put yt in a glasse. & when youe will cut or burn a man, put on sponfulle therof in a gallon of alle or wine. Yf youe will make it strong put 2 sponfulls therof to a gallon of wine or alle. and giue the partie on sponfulle ther of to drincke and he will slepe soundly, whill youe cut him or burne him with an yron for any disease. To make him to a wake—Rub the palmes of his handes and soulles of his feet with wine viniger.[21]

Both Siraisi and Sawyer, writing about different centuries and different countries, conclude that keeping surgical and medical procedures separate, while certainly done in theory, was virtually impossible in practice.[22] Perhaps a practice that was chiefly medical was somewhat easier for Forman to manage in London where surgeons were plentiful than for Napier, whose rural patients had fewer options when they needed surgical intervention.[23] Whatever the reason, after the 1592 and 1593 contretemps with the surgeons, all Forman's trouble came from the College of Physicians, and the casebooks from the late 1590s make almost no mention of wound dressing, bone setting, or surgical procedures. Forman seems to have begun with a practice that was both medical and surgical (whatever patients he could attract), and as he became more successful he gradually turned almost exclusively to medicine, the more prestigious and lucrative of the two.

The second indication of Forman's inexperience as he worked with the King's College manuscript is that he seemed to accept all forms of diagnosis and therapy with almost equal enthusiasm. The long passage on urine and its analysis in this manuscript is surprising since in manuscripts of the 1590s and 1600s, Forman vehemently denounced diagnosis by uroscopy. Edmond and Rowse have very different opinions about Forman's use of certain medical techniques because they have studied different Forman manuscripts (Rowse apparently did not examine the King's College text). Edmond comments:

> Dr. Rowse says Forman did not set much store by urinology—but it seems that in this he was simply echoing Boorde; Dr. Rowse also asserts that Forman "thought pulse-taking overdone," but one of the most carefully copied passages from Boorde relates to this subject, and Forman has added a note of his own describing how to take a pulse "with thy .4. fingars," and what to look out for.[24]

Edmond worked with the manuscript of the young Forman who accepted medical authority. Rowse worked with Forman's later manuscripts where he was skeptical of authority and vaunted his own experience. A whimsical expression of Forman's later attitude toward uroscopy, in a manuscript Rowse *did* consult, appears in a poem dated 1594:

Yf thou wilt a good phisision be
And of a sicknes judge a right
Marke wel what I do write to the
For vrine is of lyttle might
But studie wel Astronomie
The course of heauens arighte to knowe
For they will tell thee certainlye
That which the vrine will not showe
For urin is a strumpet bad
In which smalle truth is seldom had
And will the lokers in deceyue
And of the truth them clean bereaue.[25]

In the same manuscript Forman noted that he had been called to treat Lady Hawkins (second wife of John Hawkins, the great English admiral) on March 28, 1595. She received him well and invited him to stay for supper. However, "they gaue me nothing but fair wordes for my pains, but suspected me to be a magitian &c because I told her dizeas and sawe not her water."[26] Without urine inspection, a consultation was not considered legitimate, so Forman had patients bring or send their water, but continued to pay scant attention to it, occasionally even becoming histrionic about "pisspot" diagnosis.[27]

Early in his medical career, the period reflected by his dogged work on the King's College manuscript, Forman was willing to accept almost any "authority." After a decade or more of practice, he formed strong views on what worked and what did not work and was thus prepared to be scornful of pulse taking and urine inspection as primary diagnostic methods. His willingness in the early days to try all available techniques is reflected in the following comment in the King's manuscript:

> And this ought every phisition to doe to search and knowe of what complextion the patient is & whence the deses cometh & what medison is convenient for it. for yf the phisition doth it not & minister to him the contrary, to his complextion and nature, then doth he misorder the patient & is gilty of his pain, or haply deth. for this cause ought no physition to trust to his sciens nor wysdom only, but aske & enquier of the patient, or other all circomstances to what fashion ye diseas doth enclyne, he ought also to veu & se ye vrin, soe to the pulse & behould the patients phisiognimi, then may ye phisition minister to the patien the moe boldly.[28]

A physician's guilt for his patient's suffering if the practitioner failed to use the appropriate therapy is here couched in general terms, as though Forman were warning himself as well as other physicians. In later manuscripts Forman sometimes blamed other physicians for mistreatment of patients, but never again did he suggest that he, too, might make mistakes. With Forman's experience came enormous self-confidence about his medical expertise, an attitude vividly expressed in a late manuscript, an alphabet book that included both alchemical and medical lore. After a note about the elixir, Forman burst out, "yet for my selfe I never lerned anythinge of any man—neither could I say that ever I was beholding to any man for art but to on simple fellowe. but to god and nature for I was borne to find out arte & to make yt perfecte."[29] His early work on Cokkis's manuscript, however, belied his claim of self-sufficiency. Forman actually learned from many sources, but once he had learned, he refashioned his medical history, as he had done his personal history, claiming that he was "born" to be a great physician.

One final note about the King's College manuscript provides a bridge into Forman's more mature medical writings. He copied a long note on the suppression of menstruation, not from Boorde, but from Philip Barrough's *The Method of Physick*.[30] The subject greatly interested Forman; he wrote a short essay on it in 1596. The inclusion of material from Barrough, whose work was published first in 1583 and reprinted in 1590, makes clear that Forman continued to update the manuscript he had acquired in 1574 with material from newly published medical works. Nor did he neglect older texts. Partway through the note on menstruation, he abandoned Barrough to include what "Albertus & Scoto . . . sai"[31] about amenorrhea. When Forman "confessed" in the mid-1590s before the examiners of the College of Physicians that he had never "read any Author in Physick but one *Cockis*," whom Goodall goes on to describe as "an obscure English writer and of no reputation,"[32] Forman greatly understated his learning, showing the same bravado that led him to claim he was self-taught. He had sampled in part or whole a good many medical writers, classical and contemporary, writing both in the vernacular and in Latin, even on the evidence of the King's College manuscript, and his later papers demonstrate continued reading and ownership of medical texts.

☞ Forman's Medical Writings

Forman composed and copied numerous medical texts over a period of some thirty years. It is not always easy to distinguish the copied or translated from the original, although Forman often gave the source of copied texts as he did for the "7 bockes of Aurelius Theophrastus parracelsis." At the end of book three of his copy of that work, Forman wrote the date 1590 and signed his name as "scriptor sed non factor," and at the end of the seventh book he added another date, February 8, 1591, "out of the coppi I had of Willm Falowfild which he wrote 1590. July 3."[33]

Forman occasionally indicated that he was making a compendium of authoritative materials, as in a manuscript in which he headed the text "The Grounds of Physiq and Chirurgerie gathered out of the sayinges of dyuers ancient philosophers" and then listed fifty-five "authors alleaged in this boocke." His sources include Aristotle, Avicenna, *Birth of Mankinde* (Thomas Raynalde), Cornelius Agrippa, Genesis, Galen, Hippocrates, Paul the Apostle, Ptolemy, Pythagoras, and "Incertq. author," better known to modern readers as "anonymous." Forman also showed uncharacteristic humility in the opening pages of this work, writing an apology for any mistakes that the text contained:

[I] haue gathered togither out of diuers Lerned mens bockes certaine Infallible groundes and ph[ilosoph]ical reasons which I haue placed in the beginninge of this my Bocke and som of them I haue expounded. And those and the reste I put to the vewe of all: and leaue to the sounde censure of the Lerned and discreate Readers, and yf Any faulte be found herin, I yeld the Reforminge therof to those that be more lerned then my selfe and haue better discretion to Iudge of the profundity of arte.[34]

The unusually humble tone of this passage may have been an attempt to strike the conventional authorial pose of modesty before his intended readers. Whatever Forman's intention, the work remained in manuscript, available only to those readers to whom Forman's manuscripts circulated.

In addition to copying the work of other medical writers, Forman wrote medical essays based on his own experience. Among the most noteworthy is "Matrix [the uterus] and the pain thereof," a gynecological essay on amenorrhea written in 1596–97. Forman had a particular interest in gynecology. The large number of women who came to consult him about gynecological disorders suggests that he had acquired a reputation for dealing effectively with women's physical problems. Medical historians have raised questions about how directly male physicians of the period examined and carried out gynecological procedures on female patients. Forman's papers give somewhat contradictory information about this issue.

In 1592, early in his London practice when he was equally involved with both surgery and medicine, Forman reported treating "Sisselli Burton a Jentlewoman hauing the swelling & precipitation of the matrix that yt was soe sore & big that she could scant goe and worse syte." Prolapsed uterus was fairly common among women who had borne several children. Sometimes the uterus would actually protrude from the vagina (as was apparently the case here) causing terrible pain and risking serious infection. Forman first gave his patient a medicinal drink to prepare for a purge. The following day he purged her and "after twise purging, I with my owne handes did minister a cataplasme [a poultice] to her lower parte of her belly the [Sun]day morn following at 30 p[ast] 9 am & she was holle within 3 daies after but I was but badly paid for doing yt."[35]

This is the only explicit reference I have found among Forman's papers to performing such a procedure himself. "With my own hands" may be his way of emphasizing how unusual it was, or it may simply reflect the circumstantial detail we have noted in other early cases before the procedure described became routine to Forman. In a German illustration of 1559, a male surgeon is shown reducing a prolapse manually, as Forman apparently did.[36]

In his treatise on the matrix, however, it is clear that the therapies to encourage regular menstrual flow were to be performed by a midwife. In marginal notes added to the carefully written essay, Forman mentioned Mrs. Chackham, who suffered from an impostumation [abscess]. Mrs. Whip, a midwife, had put her hand into Chackham's matrix and found it clear with no superfluous humors and reported this to Forman.[37] At another point in the marginal notes, Forman again cited Mrs. Whip as responsible for providing a mollifying lotion used to bathe the sufferer.[38] The remedies that Forman recommended for amenorrhea were warm baths, lotions, pessaries, and infusions spouted into the matrix through the vulva.

The difficulty involved in this last procedure required that some skilled person perform it. A woman suffering from stopped menses must wait, Forman wrote, until the time when she felt that her menstrual flow should begin. Then she should lie down with her hips higher than her head, having drunk an "abortive" powder to force down the matrix and to open it. The practitioner then took over:

> Then take your sirindge and fill yt with your iniection, and firste put in your finger at the vulua vp into the matrix and feelle wher the mouth of the matrix be open and doe lie righte or noe for somtimes the matrix is soe weke of yt selfe that yt will not kepe open, and then youe muste haue a nother manner of Instrument that is brod at the outward end and smaller towardes the Inner end and that Instrument muste be of som 5 or 6 ynches longe somwhat bending or croked vpwardes. That muste youe put firste into the matrix and let yt staie therin to kepe open the matrix, and allwaies put your syringe with your iniection into that and thorowe that put yt vp into the matrix spouting it hard vp.[39]

The standard treatment for stopped menses was copious bloodletting in the foot.[40] Forman knew this remedy, for he explained it briefly to Napier in a letter and told him to check further "in the lyttle wryten bock I gaue youe."[41] In his own essay, Forman, who was generally conservative about bloodletting, developed an alternative treatment, working with medicines applied both internally and externally. The long passage on menstruation copied in the King's College manuscript discussed how the menstrual blood could become stopped: causes ranged from too much exercise or perturbation of the mind, to some physical blockage of the mouth of the matrix. But in that manuscript passage, Forman offered no remedy or course of treatment. In the "Matrix" essay, however, Forman paid scant attention to the causes of the condition and instead focused on a course of treatment.

The willingness Forman demonstrated in this essay to find out what he did not know and to incorporate his new information into his work was unusual in medical texts of the period and suggests that Forman, in some ways, very much deserved the label of "empiric." Speaking of the womb's power to purge or empty itself, Forman wrote that

> I haue made diligente Inquisition amonge graue matrons and midwifes and others to knowe whether the matrix doth exempte himself of any thinge that yt receyueth of man more then once in a month or noe. And they haue told me yea, that yt doth exempte yt selfe of any thing that yt receyveth of man and dothe vomite out the nature and sperme of man receiued by diuers coitions, and will alsoe belche out wind (like as the stomacke doth) at the vulua.[42]

Forman incorporated this information into his organizational scheme: the matrix empties itself naturally three ways. It empties (1) twice a day with the tide (accounting for the new information about voiding sperm received during coitus); (2) with the monthly menses; and (3) partially with childbirth, but here not all the "cells" of the matrix are opened so that complete purging does not occur.[43] How broadly (or indeed whether) Forman canvassed for an answer to his question cannot be gleaned from the text; what is clear, however, is that he acknowledged the use of sources other than classical or contemporary medical texts.

Forman appended to the body of the main essay on amenorrhea several remedies and lists of drugs that could be used, apparently interchangeably, to make the various lotions, plasters, and infusions he recommended. The first list consisted of "such thinges as cause abortion and cause the matrix to vomite out and discharge her selfe of all dead birthes and fals conceptions or of any other putrified matter."[44] The list includes marigolds, mandrake, cinnamon, saffron, and tacamahac. This last substance was an aromatic resin imported from the New World. Its first *Oxford English Dictionary (OED)* citation appears in 1577, suggesting that Forman was up-to-date in his knowledge of the pharmacopoeia. The other lists gave substances good to make injections to soften the matrix and loosen the humors (white wine, radish root, goat and cow milk); ingredients for plasters that strengthen and comfort the matrix (cloves, sumac, and again cinnamon and tacamahac); and ingredients for baths and lotions to prepare the patient for an upcoming course of treatment (carrots, cucumbers, the ever-present cinnamon, and certain oily animal products like oesyphus [a crude form of lanolin obtained by boiling sheep's wool]). All these lists are extensive; the one for baths contains 140 ingredients. Forman must have offered a great number of options in the hope that at least a few would be available. One of the actual recipes he gave for a glister [enema], for example, called for only eight ingredients, all to be boiled together in cow's milk. In another essay, after having listed a dozen ingredients for a plaster, Forman added "or the moste of them yt youe can get."[45]

These lists remind us that even when a Londoner knew of a remedy for her illness, its availability must often have been a problem. Forman worries about such things as whether to buy rhubarb (an ingredient for his concoctions), and in a letter to Napier, for whom he sometimes purchased drugs in London, Forman alluded to the difficulty of procuring the desired supplies:

> I have boughte and [sent] youe such parcells of drugs as ar specified in the note herin enclosed. but we haue no hipericon water [made from St. Johnswort] nor can get none/ Endiue water is to be had but we knowe not howe to send yt for spilling. In the mean tyme make your infusions with white wine. for every dram of rubarbe put 1 oz. of whit wine, or Rennishe wine. I haue sent you but halfe a pound of hamech because yt is somwhat old. . . . I rc. [received] xx s[hillings] of your brother towardes the payment of your druges. the which doe com to 26 s[hillings] 9 p[ence]. . . . you shall rec[eive] thes thinges of warren the carryar my boy deliuered them vnto him pacte in a candell basket.[46]

Because he was not licensed by the College of Physicians, Forman had no legitimate access to an apothecary to prepare his drugs. Instead, he grew or purchased his own raw materials and then mixed, boiled, distilled, or stewed as appropriate. In his autobiography he mentioned that his master Commins sold among many other wares "all poticary druges and grocery, wherby the said Simon learned the knowledge of all wares and druges."[47] Notes throughout the manuscripts refer to operations such as distilling aqua vita (alcohol). Though he clearly was usurping territory that the apothecaries considered their own, I have found only one reference to Forman "falling out" with an apothecary.[48] Indeed, several come as patients to consult him, and on at least one occasion he and an apothecary seem to have cooperated in a patient's therapy: for a sixty-seven year old male patient, April 20, 1597, "the apoticari gaue him a purge & I gaue him a vomit."[49] This apothecary, or any apothecary who cooperated with Forman, might have got in trouble with the London College of Physicians. Goodall records at least one case in which a search of an accused apothecary's shop by the College censors turned up "divers bills found upon the file written by Empiricks and ignorant Mountebanks." The apothecary's medicines were subsequently destroyed.[50] Given this situation, Forman had very little choice but to mix and prepare his own medicines.

As we have seen, Forman's essay on the matrix deals with a very specific problem, focusing on treatment rather than on causes. In his essays on plague, he proceeded quite differently. For one thing, he could write about plague from the perspective of a one-time sufferer. In 1592, the terrible epidemic of plague that swept London, causing the wealthy to flee the city and closing the theaters, struck Forman himself.

> The 21 dai [of June] I begane to complaine in my groin and the 6 of July I toke my bed and had the plague in both my groines & som moneth after I had the red tokens on my feet as brod as halfe pence. & yt was 21 wickes before I was well again. The which did hinder me moch. I was let blod the 10 of August.[51]

In 1593, he composed an essay on the plague, and in 1607, four years after another plague had swept England, Forman wrote a second, quite different plague treatise, although it incorporated material from the 1593 piece. His first plague essay treated the disease as astrologically determined and as God's punishment of mankind for its sins. Dividing the disease into natural plagues, plagues of the devil, and plagues of God, Forman dispensed rather quickly but concretely with his first category. Natural plagues were created by the revolution of the heavens and the influence of the stars. Distinguishing between the plague of Saturn [black plague] and that of Mars [red plague], Forman graphically described the sores each produced, the symptoms felt by the sufferer, and therapies for each. In his discussion of plague sores, Forman was at his observant best, offering a detailed disease description:

> The sores [of Mars] ar felte vnder the eare, vnder the arme pites and in the flancke or groine, as those of Saturn ar, but thes sores or carbuncles of mars ar more fierie hote, and red, and doe rise vp and com out quicklie in respecte to those of Saturne for those of Saturne when they rise they begine depe in the fleshe and ar longe before they com to any perfection, and doe seldom breke, and they locke wan & palle in respecte of those of [Mars] & therfore I haue lancte them & cut them often tymes. And ther is in them lyttle matter, but moch water, and they ar verie sore and gryvouse. But those of mars doe

rise in the superficies of the fleshe and com to a hed quickly. and will breake often tymes of them selues, or with a lyttle healpe, but let men take heed to stand by in dressinge of those of mars because they ar daungerouse and verie infectiue.[52]

Forman went on to give vivid descriptions of the marks, "God's tokens," which appeared on the sufferer's skin, drawing pictures of the black spots in his text.

In the second section of the 1593 essay, Forman wrote of the plague of the devil who either obtained permission from God (as in the Biblical example of Job) or was compelled by God to plague mankind. Here Forman offered no physical descriptions of plague, but instead recited Biblical examples of the devil's interference with mankind (Eve, Job, Ahab, the temptation of Christ).

The third and by far the longest section dealt with the plagues of God, brought on by "the sinne and wickednes" of the people. From early examples of God's punishment of misbehaving Biblical figures (among others, Adam, Cain, Saul, and David) and of the children of Israel generally, Forman slid into a critique of contemporary social conditions in England, emphasizing particularly the conditions of the poor:

> Soe yt is likwise to be fered that god in thend will heare the daily complaintes of the fatherles and wyddowes, of the pore and those oppressed with the burdeins of Egipte (which suffer moste Intollerable Iniuries with dailie complayninge, without redres, and will by the hand of som good moises [Moses] deliuer them, from oppressions from wronges and robberyes scourying [scouring] England and her Inhabitance). . . . The wrongfull oppression of mani is soe great and griuous at this dai in England whose outcries and greuouse grones . . . ar ascended vp before the Lord . . . who is the Iuste reuendger of all wronge oppression & robberie done at this dai in England.[53]

Forman continued his highly rhetorical attack, reproaching landlords who raised their rents; courtiers who bought and sold offices; lechers and gluttons; hypocritical women who looked and acted virtuous when really they painted, wore ridiculous clothes, and enticed men; vagrants who pretended to be wounded soldiers; physicians who fled when plague came; clergy who never set foot in their benefices; and merchants who had false balances and weights. He offered this massive indictment of English citizens to explain why God had sent plague. God had been merciful for years, allowing "longe peace and quietnes," though from time to time He had warned England:

by the great blassinge stars that haue byn seen within this 20 yeares. And the greate & generalle Earthquake that was in the year 1576. And alsoe by the great famin in the yers 1584 and 1585. And then by the comminge of the navie of the Spaniyeardes 1588. And nowe lately by this great and generalle plague. Thes I say ar the messengers and forwarners of the wrath of god.[54]

Worse would come unless people reformed, and Forman enumerated each profession's misbehavior. Thus, what began as a fairly objective medical description of the symptoms of plague ended as a rhetorical denunciation of the behavior of the English social body which had brought the plague upon itself.[55]

By 1607, Forman was more concerned with the physical disease, although his second essay on plague had its own moments of rhetorical exhortation. Like its predecessor, it began by describing kinds of plague, but then moved to such practical subjects as places to avoid during plague, techniques to get the disease out of clothes and bedding, ways to recognize plague sores, and advice on their treatment. Though he continued to distinguish between the plague of Saturn and what he called in 1607 the "pestilence" of Mars, in the later essay Forman was more detailed and confident about his therapy:

> But yf youe carry those sores longe before youe purge, then they will lie in the deapth of the flesh long and not goe a way. then the beste wai is to clap a hote cup on them and drawe them vp full. and then lance them with a knife, and let them Rone as Longe as they wille and to healle them vp, Take the joice of smallach [wild parsley] honny and the yolke of an egge and flower and beat them well together and therof make a salue, and with yt salue healle the sores. the botch and alsoe the blaine, with that on salue. for with this haue I cured many.[56]

Keep plague patients warm, he urged. Do not eat onions because they draw plague. Do not allow someone with black plague to be bled because it weakens the patient too much. In this essay, Forman was very explicit about his purpose: he wrote to "teatch men to heall them selues."[57] They needed to be able to heal themselves so they would not be victimized by unscrupulous or untrained surgeons. "I marvaille," Forman wrote, "what . . . such like chirurgions will say in the dai of dome, when he shall giue an accounte of his profession before god when on shall com in halte another blind, another with on leg . . . another whom they laid for the pox, that never had yt and soe died thorowe their folly."[58]

Though Forman attacked surgeons in this outburst, only a few leaves later, as he recounted how his maid Cissely was thought to be sick of plague and brought home and boarded up in Forman's house on the day his son Clement was born, he seemed to join ranks, rhetorically, with both surgeons and physicians:

> Therfore youe phisitians, chirurgians & appoticaries, take heed be wise and take example by me. Let not money buy youe to visit those that haue the plague. Leste youe take the plague into youre houses. And soe haue youre dores shote vp, and be lefte distitute and be somoch abused as I was. . . . I haue staid 2 great plagues among them to giue councell & doe good to them and to many a thousand others. But god pardon me for it. I shall not be in haste to doe yt againe, to seke my owne woe.[59]

Despite this vow to turn his back on plague victims because of his treatment by his neighbors, Forman continued for another seventy leaves to offer practical advice about dealing with plague.

The difference in emphasis in these two works on plague was probably the result of Forman's increased experience with the disease. In 1593, fresh from his own bout with plague, Forman had little practical advice to offer, although his disease descriptions were vivid. Instead he focused on placing blame on those whose behavior had provoked God. With two plagues behind him in 1607, Forman had both the experience and the perspective to write a more practical work. In fact, the 1592–93 plague had provided a turning point in Forman's career. By remaining in London to treat plague victims, he had made his reputation as a medical practitioner.[60] After 1593, he never again complained of poverty; he no longer mentioned performing surgery; and from that date on, he was the object of intense scrutiny by the College of Physicians. Their unrelenting attention suggested that he was offering their members stiff competition. By 1607, he had undoubtedly earned a reputation as one having extensive experience in the treatment of plague; his second plague essay reveals that he certainly considered himself something of an expert.

Forman's medical writings have a fairly predictable pattern. First, he defined his subject, usually breaking it into parts. Next, he described the symptoms that could be observed (such as the plague sores), and then he outlined his therapy. He always illustrated his therapeutic recommendations with illustrations drawn from his own practice or from other practitioners' cases that he claimed to have observed. He typically concluded with lists of herbs or other substances that could be used to make the medicines he had recommended.

This organization reappears in his essay on melancholy, a long section of a larger work on the four humors[61] written by Forman, "secundum Experientiam suum 1600 pro seculo futuro." Forman had been treating melancholy for at least a decade when he composed this essay. He had treated his most famous melancholiac in 1597 (though neither physician nor patient would have known this) when Robert Burton, then only twenty and mysteriously absent from his studies at Oxford, became his patient. Burton came five times between June and October; each time symptoms of melancholy were present—heaviness, wind in the bowels and belly (flatulence), unlustiness (lack of sexual desire), stopping of the veins (lethargy)—and Forman prescribed purges and pills, predicting after the first visit "he carieth death vpon him."[62] Although Forman's patient cannot be identified with absolute certainty as the Oxford scholar who wrote *The Anatomy of Melancholy*, a note from an unpublished Forman manuscript that Burton copied into his own astrological notebook lends credence to a link between these two men who both believed strongly in the stars' influence on the health and temperaments of individuals.[63]

In his essay on melancholy, Forman first distinguished several kinds of melancholy, each dependent on what other humor the melancholy mixed with. Then he offered general remedies and advice. One should always treat melancholy as quickly as possible, he urged, since it is easier to cure when caught early. The sufferer should be surrounded with pastimes and mirth, eat fat and sweet meats, and get lots of sleep. Sweating and carnal copulation must be avoided; poultry, herbs, and young white wine are to be consumed, and the patient should walk in the open air in pleasant places, climb high hills, and sail on the water.

Next, Forman distinguished the locations of melancholy in the body: if it is in the brain, don't bleed the patient; if in the whole body, bleed; and if caused by stopped menses or stopped hemorrhoids, get the bleeding started again. (Like some other physicians in the period, Forman saw hemorrhoids as a male equivalent to the menses, a natural purgation of blood, and he almost never attempted to heal them.) Other ways of classifying melancholy followed: he distinguished among desperate (suicidal) melancholy, mania, and frenzy. In each of the subsections Forman gave examples of patients he had treated; uncharacteristically, however, he crossed out the last name of each sufferer, one bit of evidence that he expected the manuscript to be read by others. Thus we hear of suicidal Elizabeth B[raddage] of London, a handsome woman of 40 years. "She wold sai she could not beliue she should be well or that she should be saued. her faith was weke. and she could read well and when she did read in the bible or any good bocke she was the more trobled."[64] Later, Forman noted that he had helped this woman twice, over a four-year interval.

Patients suffering from mania were solitary, rarely spoke, and sometimes seemed bereft of sense. Forman had seen the traditional dark room treatment:

> I haue knowen of thes, that haue bine kept darke & fastinge and bin whipte every dai, or twise a daie, to bringe them to their wites again but all wold not helpe doe what they could they wold alwaies haue a spes [species] of yt for ever after and som of them becom very foolles after and lose their wites and sences vtterly afterward, and sit lyke dum godes.[65]

Forman offered little hope of cure—"ther is noe striving with them: but to chein them in a light rome, & not in a dark rome, and let them never be without company. but haue singing dauncing pipinge & mirth"[66]—but at least his regimen was more humane than the dark room and whipping.

Forman's description of "frensy" was vivid and could have served as a subtext for an actor playing Ophelia's mad scene:

> They will singe and rime, and never leave talkinge and playing with their handes and whirring them round aboute on a nother, & will laughe moch, and will out of the bed naked and about the house and clymb vp to the top of the house yf they get loose . . . & somtimes they ar ferfull and will cry and wepe sodainly & call & kepe moch adoe, & saie com kisse me to the standersby . . . and tell 20 baudy talles. and they eat lyttle and slepe not at all. I haue seene many both men and women in this disease.[67]

The descriptions of the various forms of madness are perhaps the most compelling part of this essay. It concludes with a discussion of the anatomy of the brain and with Forman's customary long lists of remedies "to digest and mollifie the melancholy humors," to purge melancholy in general and, finally, to purge melancholy from specific areas of the body.

Forman's recommendations in this essay to modify traditional treatment—to change the dark room to a light and to substitute singing and dancing for whipping—demonstrate once more his willingness to try new remedies when old ones proved ineffective. He has altered his early reliance on "authority," as demonstrated in the King's College manuscript, to some measure of therapeutic independence.

An example of the occasional, fortuitous appropriateness of some of Forman's therapy appears in a brief essay on scurvy, in one of his alphabetical medical books. Following his usual format, he offered a vivid description of the symptoms:

> Those that haue the scurvy they haue moch pain in their heade Jawes gums and teath and their gums doe swelle and the flesh groweth over the teath and is verie sore and full of waterish blod, so that they can hardly eate or joine their teath together. Their breathe doth stincke, they haue moch pain in their stomacke, and pricking in their head like neadelles and sornes with all of the flesh, and swellinge in their Jointes and legges. and somtime they haue knobes in the flesh, and somtyme all theire bodie from the Crowne of the head to the soulle of the foote doth swelle with pain and akinge. And most Commonly they that haue or ar like to haue this disease ar spotted in the body and members with blacke spotes as though they had bine pinched by on.

Forman believed this disease was caused by bad diet, which he defined as "eating and drinkinge of grosse and evill meates and drinkes." As usual, he listed many remedies, concluding the essay on this final note: "The sirupe or Joice of lemons 4 sponfulls drunck at a time 2 a daie is excellent good against the scurvie."[68] Though it would be a century or more before scurvy was identified as caused by a lack of antiscorbutics, Forman had an efficacious remedy.[69]

Lest I seem to be overestimating Forman as a practitioner ahead of his time, let me hasten to add that his fortuitous medical successes were offset by remedies that modern medicine would find horrific and appalling. Among the most dramatic of these are some located in a manuscript that primarily contains material by Napier, but the following notes are in Forman's hand:

> Yf a mans eye be blod shote and fear a cataracte to growe. let him put a hed louse into his eye and he will eat yt out and healle yt . . .
> Yf one be trobled with a dropsie, let him drinke every dai his owne water [urine] and walke on it till he swete. Yf he wash also his belly and stomake therwith yt is the better . . .
> Yf a woman have a flux of her course [excessive menstrual flow], let her take 3 or 4 drops of the purest blod ther of in bear or win & drink yt and yt stoppeth them.[70]

Other suggestions in this group of remedies include the powder of a man's burnt turd to cure the fistula; stroking a swollen throat with the hand of a fresh corpse; and for one suffering from colic, "loke wher he may find a dog lyinge on the ground, and let him kike vp the dog and pisse on the place wher the dog lay, and he shalbe cured of the collick."[71]

Forman offered no evidence that he had actually tried these particular remedies on his patients, unlike many of the therapies recommended in the essays discussed earlier in this chapter. Nearly as futile, however, would have been the remedy for a prolapsed uterus mentioned in passing in Forman's essay on the matrix. A woman suffering this condition should wear sweet-smelling things around her neck—musk, amber, civet—and burn stinking things and take the fume of them below, between her legs. The matrix would be repulsed by the stink and attracted by the sweet smell and draw itself back up into the woman's body.[72] Forman cannot be given credit for this remedy, though he apparently used it, since manipulating the uterus by inundating it with foul or sweet smells was a standard therapy both for prolapses and for the mother (where the foul smell was worn at the neck to keep down the rising womb).[73] Perhaps the most that can be said of Forman's medical theory was that it was eclectic; he was willing to try—at least once—almost anything. Primarily a Galenist, he also incorporated bits of Paracelsian theory and, increasingly, Paracelsian drug therapy into his practice. Forman's interest in sulphur, for example, indicates the influence of Paracelsian medicine on his pharmacopoeia. Paracelsus stressed the use of both sulphur and mercury in his drug therapy. Though I have found no record of Forman prescribing mercury (he used it in his alchemy, however), in the later years of his practice minerals began to appear more frequently in his prescriptions, mixing with the herbal remedies that had been his mainstays in the 1580s and early 1590s.

In the ancient debate about whether humoral imbalance could best be cured by treatment with similar or with contrary remedies,[74] Forman took the middle ground, willing to try either method:

The nature of the Cause of the diseas being considered of. whether yt be hote or cold dri or moiste or so forth. Youe most eyther cuer him per simile or per contrarium. Yf it be per simile, then yt moste be thus. Yf the disease doe com of a hote cause, youe most cuer him by a medison that is hoter then the diseas by halfe a degre or a degre & not aboue.

Yf it be per contrarium, then yf the disease be of a hote cause then youe moste cuer him by a cold medison, that is more colder by on degre then the cause of the diseas is hote.[75]

Forman also refused to treat some patients. A necessary skill for a successful physician of the period, as Siraisi has noted, was to recognize an incurable condition and refuse to treat it.[76] In his book of astrological medicine, Forman declared that certain patients were marked by God:

> And ther for I wishe thee and every on to whose handes this my bocke shall com. that thou be wise in Iudgmente. and when thou findeste the punishments to com from God then I charge thee meddle not with the partie nor giue them any medison for yt wilbe in vaine but put them of as I haue often don. But for this cause saith the Lord I will deliuer them over into the handes of the phision. That is into the handes of Evill phisisions to tormente them and make them spend their mony in vaine & consume them selues. till he hath sufficiently punished them. Therfore I wold not haue thee on of those evill phisisions or tormenters but haue a good faith and pure and vndefiled conscience.[77]

In practice, Forman recorded rejections of patients only rarely. In the entire 1597 casebook, he mentioned two cases that he definitely turned away. One man, Anthony Slaughter, 35, whose urine was brought by his brother's wife without his consent, had been ill for sixteen months and "is not to be remadied . . . meddle not with him, he will die therof 122 dais hence." The second was apparently not dying, but uncooperative as a patient. John Heiborn would not be ruled and was "enemie to him self . . . his sickness is imposed on him by the angell of God for he was cause therof him self & yt seems he is leauing some ill physician that hath had him long in hand & let him be his own physician. Yt is not good to meddle with him."[78]

In two other cases Forman was wary but did not refuse outright: Margery Webster, 48, had a variety of symptoms including "moch pain in left arm." "Finger of god," Forman remarked, "let her com a month hence." Rowland Griffeth, 24, was very sick. "Meddle not hastily with him for he is unfortunate & his diseas is not at worste . . . in perill of death."[79] Contrary to Siraisi's findings among the practitioners she studied, imminent death did not seem to be Forman's main reason for refusing a patient. For many he predicted, and then recorded, swift death. Rather, Forman rejected patients who he thought were marked for punishment by God or were intractable.

The question of who holds the power and control in the physician/patient relationship, still of concern in modern medical practice, was important to Forman. He made clear in his accounts that a good relationship was one in which the medical practitioner was in control, and the patient submissive. The following accounts of a bad patient and a good patient demonstrate his feeling:

> 1593. 19 Jan. am 26 p 8 I began firste to dresse Emanuel Vandrath for the grife vnder his chine. . . . First I did anointe the place with my ointment mad of verveine [verbena] & the herbs of the plannetes gathered in their howars and boiled in cates grece, to mollifie and resolue the hard fleshe. And because he wold not be long in healinge he made me lai a corosiue to yt to eat awai the fleshe and I did soe. . . . This man was healed vp quite the 17 of Aprill, but I had moch a doe first with him, and was lik to giue him over twise before I had mad him wholle he was soe vmpatient, and wold not suffer me to work my will. . . .
>
> 1593 the 25 of March am at 6 first dressed Madline Ioice for her hed & disease. I did first dresse this childes hed her armes and body, and she was holle within 12 daies, & sound, I did first purge collor & flem, and did plaster all her sores & washe them, with the Ioice of lemens, allom and viniger. & did purge her euery dai almost & then did let her blod she was but 6 yers old, she was ruled and I had althinges to my owne mind.[80]

The child, despite what must have been terrible stinging from lemon, alum, and vinegar on open sores, allowed Forman to "rule" her completely and, after a horrific regimen of purges and bloodletting, healed in twelve days. The more obstreperous adult male, who expected a voice in his own cure, apparently impeded Forman and, despite his impatience, healed only after three months. Whatever the differences in their original complaints, Forman clearly saw the difference in their cures as a matter of their willingness to allow him to do his own will.

Forman almost gave up on Vandrath, the difficult patient discussed in the preceding quotation, in midtreatment. Sometimes, too, he changed his mind after first refusing to treat a patient. The following lengthy account tells of a patient he had avoided for several years.

> I did once put of a gentlewoman of good fame and credit so almost 3 yeares, from time to time as often as she send for me, and she could never get me to come to her to see her, because . . . I Judged the finger of god to be on her, and that her punishment was supernaturalle, I meane, that god did punish her with that grievous disease for some offence she had done, for she was 9 yeares in this disease, and she had spent much mony on the phisitions and Surgeons in that time, and could find neither ease nor remedie, And she sent to me from time to time as is aforesayde. And I would tell them that came my Judgement, but I would neither come at her, or give, nor prescribe

her any thinge to take, and in 3 yeares she never wente out of her doores, for she was not able.

Having established the difficulty of the case and his own unwillingness to take the woman as a patient, Forman goes on to narrate her cure.

> And yet in the end it was my lotte to cure this woman throwe the grace of god, for one a time almost 3 yeares after she did first send unto me, I cominge to the citie where she dwelte to a neighbour of hers, beinge at breakfast she was unknowne brought thither betweene two in a chaire and set downe betweene the doore and me in the parlore, that I could not get out, but I must speake to her where I would or no, and she weepte bitterly and in her conference said. O Lord! what have I done against thee that thou hast punished me so, and I acorsed above other women that thou wilt not suffer this man to deale with me, and in all this not to come unto me, and now Lord that I am brought here unto him, that he will not speake unto me. But I was so much pressed with her grievious lamentations and so were all the table that with many intreats, I promised her, if god would, to cure her conditionally, which I thanke god, in 19 weeks after, I did performe fullie, and this was in the yeare of our Lord god, 1579. and the Gentlewoman is living yet to this hower well and lustie thankes be to god.[81]

As an exemplary account of how to deal with the "finger of god" case, Forman's narrative is noteworthy for its acknowledgement of the pressure put on the practitioner by a face-to-face encounter with a suffering patient (it was easier to say "no" to the patient's messengers) and by the onlookers "all at table." The entire incident was, as were most of Forman's extended patient narratives, framed within God's will—the finger of God was on the case initially; the patient prayed to God rather than directly begging Forman for help; and "if god would," Forman undertook the cure. Missing from the narrative, however, is any information about the woman's disease or the therapy Forman used to bring about a cure in nineteen weeks. In contrast to the practical essays examined earlier in this chapter, this account is of a "miracle cure" represented almost entirely as God's will. Calling the account even further into question is its date, 1579, which puts the cure at the very beginning of Forman's practice, a decade before he moved to London. How would he have gained a reputation as a powerful healer, especially if the patient had begun to send to him as early as 1576? Forman himself acknowledged the need for documentation of this story; he commented that "the Gentlewoman is living yet to this hower well," but avoided giving her name, the city where she lived, or the name of the "neighbour" with whom he was staying when she so dramatically appeared before him. In its narrative trajectory, this account more resembles Biblical accounts of Christ's healing those carried before him than it does most of Forman's own cases.[82] How such "medical" narratives[83] are to be weighed beside the detailed but far less narrative casebook materials is another part of the Forman puzzle, reminiscent of the similar disjunction between Forman's diary entries and his narrative autobiography. Forman's medical story is as difficult as his life story to bring into clear focus.

For Forman, the good physician was born as well as made:

> To make a perfecte phisision ther belongeth 3 thinges Speculation practice and a quick conceight, inclination, for excepte a man haue a quick conceighte by naturall inclination to Ioine his speculation and practice together, well he may be accounted a phisision, but yt will be a good whill before he be a good phisision for the quick conceight by natural inclination doth Ioine the speculatiue parte and practick to gether to make a good phisision even as the Soulle doth vnite the body and the sprite to gether to make a man.[84]

Forman was confident he had the three necessary elements: study (speculation), experience (practice), and inborn talent (natural inclination) to be the perfect physician. The opinion of his contemporaries on that subject was apparently divided. Nevertheless, the details Forman recorded, the variety of the authorities he consulted, the care with which he created his vade mecum, and later, the attention he lavished on his own medical essays attest to the seriousness with which he approached his medical practice. His thousands of patients—some on the brink of death—also took him seriously.

❦ T H R E E ❦

Forman's London Practice

THOUGH FORMAN'S STUDY and practice of medicine stretched over a thirty-year period, detailed information about his daily medical routine is available only for a few years at the turn of the century. His tenure in London and, later, in Lambeth—a location close enough to his old London residence that patients from the London practice could continue to consult him after he moved—spanned two decades. Although Forman presumably kept careful casebook records for most of this period, only five casebooks covering the period from March 1596 to November 1601 survive.[1]

Forman's London practice really began to grow about 1593, after he remained in London during the great outbreak of plague. The casebooks that survive begin about three years later and continue through the period of his adulterous affair, his marriage, and his meeting with Richard Napier, ending about the time of his move to Lambeth. Therefore, most of the information about his day-to-day practice comes from the middle period of Forman's professional life. For those few years, it is possible to count patients, read lists of symptoms and diagnoses, and even to find a few records of Forman's fees.

Forman's detailed casebooks were unusual records for a medical practitioner of the period to keep. In his history of the Royal College of Physicians, George Clark traced detailed record-keeping by English physicians to the influence of the eminent French Paracelsian, Theodore Mayerne, who arrived in England about the time of Forman's death, became physician to King James I, and argued that record-keeping was part of a physician's duty.[2] In the decades preceding Mayerne, however, members of the College of Physicians had regarded Forman's record-keeping with suspicion. In

Goodall's summary of one of the College's periodic encounters with Forman, the questions Forman asked patients for his casebook records received the College's censure:

> After this, Mr. *Pelham*, a Physician, and another person acquainted the College with the notorious cheats that *Forman* made use of for deceiving the people, as his enquiring the Patient's name and place of habitation; then erecting a figure; after that, passing a judgment of the disease and event thereof; then prescribing remedies *&c.* Upon which the Censors order'd a Citation for his appearing before them; But he refusing to appear unless he might have their promise for his safe return, he was prosecuted at Law according to direction of Councell, *de mala praxi & illicta* [for bad and illicit practice].[3]

The patient's name, place of residence, and the astrological figure were information that Forman recorded in his case notes, along with the patient's symptoms and, sometimes, his own diagnosis and recommended therapy.

In his book of instruction on astrological physic, Forman explained in detail his patient records:

> I do not aske the Name for Nought.... Some come as well to try a mans cunning or skill sometyme as well as for the sicke, some bring a mans urin & say it is a maydes or womans, some bring a maydes Urin or womans and say it is a mans, some will not sticke to bring a beasts water and say it is a mans or womans, some cast out the Vrin they are send withall and pisse in it them selfes, and sometymes they breack the glasse by the way, and buy a new & take the horse pisse, or maris pisse or their owne, and so like deceiptfull knaves and cogging [cheating] mates, they come to the physicion, thinking to deceiue the physician.

In order to forestall such deceptions and to help himself keep track of patients, Forman records certain details.

> Therefore ... I ask the name of the party, his Christian name and his Surname, for by the name I know partly whether it be a mans or womans water.... And again I aske the Name for an other cause also and that is because I will not forgett, what euerie once diseaze is and what counsel I haue giuen them, for hauing their names on my booke, I can allways tell thereby, what theyr diseases be, and what counsel I haue giuen them.

In what follows, Forman describes as succinctly as anywhere in his papers the ebb and flow of his working life:

For suppose theire comes to me this day 3. 4. 5. or 6. 10 or 20, and to morrow as many more, & the next day as manie more, some of them will take physic/ and some will take none, some tymes again, the tyme doth not serue to giue physick, and sometymes men, or the parties haue no tyme to take it, because of necessarie businesse and they come again 2. 3. or 4 dayes or a weeke after. If I had not their names, and disease on my booke, how could I tell what their diseases were, or what to do vnto them, or what to giue them.[4]

In addition to explaining Forman's rationale for keeping detailed case records, these lines provide a good general overview of his busy practice: he saw multiple patients in a day; some were rushed, and some were not ready for the powerful doses that Forman was likely to prescribe. What might seem like another example of Forman's paranoia—worry that people would try to trick him with the urine samples they brought—was actually a common concern among physicians. Arnald of Villanova addressed this very issue, discussing attempts to test the practitioner by presenting a false account, or no account, of the urine's source. He suggested that the best defense against such trickery was for the practitioner to ask leading questions of the bearer of the urine flask,[5] a strategy that Forman also employed.

Forman's practical use of his casebook records appears in his instructions to the reader of his treatise, apparently assumed to be an astrological practitioner like Forman, to look back to the first figure ever cast for the patient and to see if the signifiers (important astrological markers) of the cause of the disease had altered since the patient's first visit. If they had changed, the practitioner could see "briffeste and sureste whether the sicke doth mend wax worse or continue in his sicknes."[6]

Forman passed on his record-keeping methods to Napier, whose casebooks are set up in a fashion almost identical to Forman's. Aside from Napier's, no comparable collection of early English medical records exists. One anonymous North Riding physician left his financial records for 1609, including a one- or two-word identification of each patient's complaint, written on the flyleaf of a book of anatomy.[7] The North Riding record dramatizes the difference between the practice of Forman and that of this country practitioner. In 1609, the North Riding physician saw a total of 188 patients; Forman in 1597 held 1757 consultations. The North Riding physician thanked God that he had earned 17 pounds, 6 shillings for his year's work; Forman was happy in 1594 that he had earned 50 pounds in one quarter of the year. Forman's yearly total of patients is in line with the approximately two thousand consultations held by Richard Napier in 1610 and again in 1620.[8]

☞ Nonmedical Astrology

Forman's records reveal the demographics of his practice as well as the sorts of problems for which astrologers were consulted. Although references to Forman by his contemporaries stressed his nonmedical—as opposed to his medical—astrological practice (Jonson, we remember, called him "Oracle Forman" and accused him of vending love potions), his casebooks show that nonmedical questions accounted for a rather small percentage of his workload (table 1). Of the 1819 consultations that are recorded in the 1597 casebook, 203 (11 percent) were for nonmedical advice. Of the 1183 cases in the 1601 casebook, 160 (14 percent) were nonmedical. Also surprising, perhaps, given Forman's reputation as a consultant to lovesick women, only 11 percent of his female clients in 1597 and 12 percent in 1601 came for nonmedical advice. In the same years, 13 percent (1597) and 19 percent (1601) of his male visitors came for nonmedical reasons.[9]

Nonmedical clients often made repeated visits. In 1597, for example, one Mr. Broughton hoped to be appointed dean of Chester Cathedral and came frequently to ask, among other questions, about the chances of his rivals for the position. Forman eventually treated him as something of a nuisance and simply scrawled "Mr. Broughton for Chester" on the page without bothering to sketch out a full astrological chart. Broughton alone accounted for 5 percent of the nonmedical questions asked in 1597.[10] Repeat clients also accounted for many astrological consultations in 1601. Mr. Thomas Digby consulted Forman thirty times in the eleven months covered by the casebook. Only one of these consultations was medical, an April visit when Forman recorded that Digby's stomach swelled, his gall began to overflow, and he had too much melancholy and choler. The remaining twenty-nine visits (17 percent of the year's nonmedical total) were the result of Digby's many anxieties. At the beginning of March, he wanted to know what would

Table 1: Patients who consulted Forman for astrological and medical advice as recorded in his casebooks for 1587 and 1601

	Number of Consultations	Medical	Nonmedical	
			Men	Women
1597 casebook	1819	1616	90	113
1601 casebook	1183	1023	88	72
TOTAL	3002	2639	178	185

happen to him that month; a few days later he returned to know if "there was any evil or good towards him and whether he shall get money"; soon he was back asking whether John Worborn would betray him or not; a few days later he repeated the question about Worborn. He visited twice more in March, but Forman did not record what he asked. Most of his remaining visits during the year were unexplained, though once Forman noted that Digby was "turba" [upset], and once he seemed to be inquiring whether to rent a particular house and whether he had a chance to be appointed Master of the Robes.[11] Such persistent clients swelled the statistical proportion of Forman's nonmedical consultations in ways that do not really reflect the proportion of individual astrological clients as compared with medical clients.

Another repeat client from 1601 had quite different concerns. Eusebius Andrews, twenty-four, first appeared in February to ask whether he should marry Lettice Rodish. Forman advised him against it, since "she is entangled."[12] Two days later Eusebius returned to ask whether to marry Dorothy Walsingham; this time Forman told him to go see her on March 7 at 9:00.[13] Apparently the visit was not successful, for in late March Eusebius returned twice to ask about marrying Mary Curson.[14] Forman did not record his advice on these occasions. In early April, however, Andrews returned once more to ask about Mary. On the preceding Sunday night at 8:00, he had spoken to her and kissed her. Now he wanted Forman to tell him what would happen next in their relationship.[15] By May, however, Andrews's problems had changed from the romantic to the physical. He consulted Forman for pain in the head, great heaviness, and dryness.[16] Next, his brother appeared to ask about Eusebius's health; he had a fever, was idle-headed [delirious], and could not sleep.[17] These symptoms are, of course, classic to those suffering from love melancholy[18]; however, they could also have been symptoms of serious illness. Forman predicted that Andrews would have a "hard fit" [a crisis in his illness] before twenty days had passed. With that, Eusebius Andrews disappeared from the casebook. Whether he died or recovered and found a wife, Forman did not report.

Many of Forman's male clients came to ask about travel, especially about going to sea. Sir William Monson, about to undertake a voyage in the spring of 1597, came to ask Forman about the success of the venture. His wife and members of his crew also inquired about this voyage.[19] John Flowers came in 1597 and again in 1601 to ask about sea voyages. In January of 1601, in response to his query about the fate of a ship called the *Speedwell*, Forman warned him that its voyage would face great danger. Flowers apparently looked for another ship, because he returned later in the month to ask whether he should send his goods to Bordeaux in the *Marigold*. Forman assured him that this ship would be safe.[20]

Ships continued to be a source of anxiety once they were on the high seas. A number of questions from both men and women concerned the safety of a particular ship, when it would come to port, or the safety of a particular crewman. In the summer of 1601, for example, Ellen Flowers came several times to inquire about her husband (probably John who had questioned Forman so carefully in January) who was on a sea voyage, wanting to know when he would return home.[21]

Astrological clients consulted Forman for a variety of other purposes. One client brings to mind Abel Drugger, who visited Subtle and Face in Jonson's *The Alchemist* to ask about the best location for his new apothecary shop. In February 1597, Mr. Woodward consulted Forman "to knowe which waie from his master is best for him to dwell to thriue." Newly released from his apprenticeship, Woodward was ready to set up in the same business as his former master. But where? "Goe este," Forman advised, "or south est or flat west to the stron [strand]."[22] A couple returned repeatedly for help in finding their lost dog, a bitch with a blue and green velvet collar decorated with bells.[23] Yet another couple consulted Forman several times about a stolen doublet.[24]

Because a client's age was unnecessary in casting a nonmedical horoscope and because no medicine or therapy needed to be prescribed, Forman usually provided less information for nonmedical consultations than for medical ones. Disappointingly, he frequently did not even record his own answer or advice. Of the nonmedical questions in the 1597 casebook about which Forman recorded enough information to make the client's question comprehensible, 16 percent of the men and 40 percent of the women asked about love and marriage. Whether a particular person loved the client or whether the client (like Eusebius) should marry a particular person constituted about 25 percent of all the nonmedical questions Forman's clients asked.

Because of Forman's reputation as a consultant to lovelorn women, I have examined in detail the nonmedical visits by women for the period covered by the 1601 casebook. Of the seventy-two nonmedical visits by women, only fifty-eight include enough information to make the purpose of the visit clear. Eighteen women wished to know whether they should marry particular men. Another nine asked about a particular man without specifically asking about marriage. Did he love her? Was he worth thinking about? were frequent questions.

Eleven wives came to ask about absent husbands. Some may have been at sea, but the case note usually says simply that the husband left on a particular date. Would he return? Or when would he return? Forman told one wife that her husband had been back in town for four days but "coms not at her."[25] One woman asked what would happen to the earl of Essex (then awaiting trial for treason); another wanted to know what had happened in a quarrel between two men. Two women came to ask whether particular individuals would keep their word. Four inquired about the fate of particular ships; two more wanted to know how their lawsuits would fare. Four came for information about stolen goods. In one of these cases, Forman recorded the outcome: the thief had already been captured in bed with two "wentches" and sent to Bridewell Prison.[26] The circumstantial detail that Forman supplied here and elsewhere must have come from sources other than his astrological cast that could provide only a general description of the thief (gender, age, complexion) and the direction in which the stolen goods had been taken. Forman was a careful gatherer of information as he gossiped with his clients and acquaintances, remembering details that might help him respond to subsequent questions.

Other women were interested in their future. One wanted to know whether to take a trip; another whether to buy a house; and a third asked what her dream about an old man portended. Three came for more general information. One of these asked whether there was "any evill don against her for that she prospereth not" and demanded that Forman tell her "why the crowes doe followe her."[27]

Among the female nonmedical clients in 1597 and 1601, none asked for love potions, aphrodisiacs, or anaphrodisiacs—the substances Forman was reported, during the Turner trial for Overbury's murder, to have sold. The final decade of Forman's practice, of course, is represented by few records and might have branched off in new directions. Moreover, Forman might have left such requests unrecorded—although he did record details about his occult practices that would seem to be just as dangerous. As we will see in chapter 5, he made sigils or amulets that, among other functions, could win the wearer the affection of a loved one. The manufacture of these charms was recorded in great detail and with no attempt to disguise their function.

In general, nonmedical astrological consultation was not particularly important to Forman's practice. I have found no record of what Forman charged for such consultations, but it cannot have been a great deal. Clients like Mr. Broughton and Mr. Digby, who returned so frequently, were unlikely to have spent much for each visit. The couple who came six times for help in finding their lost dog were surely not paying large sums. The frequency of visits for rather minor advice suggests that Forman's fees for astrological consultations must have been fairly low.

☞ The Medical Practice
Patient Profiles: Women and Children

The backbone of Forman's practice was medical.[28] He recorded more information about his sick patients than he did about those seeking astrological advice, information which allows us to glimpse the social and demographic range of his practice. For example, he usually recorded the patient's age. In 1597, 132 (9 percent) of his medical consultations were for children under sixteen; in 1601, 110 children's consultations accounted for 11 percent of his medical practice. Sixteen percent (241) of Forman's patients whose ages he recorded in 1597 were fifty or older, and in 1601 again 16 percent (156) were fifty or older. In 1597, 18 percent of the women and 17 percent of the men fell into this age group; in 1601, 23 percent of the men and 15 percent of the women were fifty or over. Because these figures are based on the patients whose ages Forman specified in the casebooks, they exclude both the nonmedical consultations where age is rarely recorded and some medical cases where Forman did not record age (table 2).

Clearly, the large majority of Forman's patients were between sixteen and forty-nine. This pattern differs from what we expect today, when children and the elderly account for the majority of medical visits. The difference in life expectancy, of course, goes a long way toward explaining the relatively small number of elderly patients who consulted Forman. As for children, they surely got sick just as frequently, or more frequently, than they do today. The question of why children form such a small segment of Forman's practice (Napier's casebooks show a similarly small percentage of child patients[29]) is related to other questions about the treatment of children in the period which have puzzled twentieth-century historians. Several scholars have argued that

Table 2: The age and gender of the patients who consulted Forman for medical advice as recorded in his casebooks for 1597 and 1601

| | Medical Consultations for which Age Is Recorded | Age | | | | |
| | | 1–15 | 16–49 | | 50 and Over | |
			Men	Women	Men	Women
1597 casebook	1479	132	449	657	95	146
1601 casebook	954	110	276	412	81	75
Total	2433	242	725	1069	176	221

early modern parents tried not to invest too much emotion (or money) in a child until it reached an age where survival was indeed fairly likely.[30] If they are right, it is easy to understand why parents would not wish to consult a medical practitioner whom they would have to pay. Yet numerous examples of extreme grief over the loss of children survive in the texts of the period, and MacDonald explains that the loss of a child was one of the triggers of both physical and mental illness among Napier's patients.[31]

A more likely explanation for the relative infrequency of medical consultations for sick children is that the favored medical treatments of the period—rectal purging, forced vomiting, and bleeding—were generally not recommended for children. They were simply too harsh.[32] Parents may have felt, quite justifiably, that there was little that physicians could do for a sick child.

The children Forman did see had a wide variety of problems ranging from the standard fever, pain, and vomiting to wasted limbs, skin diseases, and being "fairy-pinched"[33] all over the body. Forman frequently noted whether the child was present during the consultation or whether the parents came to inquire about the child without actually bringing him or her; whether the child was present made a difference in the way Forman calculated his astrological cast. Of 132 consultations for children in 1597, Forman indicated that forty-five (35 percent) were visits by a parent on behalf of a sick child. In thirty-three cases (25 percent) the child was present for the consultation. Comparable figures for the year 1601 show that of 110 cases, in forty (36 percent) the parents came without their sick child (in two instances women came to inquire about their young maidservants), and in twenty-six cases (24 percent) the child was present. For the remaining consultations, Forman failed to note who was present.

The parents did not always expect Forman to help their child. Sometimes they just wanted his prediction of what would happen to it. In a number of the consultations the parents simply asked whether the child would live or die. For example, in January 1597, Forman's first child patient was William Carter, six months old. His mother reported that he was frantic and asked whether he would live or die. Forman noted that he died three days later. Another example was Katherine Waldorn, two years old, whose mother came in March 1597 to ask whether the child would live or die. Forman answered that she would die "10 dais hence" but added in a note that the child died five days after the consultation "and had the mesells [measles]."[34] There is no indication that these parents expected Forman to do anything about their children's illnesses. They simply wanted a prognosis.

Many parents, however, hoped for help for their children. A sample of the children Forman treated in the two years here studied in detail gives some idea of the medical problems that Forman faced and the limited medical help he could give. In June 1597, Forman saw Lence Spensar, thirteen. He recorded that she was much swollen, had pain in her throat, was idle-headed, and had been starved and beaten. He commented, "she will hardly live." His next child patient, three-year-old Joan Smith, had a fever, pains in her belly, and fits. His comment this time was more cheerful: "this child mended and did well deo gratias [thank God]." In October, the mother of William Commin came from the Isle of Dogs to ask about her son, only three months old. It had "great crying," was "griped in the belly & had stomake worms," and shook as if it had the falling evil. Forman said it would live and told her to anoint it (with what substance he does not say) at 7:00 P.M.[35]

In March, 1601, Forman saw John Bigs, six, from Bishopsgate Street. His problem was "a cholorik humor in his nose that eats then [the end] of his nose lyk a worm." Forman offered no more information. In April, another six-year-old boy, William Palmer of Fetter Lane, came to Forman: "Videtur per venificium [it seems by witchcraft] and yt prospereth not nor groweth not . . . cold and chilly in the body & a saltesh humor comes out on yt lik a leprosy. Yt will be worse for 16 days, after that purge it well & lose [loosen] the enchantment." In September, he saw a two-year-old boy, James Campion, who pined away. His legs were consumed; he had a fever and was "sometimes hot, sometimes cold." For him Forman prescribed a drink composed of polypody [a common fern], red rose leaves, violet leaves, ginger, and whey. A final example was one-year-old Charles Kelly, also present for the diagnosis; Forman reported "it is feri [fairy] blasted & pineth away." His hands and feet swelled and looked very black. No therapy was recorded.[36]

In this record of remediless suffering, Forman did not usually distinguish between male and female patients until they reached the age of ten or so. In several of the examples above, Forman used the neuter pronoun "it" to refer to his patient. He apparently did not think of children as gendered until they approached puberty, when the pronoun by which he referred to them became "he" or "she."[37]

Though Forman treated proportionally few children, the range of their symptoms was enormous and the alleviation of suffering which Forman could offer was limited. (I discuss Forman's range of treatment below.) Perhaps his chief function for many of the parents who came to see him was to allay their uncertainty. He made definitive statements: the child would live; would die; would have a crisis in ten days. Of course, he also had certain formulaic responses that avoided the too-definitive; one of his favorites, used repeatedly with both children and adults, was "will die or scape hard." This prediction acknowledged a serious, probably fatal, condition but allowed Forman an out should the patient recover.

Another category of Forman's patients that deserves special comment is women of childbearing age, defined for my purposes as women between the ages of sixteen and forty-nine. While the ratio of males to females was roughly equal among patients under sixteen and over forty-nine, in the group aged sixteen to forty-nine, female patients consistently outnumbered males. In 1597, Forman saw 1106 patients in this age group; 657 (59 percent) were women. In 1601, of 688 patients between sixteen and forty-nine, 412 (60 percent) were women (table 2). The predominance of women is explained by the number who came with complaints or questions related to childbirth or to their reproductive systems. About 12 percent of the women in this age group came to ask whether they were pregnant or were diagnosed by Forman as pregnant during the consultation. Many others reported gynecological problems: some had not menstruated for years or were experiencing extreme menstrual irregularity; others reported what were apparently vaginal infections involving itching, "mattering" [discharging a viscous fluid], and burning. Some reported having been sick since their last childbirth—which might have been as much as five or six years earlier. Over 50 percent of Forman's female patients in both 1597 and 1601 reported some female-specific symptoms, although in a number of these cases it is difficult to determine whether the symptom was a primary or secondary part of the complaint that brought the woman to seek medical help.

By contrast, only 5 percent of Forman's male patients reported male-specific symptoms: swollen genitals, "wasting of nature" [shrinking or atrophy of the penis], genital itch or pimples, or infection of the penis. Robarte Turner, twenty-two, was one such patient. On May 12, 1601, he was described as having "weaknes of natur and acte of generation by reason of overmoch wast of nature and many cold humores in the muscles of the yerd [penis] & back."[38] Forman may have attempted to draw a picture of Turner's problematic genitalia in the margin of his casebook, but it is difficult to determine exactly what his little drawing is intended to represent. Forman recommended purging in this case. For swollen cods [testicles] the treatment was different: "take horsedung with vineger."[39]

Among women from sixteen to forty-nine, the complaints ranged widely. Jone Hil, for example, had delivered a child some six weeks before she consulted Forman and had not been well since that childbirth. Forman noted that she had a noli me tangere [facial ulcer] on her lip and that she was full of corruption. Bridget Starker was seen by Forman on March 20, 1596: "she was deliuered of a child the same dai within 5 howers after, and the after birth remayned behinde. The child died and the woman waxed frantick but cam to her self again after a few days & was lyuing the 3 of Aprill & reasonable well." What Forman's role was in this case is unclear; there is no evidence that he ever assisted at childbirth, so he probably saw this patient just before she delivered and again when complications developed a few days later. Similarly, he reported of Elizabeth Heiborne, thirty-four: "she was with child and brought a bed of a ded conception of some 14 or 16 wick [weeks] & the back of yt was blacke & the fingers rotton."[40]

Forman was occasionally called on to treat an attempted abortion, as with Joan, Mr. Borace's servant: "yt seems she is grauida [pregnant] by her master [Borace] & hath giuen her som ill medison & gon to sombody to bewitch her that she should die & the fetus perisheth."[41] Forman's records show no evidence that he himself helped women rid themselves of unwanted pregnancies. In fact, most of the women who consulted him seemed anxious for pregnancy rather than disturbed by it. Most frequently the women who came were in pain. Their heads ached; stomachs were "stopped" [indigestion]; their menstrual courses had stopped or were irregular. The inclusion of menstrual troubles along with other symptoms makes it difficult to tell in many cases whether patients' problems originated with their reproductive systems or whether they were ill from some other cause of which menstrual irregularity became a symptom.[42] Forman regarded a woman's menstrual history as a vital piece of information. When women come "to know their dyseases," he remarked in one text, "the first and chifeste thinge, a man should loke into in such is firste to knowe howe they haue their menstrualle course."[43] His own emphasis on this part of a woman's medical history may be responsible for some of the emphasis on menstrual disorders in the casebooks.

Patient Symptoms

The cases involving reproductive systems aside, both men and women had similar complaints. The most frequent symptoms included general pain; gravel in the reins [kidney stones]; fever; vomiting; scouring [diarrhea]; costiveness [constipation]; cough; being "stuffed" in the stomach and lungs;

idle-headedness [delirium]; fearfulness; and what Forman termed "taken cold" or "grief" or "thought." Many of these symptoms are fairly straight-forward; we recognize them from our own physical problems.

The casebook records make no distinction between symptoms the patient, or the patient's messenger, described and those Forman deduced from the horoscope he cast for each patient. Some complaints are so specific that they must reflect a particular patient's visible condition: a dead palsey in a man's left arm and leg; urine that was red as blood; buboes [plague abcesses] swollen in a patient's groin; a woman who surfeited [fell ill from eating to excess] from eating raw roast beef; another who vomited a worm a yard long. Other symptoms are formulaic and might have come from an astrological cast.

Elsewhere Forman addressed the issue of receiving too little or inaccurate information from his patients when he explained how to determine astrologically whether a woman "hath her naturalle course or menstrues. . . . because many tyms som of them will dissemble. and again at other tymes the parties them selues be not presente neither can the messanger tell. I thoughte yt alsoe good and necessary to write some what also her of."[44] Forman goes on to explain how to diagnose from the horoscope in such cases. After examining several thousand Forman cases, I conclude that most of the symptoms he recorded were relayed by the patient.[45] But when he had too little information, either because the patient had sent an uncommunicative messenger or because the patient presented few specific symptoms, Forman fell back on the formulaic patterns he determined from the horoscopes.[46]

The problem of understanding what illness or condition the symptoms of Forman's patients indicate is most difficult in the cases where patients may have been mentally ill. The line between physical and mental illness, sometimes difficult to determine in our own period, was undefined in the early modern period. In *Mystical Bedlam*, Michael MacDonald has analyzed cases of mental illness among Richard Napier's patients on the basis of Napier's casebook records. To select the appropriate patients, MacDonald established a list of key terms among the symptoms Napier reported.[47] Forman used most of those terms in his own patient descriptions, including most frequently the following: troubled in mind, melancholy, light-headed, took grief, fearful, frantic, distracted, and grieving. Napier saw a larger percentage of mentally disturbed patients than Forman; indeed, MacDonald has argued convincingly that Napier had a reputation for dealing effectively with such patients and thus was something of a specialist in mental illness. But Forman also reported these symptoms in a large number of his patients, perhaps as many as 50 percent if MacDonald's whole list of identifying terms is applied.

In Forman's cases, however, these terms were frequently part of a list of symptoms, many of which referred to physical conditions. In cases of high fever or serious physical illness, the presence of melancholy or a description of the patient as "fearful" or "idle-headed" did not necessarily indicate mental illness. For example, Richard Kingson, twenty-nine, had a fever, vomited blood at the nose and mouth, scoured [had diarrhea], was light-headed, and had taken great thought. Though the last two symptoms suggest mental disturbance according to MacDonald's list of terms, Kingson's physical condition may have explained the presence of those symptoms. In other cases, of course, the mental disorder seems primary, as with Lewis Evans, thirty-six, who had heaviness, "distemprature of mind," heat, fearfulness, and trembling.

Forman's most detailed description of a patient who was mentally ill appears as an example in his book on casting nativities. He had evidently been asked, by whom is not made clear, to cast a horoscope for the woman he described, but he recorded what he knew of her past, not what the horoscope predicted about her future.

> Susan Cuckston (born 1560) This woman in the 40th year of her age fell into a melancoly dispair and was moch vexed & trobled in mind and possessed with a sprite for oftentymes the sprite wold speake & talke to her. & prouoke her to kill & drowne her selfe. & byd her cut her owne throte when she toke a knife in her hand. Yf she cam by a well or by any water he wold byd her drown her selfe, and twise she hanged her selfe, and was cut down still before she was ded & so saued & once she was drowned, and yet they got life in her again. and the sprite that was in her said to her, he was a sprite of the water but had his being in the ayer, and she could not a byd any pines [pins] about her, but she moste thruste them in her fleshe, and this continued long on her. 1603.[48]

Though the present century would judge that Susan Cuckston was mentally ill, her early modern physician might not have agreed. Elsewhere Forman made clear that he believed in the existence of malevolent spirits, and his account of Cuckston's case reveals no obvious skepticism about her indwelling demon.[49]

In the case of Agnes Foster, twenty, whose mother came to consult Forman about her daughter, Forman seemed less convinced of the interference of a spirit:

Full of coller and moch pain at her harte, and moch sand [fine particles in the urine] a feuer hote and burninge & when the fit coms on her she is as yf she wer possessed with a sprite & lilleth [hangs] out her tonge making mockes and mowes [grimaces]. & 4 folk cannot kepe her in her bed.[50]

Foster had a physical illness which may have produced symptoms of a disturbed mind, "as yf she wer possessed with a sprite." As these examples demonstrate, the number of Forman's patients who can be identified with certainty as mentally ill, using MacDonald's terms, is relatively small. Though madness was clearly a condition recognized by sixteenth-century physicians and one that Forman wrote about in his discussion of melancholy, he rarely used the term to describe a patient and did not seem particularly interested in those few cases in which the symptoms seem to warrant such a description.

Diagnosis and Therapy

Forman's diagnoses are just as difficult to interpret as his lists of symptoms. As was common in the period, most diagnoses were humoral: melancholy mixed with red choler; tough phlegm; a venomous humor. Quite often Forman mentioned a specific condition or disease: plague, pox, measles, gonorrhea, sciatica, pleurisy, jaundice, dropsy, strangury [slow and painful urination]. Even though many of these names are familiar, they may not have indicated to Forman the condition that the present-day reader associates with these terms.[51] "Pox," for example, could refer to both smallpox and venereal disease, while "gonorrhea" was applied to any infection of or unusual discharge from the genitals. In cases in which Forman gave a full list of symptoms, his diagnoses can be evaluated fairly well, but often he recorded his diagnosis without noting symptoms, or listed symptoms but gave no diagnosis. Therefore, it is impossible to compile accurate statistics about his patients' symptoms, his diagnoses, and the therapies he prescribed.

Even without statistical accuracy, however, study of his casebooks produces a general understanding of Forman's therapy. He recorded his treatment in roughly one-third of his medical cases. Like most practitioners of the period, he responded to illness by ordering purges, dietary drinks or pills, and bloodletting. Only in children's cases did he prescribe pills or liquid medicine more frequently than purges. He ordered purges in about 13 percent of his juvenile patients and bled only 4 percent of them, almost always teenagers.[52]

Among adults, men were bled and purged more frequently than women. He purged about one-third of his male patients and one-fourth of the females. He bled about 19 percent of his male patients and about 5 percent of the females. Because women bleed naturally as part of their menstrual cycle, they received phlebotomies less frequently than male patients. If a woman was having regular menstrual periods, bloodletting was unnecessary, and most of the bleedings that Forman prescribed for women were for those whose menstrual periods had stopped. Frequently before purges and phlebotomies, Forman prescribed a preparative diet or drink, and sometimes the invasive procedures were followed by a course of pills or liquids.

John Weston, twenty-three, in January 1597, complained of "itch" and pimples on "his yerd." Forman diagnosed his problem as a venomous humor: "he hath dealt with som vnclean woman" and predicted he would have pox or plague. His therapy was to prepare for two days and purge "and washe his yerd with aqua salse [salt water] & let him blod." Thomas Carde, forty-six, came in April, 1597. He had taken cold, was short-winded, faint-hearted, feverish, sore in the breast, and had "an ague cake [lump] in his left syde." Diagnosing a surplus of melancholy and choler, Forman ordered Carde to prepare and purge, and made a plaster for his side "to resolve the matter & clear his lungs."[53]

Occasionally, Forman recognized a patient's problem as related to his or her behavior. Thomas Cole, fifty-six, in July 1597, had a dead palsey in his limbs and speech and "bonoshawes"[54] that rose like knobs on his shins. Forman said he had a venomous humor; Cole's body was dry because he used "ill diet" and corrupted his body. His heat and moisture were spent in "wine, women, and watching [staying up late and not sleeping]." Forman writes elsewhere of Margaret Bull, daughter of Thomas Bull and An Atkinson of Hagerstore. This twelve-year-old girl lived, probably as a maid, with Goodwife Dibble at Bartholomew Lane. She got up at night, laughed, and kept much ado as though haunted with spirits. Forman remarked that her problem came from ill diet and drunkenness and surfeit and that she was "cause of her own diz [disease]."[55]

Forman sometimes prescribed a change in diet or behavior (regimen) rather than any specific medical intervention. When Ellen Hillar, fifty-nine, came from Surrey in June 1597, she thought herself bewitched. She complained of extreme pain on Fridays and Saturdays. Forman wrote that she seemed to be forespoken [bewitched] and that he would give her something against forespeaking and witchcraft. He went on to record second thoughts: "She is not bewytched," he wrote, "she must haue comfortable things and be merry and give her sweete & comfortable meat."[56] (This was his frequent recommendation for melancholy.)

Instead of recording a therapy, Forman sometimes offered a prognosis about the course of the illness, as he did with several of the children discussed earlier. When Eusebius Andrews's brother asked about Eusebius's health in May of 1601, Forman predicted that he would have a hard fit within twenty days. When Allis Lester, thirty-eight, came in April 1601, complaining that she had not been well since she lay in, Forman diagnosed corruption in her matrix and precipitation [prolapsed uterus]. "Surgeons & phisisions have spoyled her," he went on, "she will di on [Mon]day morne."[57] As Siraisi points out, "In a medical system in which diagnosis was often problematic and the ability to cure was very limited, prognosis must frequently have emerged as the most valued and actually most useful aspect of medical attendance."[58] In Forman's practice, prognosis seemed to be all that some of his patients expected.

Forman made attempts to keep his records up-to-date by adding additional information about patients to the original case note. James Hoon, fifty-four, complained on June 14 of much pain; he returned on June 28 with a fever, scouring, and melancholy. Forman bled him and predicted "he will end or mend." Hoon sent a messenger again the next day, but Forman's note says, "died first of July." Perhaps the most dramatic example of adding later notes to a consultation record occurs in the 1597 casebook. Susan Bolter, twenty-five, in July complained of a problem with her legs: "she took it in childbed. . . . hath taken much ill phisicke." She was weak and would "scape hard." Nearly three years later Forman added, "She did escape and liue & cam to me & showed herself 1600 the 29 feb & told me of it."[59]

Conduct of the Practice

Other information appears in the casebooks. Forman saw patients every day of the week, with the length of his workday varying according to the season (and with patient demand). In January, for example, consultations began around 9:00 A.M. and were usually over by 4:15 P.M. In June, consultations began at 7:00 A.M., and Forman saw some patients at 7:00 or 8:00 in the evening. Adult patients, like the child patients discussed earlier, either came themselves or were inquired about by a relative or friend. Sometimes Forman noted which was the case. In March 1597, Forman was consulted 130 times. Of these, he noted that fourteen patients were present, seventeen sent messengers, and ten patients were asked about by someone else, a relative or a servant's mistress. Forman did not indicate how the other eighty-nine made their consultation, though most probably came to Forman. He always noted if someone asked about another person without that person's consent because that changed the way the horoscope was drawn. In this particular March, Forman averaged slightly more than four consultations a day, and this is a good estimate of his daily caseload for 1597. In 1601, he did not see quite as many patients, but still averaged close to four a day.

Sometimes patients came together to consult Forman. Sawyer notes similar patterns among Napier's patients:

> Then, as now, in many cases there was a small initial block that might have to be overcome before a sick person sought help. Once the door to a consultation was opened, though, it was common for a number of related or neighboring people to rush through it, seeking advice for maladies that might have troubled them for quite a long time.[60]

Husbands and wives came together quite frequently, as did Thomas and Isabel Conyears, thirty-six and thirty, respectively, who came on May 6, 1601. Thomas had salt water and melancholy in his stomach, faintness, and flushing heat. He was told to prepare three days and purge twice. His wife was troubled by the whites [a vaginal discharge] and a sciatica. For her, Forman also prescribed three days of preparation and two purges.[61]

Relatives sometimes came together. In May 1601, Grace More of Heighton, thirty-three, consulted Forman. She was full of melancholy, unlusty, with a fever and swollen legs. Forman purged her and gave her a dietary drink. Apparently satisfied with her treatment, she returned in August, complaining only of overflowing gall. She either brought with her or brought the complaints of Mari More, sixty-eight, and An More, forty-eight. Forman cast their horoscopes in turn at 11:00, 11:15, and 11:30 A.M.[62]

One of the oddest groups to consult Forman arrived on June 1, 1597. It included Edward Kynnerstone, thirty; Judeth Bathurste, forty-six, and Charels Hussi, fifty-six. Each wanted medical diagnosis, and they asked "which of thes too men shall marry this wyddowe." Charels was grieved in mind and belly, stuffed in the lungs, "et est amore cum Iudeth." Edward was also troubled in his mind and suffered from gravel "et est in amore cum Judeth." Judeth herself "hath no gret dizeas but she is ferfull & gryued in the mind." She was, according to Forman, "a black hard fauored woman." At the end of the consultation, Forman noted, "The yong man maried the said Judeth the 16 of Jun folowinge,"[63] but the records do not say what Forman advised the trio about their amatory difficulties. Clearly such groups of patients gave moral support to one another or efficiently disposed of several issues at once.

Occasionally Forman made reference to visiting a patient or even to staying in a patient's home. But these notes almost never appear in the casebooks. Perhaps when he traveled he left his notebooks at home. In the pre-London period Forman traveled to see a higher percentage of his patients than he did in the London period. Once he had a consulting room, most patients came or sent to him. Occasionally he did make house calls, and his casebooks contain a few notations of directions to patients' homes. Like his nonmedical clients, some patients returned repeatedly. In some cases, a reader can trace the progress of a cure (or its failure), and patients recovered from one illness sometimes reappear months or years later suffering from a new complaint.

Status and Location of Forman's Patients

Since Forman noted an address in about one-quarter of his cases, we can estimate the geographical area from which he drew patients. Most frequently, of course, the address is a street or location in or around London. In March 1597, clients came from Aldgate, East Smithfield, Holborn, Southwark, Lambeth, the Strand, St. Nicolas Lane, the Kingsbench, Gravesend, Bishopsgate Street, St. Mary's Hill, Paul's Churchyard, Sherburn Lane, Copping Yard, and Lyon Street. But they also came from areas outside London proper: Barksted, Eltham, Coulson, Bridgrow, Enfield, Raffish, Yssington, and Northampton. In other months, Forman saw patients from Kent, Buckinghamshire, Surrey, and Essex. What cannot be determined, of course, is how many of the non-London patients came to the city in order to consult Forman and how many were travelers to London who found themselves in need of medical attention while visiting the city. There is enough evidence, however, to conclude that, like Napier, Forman attracted clients from a broad territory; he was not simply a local practitioner for a particular section of London or Lambeth.[64]

Similarly, we can make some judgments about the social status of Forman's clientele. Rowse identifies many of Forman's most prominent clients. Despite Rowse's impressive enumeration of the elite or economically comfortable, however, a great many of Forman's patients were working people: sailors, servants, tailors, butchers, and actors.[65] Forman identified less than 10 percent of his patients by rank or profession, and his own social ambitions might well have led him to record those ranks and professions that he felt were important. Many of the 90 percent of Forman's clients whose professions the casebooks do not mention were probably patients of lower status. Of the 160 patients seen by Forman in March 1597, he recorded the professions of only seven. Five were servants identified in relation to their employers as "a maid at my Lord Keeper's" or "Mrs. Clifford's man"; one was the son of a coroner; another was the wife of a joiner. Seventeen were called "Mr." or "Mrs." by Forman; one was referred to as "Madam" and another as "Goodwife." The occupation Forman most consistently recorded in all his casebooks was that of servant in a particular household.[66] He may have hoped to attract other patients from the same house, perhaps even the master and mistress themselves.

Although Rowse assumes that Forman's practice was primarily peopled by well-to-do tradesmen and courtiers, I suspect rather that Forman chose to record the professions of such people more often than he recorded the professions of social nobodies. He himself disagrees with Rowse's assessment in his poem, "Forman his Repetition of the troble he had with the Docters of Phisick in London and of his delivery in the plague. 1592," where he emphasizes not his patients' wealth but their poverty.

By docters ofte I was assailed
And ofte in prison to
Not for the wronge I did to them
But good which I did doe
Vnto the poore of gods electe
That trobled were with paine
I did imploy my selfe and skill
To cuer their grifes again.
And this contynued many a yere
As god appointed me
That when diseasd and sick they were
To cuer their malladie
And in the tyme of pestilent plague
When Doctors all did flye,
And got them into places far
From out of the Cytty,
The Lord appointed me to stai
To cuer the sicke and sore
But not the ritch and mighti ons,
But the destressed poore.[67]

Forman prided himself on his dedication to the poor, though his actual devotion to them must be taken with a grain of salt, since he was very impressed when rich or important clients sought him out. In fact, his practice seems to have been dominated by no single status or income level.

Forman depended on word of mouth to increase his clientele. How this worked is clear in the following note, which records a case in which he left his own consulting room and traveled to his patient. On February 9, 1596, he was called to Mr. Whitbrede's to see Mr. Watkins, who was "sicke of the stone & strangury."

> At this time I went to him. he paid me well for my paines. I gaue him [an ounce] of my strong water the next morning at 6. And at 9 he could piss well & the same dai came downe a stone as byg as a beane. And the next day another. and he was well & profitable to me. for he caused me many patientes and reported well of me.[68]

Mr. Watkins paid Forman well for relief from his painful kidney stones and recommended Forman to others. Such testimonials from satisfied patients were especially important to Forman in the decade of the 1590s when he was building his practice.

Fees

To understand the value of Forman's fees in modern terms, we must consider wage and price scales in London during Forman's years there. The following estimates, derived from Steve Rappaport's *Worlds within Worlds*, provide some rough standards by which his fees can be judged. For the year 1600, in London, skilled construction workers, bricklayers, carpenters, plasterers, and tilers would earn approximately one shilling six pence a day, which works out to twelve to nineteen pounds a year. Semiskilled workers, described in contemporary accounts as assistants, servants, or laborers, would earn about a shilling a day, or eight to twelve pounds a year. Journeymen (those who had served an apprenticeship but still worked for a master and had no shop of their own) earned about five pounds a year, in addition to room and board. A clerk received about fifteen pounds a year, "sufficient for the maintenance of any single man of modest carriage."[69] Merchants and members of the nobility often had incomes many times greater than these figures. For example, some householders (men who ran their own shops) paid more than twenty-five pounds a year in fees and fines alone when they were promoted to the livery (an elite circle who managed the affairs of their company).[70]

An alternative way to understand Forman's fees is to consider the cost of common consumables. In London, estimated food and drink prices in 1600 include, for example, the following: a chicken, seven pence; a joint of mutton, one shilling four pence; a barrel of ale or beer, eight shillings one pence; and a bushel of flour, four shillings three pence. Fuel, in the form of faggots (small bundles of sticks bound together), would have cost six shillings nine pence for one hundred bundles.

Even these few examples of wages and prices indicate that Forman was far from inexpensive. Although the cost of consulting him depended on many variables, his casebooks, supplemented by jottings in other manuscripts, do provide some sense of his fees. Forman did not regularly record his charges.[71] Occasionally, however, when a client was unable to pay at the consultation or offered a pawn arrangement—leaving a ring as assurance of future payment, for example—Forman noted the amount he was still owed. In my exemplary month, March 1597, Forman made fee notes on only three cases. He charged An Smallwood—who had chills and giddiness, was faint and fearful, and hoped to have a child—five shillings. It is not clear what medicine he gave her, but he did comment that it was possible for her to have a child if her body were corrected and her matrix [uterus] scoured, so he probably charged for medicine as well as judgment in her case. James Mitchell left nine pence in pawn in return for his consultation. He was told to return on Monday for a purge and bloodletting, so the nine pence was probably Forman's charge for the judgment alone. His only other financial note for the month concerned Henry Boes, who sent a messenger. Diagnosed as having excessive choler and melancholy, Boes was told to prepare two days and then to purge. Forman noted, "she [Boes's messenger] gave me nothing for my judgment."[72]

In the 1601 casebook, Forman listed a number of his fees, crossing them out as they were paid:

> Mrs. Jefferies she began the 31 of Aprill she must take yt 24 dais & must paie me 6 pounds 13 shillings 4 pence, and of that I rec[eived] in the begining 3 pounds 6 shillings 8 pence, and the rest she must pai 12 dais after.

> Mr. Fardinando Clutterbac began the 5 of May and must tak yt 15 dais and must pai for every glasse for 3 dais 8 shillings. oweth 2 shillings for a purg & 8 shillings for a glass dietari. . . .

> Mr. Shawe thelder for his man Raph Holmes 6 of June a preprative 2 dais & a purge—5 shillings. Judgment—6 pence

> Mrs. Shawe a preprative for 3 dais 5 of May—5 shillings.[73]

Such details make possible the construction of a tentative fee scale for Forman's services, though since all these clients are called "Mr." or "Mrs.," they are probably all in the upper social range of Forman's patients. I have no evidence about whether he used a graduated fee scaled to his patients' ability to pay, as Napier did.[74]

Purges generally cost two shillings, but the preparation to be taken for two or three days before the purge was five shillings. A "dietary drink," prescribed by Forman to strengthen the body after purges or bleeding, cost eight shillings for a three-day supply. The consultation (judgment) itself was the cheapest part of the visit, ranging from six to nine pence.

The fee scale became more complex when Forman had to travel to the patient, as in the case of Mr. Osborn and his son:

for councell mr. Osborn	3 shillings four pence
for councell for his son	3 shillings four pence
Mr Osborn a preparation 3 dais the 5 of May	5 shillings
or going thether to see him	5 shillings
item 1 ounce strong water	5 shillings
a purge—the 8 May	2 ″ , 5 d
Item. for going to see him the 8 of May [something illegible]	5 ″
Itm. a comfortable drink 13 May	3 ″
Itm. for going to him from Lambeth	10 ″
a preparation for 2 dais for his son	3 ″
a purge for his son	2 ″

Som 39.4 shillings[75]

On May 12, Forman prescribed for Thomas Osborn (age seven) a purge for melancholy and choler. The only other Osborns listed among Forman's casebook patients for May 1601 are Edward Osborn, sixty, and his wife Mary whom Forman saw on May 5.[76] He had stone and a fever, ailments for which the strong water, a brew of Forman's own manufacture that he used repeatedly to treat kidney stones, would have been appropriate. No address is given and no son mentioned, so we cannot determine whether these were the same patients referred to in the itemized bill. When Forman had to leave his own consulting room he does not seem to have recorded the case among his day's casebook notes. Instead he commonly made a note on a separate piece of paper, as he did for the Osborns and for Mr. Watkins.

Another method of charging that Forman sometimes used was a lump sum for a cure, part to be paid at the beginning of treatment with the balance due only if the patient recovered. Hester Billey, twenty-nine, had the falling evil, which took her "first in the toes & soule of the fote and soe goeth to the calfe of the leg & from thence to the stomake & soe to the head & then falls & defilles her self. Yt cam by dronkenes." Forman ordered this patient to prepare three days and purge and then take diet for twenty-two days. "She muste pay 6 pounds, 3 pounds down and the rest 30 dais after she is well."[77] If she were not cured, she would not be obliged to make the second payment.

A variation of this kind of fee negotiation appears in the casenotes about Katherine Barnes who sent to Forman to see whether she was pregnant. "She is not with child & she saithe the doctors sai she is with child of 14 wickes & she hath 6 wickes to tri yf she proue with child she must have 5 shillings again." Forman was mistaken in this case, for about six weeks later, he wrote, "This was the woman that this dai had her 5 shillings again, because she said she was quick with child & I said noe."[78]

Among Forman's papers is a document recording a payment arrangement in which part is paid in advance and the rest is to be paid upon evidence of a cure. He first saw Margaret Sims on August 2, 1599. On August 4, an agreement was drawn and signed about terms of payment for her treatment.

> Be yt knowen vnto all men by thes presente that we Willm Sims of Ash-stead in Surrey yeoman and Nicolas Morton of Wodsyd in the parish of Croyden . . . bind our selves in the som of 40 shillings of english money to Simon Forman of London gentleman and phisision, to be paid vnto the said Simon the sum of 20 shillings at such tyme and as sone as Margaret Snowe the wife of Willm Sims shall find her self or be sufficiently recured of a diseas that she nowe trobled with all. vz of a vexation of her mind. . . . And her vnto in witnes therof we haue set our handes. The mark of Willm The mark of Nicolas[79]

On the pattern of Forman's other prearrangements, twenty shillings had been paid up front. The remainder would be paid upon a cure.

The setting of fees in advance, to be paid in full only if the cure was successful, was apparently widespread enough among medical practitioners to cause the London College of Physicians expressly to forbid the practice.[80] Forman used this method of setting fees infrequently, though in his 1593 diary entry, he reported that his failure to bargain first had resulted in a loss of payment:

> This yere I liste [lost] moch money that I should haue had for diuers cuers that I did, & was besides that slenderly paid for many cuers that I did because

I did not bargain with them first. . . . Alsoe yf I did take any on in hand to cuer and did bargain with him first, then eyther I did not cuer him, or ells I was not paid for yt when yt was done.[81]

Forman seems to have lost money in 1593, the year of the plague when he made his reputation, no matter which method of charging for his services he used.

This method of advance payment insured that the physician would receive something for his time and trouble whether or not he cured the patient, but it also insured that the patient would not have to pay excessive fees unless a cure resulted. This system eventually became more common in Jacobean London. In statutes written at the beginning of the seventeenth century, the College of Physicians removed the penalty for bargaining in advance with a patient, provided the patient desired the bargain.[82]

Forman's casebooks reveal a busy urban practice, primarily medical but also serving those who desired to find lost belongings or to check on a ship at sea or to consult the stars about a prospective marriage partner. Limited in his range of therapies, Forman nevertheless provided a ready ear for his patients' troubles; he gave them a prognosis and frequently intervened physically by purging, bleeding, or administering medicine. This kind of intervention left no doubt in the patient's mind that something was being done, however futile it might finally prove. By and large his therapies were conservative for the period; if they frequently did not cure, they probably did not do much harm either. Despite his frequent characterization as a quack, he was not an itinerant wanderer who preyed on a neighborhood and then moved on. Instead, Forman practiced in just two locations for over twenty years and, when he moved from London to Lambeth, a number of his loyal patients continued to consult him in his new location. His practice was comparable in its size and nature with that of the respectable Napier (who also had no formal medical training). Like Napier, Forman attracted clients from far away and from wealthy and even noble families, but more often his patients—again, like Napier's—were the ordinary people among whom he lived. In fact, Forman's passion for recordkeeping has produced a fairly detailed picture of how a relatively ordinary urban medical practice functioned in the early modern period. To say that, however, we must accept (as the College of Physicians could not) that an astrological physician who had no formal medical training and no university degree could actually *have* a flourishing medical practice. The casebooks provide considerable evidence that Forman did.

❦ F O U R ❦

Troubles with the College of Physicians

FORMAN'S SUCCESS IN ESTABLISHING his astrological medical practice in London brought him both legal and financial trouble. He attracted the attention of the London College of Physicians in 1594, several years after he had moved to London, and they continued to investigate, summon, fine, and sometimes imprison him for nearly two decades until his death in 1611.

The College had been established by royal statute in 1518 and was charged with overseeing medical care in the city of London and for a seven-mile radius around the city. In practice, this meant that the College had the power to license medical practitioners working within those geographical boundaries and to fine or imprison anyone practicing medicine without the College's license, which was granted only after a formal examination by a committee of its members.

King Henry VIII and his court physician Thomas Linacre, who was chiefly responsible for the College's foundation, had intended that this overseeing body would improve the quality of medical care available to London citizens. The number of physicians who were members of or were licensed by the College was very small, however, in proportion to the rapidly increasing population of London, with the result that the College had only limited success in restraining the sizable number of unlicensed medical practitioners in and around London.

Indeed, had the College been successful in suppressing all "unqualified" practitioners, vast numbers of Londoners would have had no one at all to consult about medical problems. As Margaret Pelling and Charles Webster note, "The Fellows showed little interest in adapting the College to the needs of the expanding metropolis. Their primary concerns related to fastidious details of internal management and the protection of their monopoly against the swelling tide of unlicensed practitioners."[1] The College was able to restrain some of the most notorious and the most financially successful among the unlicensed practitioners, but many went unnoticed by the College. Also, some of those examined and punished for unlawful practice were singled out more for political and social reasons than because they were less medically competent than others whom the College tolerated.[2]

From the time of its foundation with six members, the College had restricted its size. By the 1590s it admitted thirty members. The monarch's physicians automatically became members. Other members were urban physicians practicing in and around London. Candidates for membership could be selected even though the College had no openings but, if approved for membership, the successful candidate would have to wait until one of the thirty places became vacant. In 1599, a new limit of six was placed on those who could be admitted even to this outer circle of the elect. Therefore, medical practitioners in London formed an informal hierarchy, composed of a small elite body that strictly controlled and limited its own membership, a larger group of licensed practitioners approved by the College, and a much larger number of unlicensed medical practitioners who went about their work in defiance or ignorance of the College's "privilege."

Though medical practice and theory changed very little in England during the two decades in which Forman practiced in London, the College of Physicians made changes during this period that increased its power and exclusiveness. Not only did the College restrict the number of candidates approved for admission to its ranks, but the members of the College also voted for themselves a new dress code that would give them a distinct and recognizable appearance as they went about their professional and social duties: "agreement was reached on scarlet for feast-days and solemn meetings, purple for other occasions, and on caps, either woolen or silk, or other suitable material, for comitia [meetings], funerals, anatomical demonstrations, and 'honorable consultations.' "[3] In 1600, Forman reported buying "my purple gowne my veluet cap my veluet cote my veluet breches my taffety cloke my hate."[4] His attire seems to be closely modeled on the official dress of the hated "doctors."

Charles Goodall, a College member during the mid-seventeenth century, abstracted and summarized from the College's records a number of the cases against unlicensed practitioners. These he published in 1684 as *An Historical Account of the College's Proceedings against Empiricks and Unlicensed Practisers.* Goodall's account makes clear that even the exceptions to the College's broad licensing power—holders of Oxford or Cambridge degrees in medicine and those given a license by certain clergymen, such as the archbishop of Canterbury—were not always honored by the College Censors.[5] In 1590, for example,

> *Robert Tanner* appeared before the College and brought along with him the Archbishop of *Canterbury's* license in justification of his practice; but being found by the President and Censors a very ignorant and illiterate person, he was interdicted practice for the future.[6]

In 1592, "*William Forrester, master of Arts* and *Clergy-man*" was summoned, examined, and refused a license. He continued to practice, however. After more complaints, including "that he had bargain'd with them for their Cures, taking part in hand and reserving the other part till the Cure was performed" (a practice Forman occasionally used and that the College itself grudgingly permitted in its revised code of statutes approved in 1601),[7] Forrester was again summoned before the College, "but having obtained a Licence for practice from the University, he sent that to the College, and refused to come: Wherfore Orders were given for a speedy prosecution of him according to Law, for his evil and illegal practice."[8] Neither the archbishop's license nor a university license gave a practitioner absolute immunity from the College in the 1590s. Not even letters "from the Queen" in the case of Roger Powel could save him from being forbidden to practice in London, though Powel was released from prison.[9]

In this environment Forman, newly successful in his London practice after the plague of 1593, came to the notice of the London College of Physicians. Two accounts of their antagonistic relationship are available. One is Goodall's; he devoted several pages of his "proceedings" to the College's dealings with Forman. His account contains no dates, partly because he consolidated the skirmishes of many years into a single narrative, which he ended on a note of triumph with events that occurred about 1601. The other account, Forman's own, must be pieced together from his notes. Though there is ample evidence of his continuing anger at the "doctors," he nowhere gave a coherent narrative account of his seventeen years of conflict with them, a period from 1594 until his death in 1611.

Initially, Goodall's and Forman's accounts jibe fairly well (if Goodall's judgmental vocabulary is discounted):

> Simon Forman, a pretended *Astrologer* and great *Imposter*, appearing before the President and Censors confessed that he had practised Physick in *England* 16 years, and 2 years in *London*. He pretended that he had cured many Hectical [feverish] and tabid [wasting] people by the use of *Elect. e Suc. Ros.* in Wormwood water. He boasted that he made use of no other help for the discovery of distempers but his *Ephemerides*, and that by the heavenly Signs, Aspects and Constellations of the Planets, he could presently know every disease. Being examined in the principles of Astronomy as well as in the Elements of Physick, he answered so absurdly and ridiculously, that it caused great mirth and sport amongst the Auditors. He was interdicted practice and punished *propter malam & illicitam praxin* 5 *l.* which he readily and faithfully promised to pay.[10]

According to Forman's notes, these encounters took place in February and March 1594. He paid the five pound fine to Dr. William Gilbert, then treasurer of the College and one of the queen's physicians, on March 30.[11] Forman did not mention the laughter that his examination by the College Censors occasioned. Of all the records Goodall summarized, Forman's was the only examination at which he recorded general mirth. Surely Forman, whose pride and sense of dignity were strong, must have been humiliated by the doctors' laughter, and this may account in some way for his behavior in subsequent encounters.

Forman recorded being imprisoned from November 7 to November 25, 1595, by Dr. Barnsdell, and in 1596 he records being regularly in conflict with the College. On January 19 he was warned before Dr. Stamp; on May 7 he was bidden to the College hall by the "doctors procter."[12] On September 15 he was sent to the Counter, a London prison, "by my l. maior" at the urging of "the doctors" and bailed out on September 24, only to be reimprisoned on September 30 and held until October 12.[13] During this prison stay, Forman was offered release by the College provided that he would seal to a bond promising that he would leave London and forgo practice. "Beste to be bound to the doctors to forsak London yea or noe 1596 7 Octob. pm at 5. . . . At this tyme their officer cam to me to knowe whether I wolde." On the basis of the astrological cast, Forman advised himself not to sign "but to stand to the Lawe and try all therof. for thei ar also weke and haue as lyttle powar as my self."[14] Despite this advice to himself, however, Forman did make a bond, which he promptly violated, and a year later he reported, "I was arested vpon that bond by the docters 1597 the 20 of decemb."[15]

Matching Goodall's account with Forman's is difficult, but the following passage from Goodall must refer to the 1596 period:

> About 2 or 3 years after he was examined a second time, and found very ignorant. He confessed that he had never read any Author in Physick but one *Cockis* an obscure English writer, and of no reputation. He then acknowledged (as before) that he onely practised Physick by his skill in Astrology, in which Art being again examined, he was found not to understand the common principles of it. Wherefore he was committed to Prison and fined 10 *l.* to be paid to College uses, *propter illicitam praxin & insignem audaciam.* After a month or 6 weeks imprisonment, he was released by an Order from the Lord Keeper; upon which, the College order'd that the 4 Censors with Dr. *Smith* should wait upon his Lordship to acquaint him with the cause for which they had committed so notorious an Imposter to Prison, and to Petition his Honour that he might be recommitted by virtue of the former Warrant signed by the Censors of the College.[16]

Already Forman was "notorious," enough of a thorn in the College's side that it was willing to send five of its members to explain to a prominent member of the Court why this man should remain in jail. Their intercession with the Lord Keeper may explain the back-to-back sessions in prison that are recorded in Forman's notes in 1596. He never alluded to being examined by the College in any of his notes, but some of Goodall's details are persuasive. Over and over Forman asserted that only through astrology could a physician properly diagnose and treat a patient. As we have seen, Cokkis's medical manuscript was certainly a text from which Forman had learned much,[17] but why he would not speak of all his other medical reading and how he failed an examination in astrology remain mysteries.[18] Perhaps the College's view of what constituted the "common principles" of astrology was different from Forman's. Perhaps humiliated by his earlier encounter with the laughing Collegians, Forman had determined to say nothing that would give the assembled doctors opportunity for further mockery.

Whatever the circumstances, Forman's record of legal battles with the College is complicated by a different sort of trouble, one which Forman believed was very serious. In Forman's chamber on October 23, 1596, just eleven days after he was freed from prison, "Jarvis stabed Atkins . . . and then began he his villaini against me." The next day, "they had out a warrant for me and I forsoke my house & went to Kates."[19] Forman hid for a few days at "Kate's" house, gathering up a bit of money: "October 26, I had out of my bag 3 [pounds] 15 [shillings] 8 [pence]. and before I had of Avis Allen that she toke forth whill I was in the Counter 40 [shillings]." On October 31, with his small traveling fund, Forman left London for "Sandwidg & did trauaill & spent moch." After several weeks he returned to London (his 1596 casebook shows no cases between October 31 and November 24), but he was still cautious. Not until December 10, after casting to see whether it was safe, did Forman return "hom to my chamber."[20] Forman seemed to believe that the stabbing incident in his rooms was planned by the College to get him into more trouble. He talks about such schemes in his poems and letters. Not enough details are clear about the incident for us to draw any conclusions about whether Forman's suspicions were justified or whether, as seems more likely, this was simply paranoia on his part.

After the troubles of 1596, 1597 was quiet until Forman's rearrest in December. Goodall's version of that episode is as follows:

> Nine months after, this bold and impudent Imposter appearing before the College, confessed that he had prescribed a compound water to a Gentleman in a burning Fever, upon the taking of which he immediately died. Being asked upon what grounds he practised Physick or durst adventure to give medicines to the sick; he answered that he understood the nature of diseases and proper remedies onely by Astrology. Being then examined a third time in that Art by the Queen's Physician [probably Gilbert], he was again found a mere Imposter and ignorant in that as well as in Physick. Wherefore he was by a Warrant from the Censors committed again to Prison.[21]

According to Forman, he and the College countersued each other at this time over the 1596 bond. In 1598, he cast for "how the suit shall go" and in the 1599 diary entry, he remarked that he had not been imprisoned that year and had "put them to silence for a whole yer after & a halfe."[22] But he was still apprehensive, casting on October 10, 1599, to "knowe whether the docters will doe any thinge against me this terme, or whether they can do me any harme."[23]

Not until late in the year 1600, however, did the College move against Forman again. On November 6, Forman cast to know whether it were "Best to go to the Colledg of phisisions or no tomorrowe . . . their officer was here for docter Gelbarte" [Gilbert had been elected president of the College in 1600]. The stars advised Forman "Goe not," and he took this advice.[24] In his diary, he wrote: "About the latter end of November the docters sent for me to their halle again but I went not but wrote vnto them. . . . Many sclanderouse speaches wer by the docters and others used secretly againste me, yet I thriued reasonable well I thank god."[25] Forman presents himself as becoming bolder in his dealings with the doctors, refusing their summons and prospering in spite of all that they "and others" could do.

Goodall's perspective on Forman's position in the struggle was quite different:

> This [another arrest] so humbled *Forman* that he fled to *Lambeth* as a place of protection from the College Officers; wherefore the College presented the following Letter to the Most Reverend the Arch-Bishop of *Canterbury* against him.[26]

Before we examine the College's letter to the archbishop, which both Goodall and John Strype (Whitgift's first biographer) reprint, we should look a bit more closely at Forman's move to Lambeth (figure 4).

Carefully planned and carried out between the lease signing in March 1601 and May 20, when the move was completed, Forman's shift of location was not quite so precipitate as Goodall implied. Clearly Forman had had enough trouble from the College and was anxious to flee their jurisdiction. Lambeth seemed a natural choice, not only because he hoped for the protection of the archbishop, but also because it was close enough to his former location to permit faithful patients to visit him. He had been married in Lambeth, where Dr. and Mrs. Blague, two of his most constant patients and friends, lived.[27] Therefore, Forman's choice of an alternative to London, especially given the growth in the size of his household after his marriage, is not surprising. His sensitivity about the reason for his move, a sensitivity that led him to change its date in later manuscripts, suggests that Goodall was probably correct in attributing the move to the attacks of the College, though Forman did not make such an undignified, pell-mell flight from London as Goodall implies.

What is more remarkable than Forman's retreat from London is the political maneuvering that it prompted from the College of Physicians and from John Whitgift, archbishop of Canterbury. Because of an ancient right passed down from medieval bishops, the archbishop had the power, within Lambeth, to grant physicians license to practice, no matter what the position of the London College of Physicians, although I have noted earlier that this power was not always recognized by the College.[28] Forman hoped to forestall the College's pursuit by moving to Lambeth and enlisting the support of the archbishop.

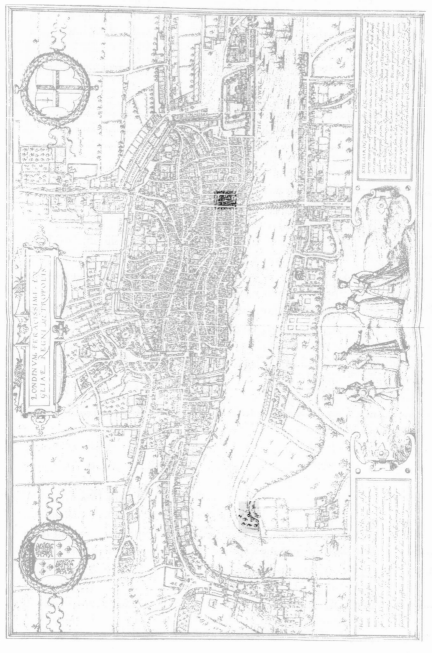

FIGURE 4: A view of mid-sixteenth-century London marked to indicate the approximate locations of Forman's homes in London (right) and in Lambeth (left). From a reproduction of the map of London first published in Georg Braun and Frans Hogenberg, *Civitates Orbis Terrarum*, 1572.

The College was in no mood to be circumvented, however. Just one month after Forman's removal to Lambeth, it addressed the following letter to Whitgift:

> May it please your Grace to be advertised, that one *Simon Forman* an intruder into the profession of Physick, hath of long time in this Cytie, as well to the great prejudice of privileges as also to the intolerable abuse of her Majesties Subjects, been a great Practitioner in the same. . . . The said *Forman*, as we are informed, hath now placed himself in Lambheath, being a Town under your Grace's Jurisdiction, mynding thereby as yt shoold appeare, to abuse your honorable protection touching the premises. In consideration whereof, we humbly beseech your Grace, that as well in regard of the insufficiency of the man, as also for the better maintenance of our auncient privileges, he may be frustrate of his expectation in that behalf: and that by your Grace's favour we may be ayded and permitted, without any lett or impediment, to use such lawfull and ordinary coorse, as both holsom Lawes and our Privileges have provided for the suppressing of him and the like offenders. . . . 28 June, 1601.[29]

Strype reprinted the College's letter in his biography of Whitgift and added, "What little countenance the Archbishop gave such empirics, and what course himself had thought on to take with this man, and what a respect he had for that learned College will appear by his answer."[30]

Several days later, the archbishop returned a polite but brief letter to the College, which is printed by Goodall and paraphrased by Strype:

> *Forman* neither is nor shall be countenanced by me: nether doth he deserve it any way at my hands. I have heard very little of him: insomuch, as I had a meaning to call him by vertue of the commission Ecclesiasticall for divers misdemeanors, if any man woold have taken upon him the prosecution of the cause against him. In which mynd I remaine still: And therefore use your authorytie in the name of God. My Officers shall geve you assistance, or els they shall be no officers of mine. And so I commit you to the tuition of the Almighty God. From my house at *Croyden*, the 4th of July, 1601.
>
> > Your loving freend,
> > Jo. Cantuar.[31]

The archbishop did not inform the College that on the day its letter to him had been written, June 28, 1601, at 11:30 A.M., he had consulted Forman. Forman's casenote reads: "Jhon Whitgifte bishop of Canterbury . . . moch cold, a pain in the syde, in daunger of the Jaundez" (figure 5).[32] Rowse also noted this casebook entry: "[Forman] naturally was interested in the condition of his eminent neighbor . . . (The Archbishop had no jaundice; however, no matter, to a true believer)"[33]—but implied that Forman cast for Whitgift's health on a whim, out of personal curiosity, and not because Whitgift had consulted him. Forman entered the case in his casebook in a perfectly straightforward way, however, among other consultations for the day and, if we doubt that Whitgift consulted him, we must doubt as well all the casebook entries.

Moreover, Whitgift *was* afflicted with jaundice. In the summer of 1603, in a letter written to the earl of Shrewsbury and paraphrased by Strype, he mentioned being "somewhat affected with the jaundice, his old disease," and again, in December 1603, Strype recorded that Whitgift was troubled with jaundice.[34] It does seem likely that Whitgift's consultation was prompted by his receipt of the College's letter, though that explanation requires both a remarkably efficient messenger and an archbishop ready upon its receipt to act immediately, since the consultation occurred at 11:00 A.M. on the day the College's letter is dated.

Whitgift appeared cooperative in his response to the College, but he was also encouraging Forman to continue to hope for his favor. This delicate balance was maintained for some time. On December 28, 1602, Forman recorded a dream about a bridge over a dried-up stream. As always, he associated the dream with what happened the day after. His note reads: "but that dai nothing hapned worth the notinge. but at night on came to byd me to diner to my L of canterburyes the next dai."[35]

Whatever help such a dinner invitation may have led Forman to expect was not forthcoming, however. How frustrated Forman had become in his search for protection against the College is revealed in a letter to Napier dated March 16, 1603. Written in a studied hand and in a tone quite unlike that of his other letters to Napier, Forman is highly rhetorical in his indignation over the College's latest attack:

> Howe I haue hether to passed the mightie stormes, of soe greate a tempeste, the bellowinge of such a Company of Basan Bulles,[36] and the Raging waves of soe mighte a Sea which in their fury have Risine aboue their Bankes and lifted them selues Even up againste the heauens, whose furie non could tame, and whose displeasure non could quallifie noe not any humble Entreaty of my frindes, no offers of peace noe giftes nor Rewardes, noe conditions, noe submission nor yet any sacrifice offred to such a leude company of infernall godes, no nor yet the combat yt selfe could end their furie, nor in

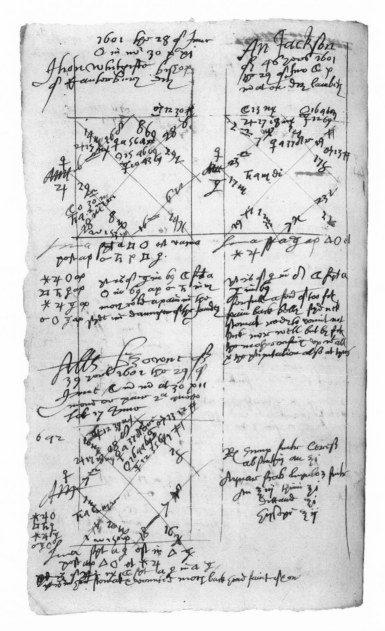

FIGURE 5: A page from Forman's 1601 patient casebook recording his consultations with three patients, the first of whom was John Whitgift, archbishop of Canterbury. MS. Ashmole 411: 110v. Courtesy of the Bodleian Library, University of Oxford.

any wise asswage the inextinguible mallice of such fierce Tygres, nor Satisfie the gready panches of such a sorte of devowring wolves.

If we take the letter literally, we hear a desperate man who has tried every trick he knows: intercession by powerful friends, gifts, and bribes. After casting himself in the role of Christ suffering while the mob calls for his crucifixion, Forman continued in a somewhat calmer tone:

> I caused both my honorable L. of Hartford and my Lady also to write most effectually vnto my Lordes Gr. [the archbishop] in my behalfe to giue me his licence but yt will not be. but he giues me fair wordes and soe dryues me of with delayes sayinge the docters haue written vnto him, desiring him moste instantlye not to take parte with nor graunt me any Lycence for yf he should yt wold be moch preiudiciall to them. to their privilege and alsoe to their proceadinges which makes his Gr. cold in that he absolutly of his owne Clemency promised me at first.

The language of this letter suggests that Whitgift had discussed the College's letter with Forman since he seems to know its contents. Forman goes on to tell Napier that Lady Hertford had written to the chief justice and to Sir Francis Popham, his son, to urge the archbishop not to take sides with the doctors:

> He [Whitgift] retorned an aunsware, that he knewe me not, neither did he graunt any warrante that he knewe of againste me, but the docters came to him indeed, to haue his hand to a generalle warrante & therto he set his hand, but henceforth he wold be better aduised.[37]

The incident that occasioned this epistolary outburst was the arrival at Forman's Lambeth home of officers with a warrant allowing the doctors to arrest him. His letter to Napier was written after he had been out of jail for ten days. He was seeing patients again, he reported, and the district attorney had been with him, "to whom I declared my mind at full."

Forman's most complete account of this period in his struggle with the College appears in an autobiographical poem, which reveals his paranoia about the College and its pursuit of him. If he really did believe his life was threatened, as he claims in the poem, then the hysterical note in his 1603 letter to Napier is easier to understand.

> And when they could not so preuaille
> They rose fals sclanders then
> One me, without iuste cause to make
> me be dispised of men
> And seinge that wold not take place

They soughte to haue me slaine
or poisoned by som stratagem
And therto ofte did fain
That certain men should com to me
To rid forth to the sicke
That by the way I might be kild
by som Inuentiue tricke

. . . .

And in the yeare of syxtie thre [1603]
Twise was I like bin kild
by their falls officers and knaues
That thoughte my blod haue spild.
from Cambridge and from Oxford both
I bid them Chuse the beste
And throughe all Europe to dispute
To set vs all at reste.
Yf he in acte did vanquishe me
My selfe wold then giue place
And leaue their Cytty and pryuiledge
And they should haue the grace
But yf my self did vanquishe him
Then I to beare the sway
Them selues to leese their pryuiledge
Or ells to Learne my waie.

. . . .

This did I offer them ofte tymes
Before the arch bishope
And in their Colledge before them
But none wold take me vp.

. . . .

In thend to Cut of all thes brawlles
To Cambridg acte [?] I wente
To trie my skille to wyne or leese
was then my whole entente
I did preuaille I thanke still god
and gracet for docter was
To practice in great phisickes arte
god broughte yt soe to passe.[38]

God had preserved Forman from the plots of the College, and he rose to the occasion, offering to meet in single medical combat any doctor whom the

College might select.[39] The grounds on which Forman would have preferred to fight are clear. Rather than an examination on classical medical theory, such as the College gave, where he stood alone to be judged before an audience, Forman preferred a dramatic confrontation with another medical champion. Clearly such a test was not to be, though Forman did receive an invitation to be examined for a license at Cambridge University.

Forman gave God and himself all the credit for his Cambridge success, and thus his poem does not help us to understand the political moves that made possible Forman's receipt of a degree from Cambridge. I suspect that Whitgift, constrained by politics from direct opposition to the London College in this matter, nevertheless wished to help Forman and—as a great benefactor of his alma mater, Cambridge—pulled the strings that enabled Forman to be examined by the university.

Whether or not the exam was pro forma is not clear.[40] The poem's words "to trie my skille to wyne or leese" imply that Forman was given a serious examination at Cambridge before the license was issued (this was standard practice for licenses granted by both Oxford and Cambridge). But if he was able to pass the Cambridge exam, why had he three times failed the College's licensing exam, exams that appear only in the College's records and are never mentioned by Forman himself? Was the College so incensed against this practitioner who would not bow to their authority that they would have refused to license him under any circumstances? Harold J. Cook describes the College at the period of its dispute with Forman:

> It . . . had the reputation of being an institution of ceremonial ritual, of Latinate discourse, of 'monopolistic' behaviour, and of a membership that was mainly conformist but leaning towards Catholicism. The conservatism of men who devoted long years of their lives to study in authoritative texts tended to cause them to favour learned hierarchies and traditional ways.[41]

Forman is unlikely to have impressed the Collge, but it is not possible to judge whether they gave him a fair examination. Nor can we determine how much influence Whitgift (if indeed he was Forman's intercessor) brought to bear in Forman's Cambridge examination. All we can be certain of is that Forman received, by some means, what he needed: a university license to practice medicine.

With his Cambridge degree, Forman expected to be free of trouble from the College. Yet in the few notes that remain from the post-1603 period, the College reappears with surprising regularity. In 1607, after a case brought against the College by a university-licensed doctor who had been imprisoned for illegal practice, a panel of judges awarded the College the right to examine and license even those doctors with Cambridge and Oxford degrees.[42] This decision made Forman vulnerable once more to their attack.

In the 1607 diary fragment, in fact, Forman wrote that "the 4 aug the docters sent their warrant to me to com befor them"[43]; and in another manuscript of the same year he recorded an astrological question: "1607. 31 Aug. the docters sent a second warrant for me to appear befor them . . . best to go to them or no . . . Noe goe not. I went not neither did they sende for me again."[44] Clark notes: "In June [1610] the College was to collect evidence against Forman, Forrester and Tenant, and again in October when the president had to make a speech against empirics."[45] Less than three months before his death in 1611, Forman cast to find out whether the College "will procead any farder againste me or no."[46]

The London College of Physicians's aggressiveness and tenacity in pursuit of Forman suggest that he must have been competing very successfully with these elite physicians. Goodall ends his account of the College's dealings with Forman after the exchange of letters with Whitgift, not mentioning Forman's acquisition of the Cambridge license. But harassment, if not actual fines or prison terms, clearly continued. Forman was one of the few targeted by the College who simply would not go away. Most of those whose examinations Goodall recorded, after their first or second encounter with the College, paid their fines, agreed to leave London, or humbled themselves before the College. Some of the humbled were eventually granted College licenses.

Forman presented a real challenge to the College's authority or "privilege." He grew wealthier and more successful each year; he had important supporters; he called the College's power into question because he was so widely known and because he refused to acquiesce to their authority. The issues at stake in Forman's struggle with the College moved rather quickly beyond medical expertise, and their conflict became instead a power struggle, something that Forman's poetic portrayal of a contest recognized. The College's records, as presented by Goodall, were careful to represent the issue as medical incompetence except that, in the letter to Whitgift, their grievance over Forman's challenge to their "privilege" clearly emerges. Forman's own repeated use of "privilege" when talking about his disputes with the College suggests that this was the rhetorical way in which the College approached him. His ability to qualify for the Cambridge degree, supported by evidence in his papers of his astrological and medical knowledge, also suggests that the College may not have given him an objective licensing exam. Though Goodall's account makes it seem as though the College had effectively dealt with Forman by 1601 or 1602, Forman's own notes reveal that he was never satisfactorily "dealt with" and that the College's harassment continued until his death. How much of his notoriety in his lifetime came from his battle with the College, whom he accused of spreading "fals sclanders" about him,[47] and how much arose from his personal behavior are difficult matters to determine. Certainly his battles with the elite physicians of London can have done his reputation no good.

Forman's Occultism

They have their christalls, I doe know, and rings,
And virgin parchment, and their dead-mens sculls,
Their ravens wings, their lights, and pentacles,
With characters; I ha' seen all these.

—Jonson, *The Devil Is an Ass*

ALTHOUGH FORMAN FOUND NO comradeship or common ground with the physicians, he certainly shared interests and ideological commitments with a number of men who can loosely be grouped under the heading of "occultists." Writing about an Italian occultist and physician of the earlier part of the century, Nancy Siraisi could almost be describing Forman himself:

> The story Girolamo Cardano (1501–76) told most frequently was his own. He was not only the author of one of the most striking of Renaissance autobiographies but also recounted fragments of his own history throughout his voluminous writings. . . . in sample horoscopes, in astrological treatises, in case histories in medical works, in examples in a treatise on dreams, as inspiration in moralistic treatises, he told and retold of his wretched childhood, his rejection by medical colleagues, his successes as a medical practitioner . . . and astrologer, his prolific career as an author.[1]

Repeatedly in this study, I compare Forman to John Dee, "the Queen's astrologer," who also kept a private diary, collected books, practiced astrology and alchemy, summoned spirits with the help of a scryer (crystal gazer), and was interested in British antiquities. Francis Thynne (1546–1608) was another Englishman who shared many of Forman's interests: "the occult, principally alchemy; British antiquities; and heraldry." According to David Carlson, Thynne also copied many manuscripts: "Thynne's collections of occult writings run to some one hundred carefully copied and extensively illustrated manuscript folios."[2]

Additional names could be mentioned, but these few are already sufficient to suggest that Forman, far from unique in his combination of interests, resembled several other men living in his century who were caught in similar intellectual crosswinds. Nonetheless, this fact does nothing to diminish the sense of Forman's personal and professional isolation that his surviving papers convey. Thynne and Dee lived primarily by patronage. They made themselves useful and agreeable to the noble and powerful (although patronage was not always a reliable financial support: both struggled with debts). Forman earned his living by selling his knowledge directly, mostly to medical patients but also to those who needed his astrological services. I find no evidence that he interacted with anyone other than Napier who shared his intellectual and professional interests. MacDonald believes that Forman was strongly influenced by Dee and, given their similar interests and Dee's fame, I suspect he is right:

> There is a direct line of descent from [Dee] to the most prominent Eliz-
> abethan and Jacobean medical astrologers, Simon Forman and Richard
> Napier. Both knew Dee and were strongly influenced by his work. Like
> him they studied magic as well as alchemy and astrology, but unlike him,
> they also established huge medical practices.[3]

Influence is one thing; that Forman and Dee also *knew* one another, however, is by no means clear. I find no references to Dee in Forman's manuscripts (though he does mention the work of Dee's scryer, Edward Kelly). Even the dinner that Rowse says Forman and Dee shared,[4] was actually attended by Napier, not Forman. Forman must have known about Dee and his work, yet he never touches on the subject in his manuscripts.

Lack of interaction was not unusual among occultists. Peter W. G. Wright has argued that it was because astrologers failed to get together and present an organized system of knowledge that they fell behind the physicians when medicine and astrology separated in the seventeenth century. Physicians successfully organized themselves and developed forms of professional regulation and control.[5] As part of this professional formation and regulation, physicians regularly used print publication both to attract clients and to attack their less-educated rival practitioners.[6] In contrast, "with a few notable exceptions, students of the occult rarely divulged the fruits or the sources of their researches in print."[7]

Sharing this widespread inclination to secrecy about occult information; well aware of the dangerous nature of some of the books he collected; convinced that the "doctors" were spying on him; perhaps, indeed, innately paranoid: Forman had many reasons that, separately or in combination, would make him both secretive and reclusive with his intellectual equals or superiors. While he seems to have interacted comfortably enough with patients, servants, women, everyday acquaintances, and with a man like Napier whom he felt he could "instruct," Forman kept his distance from those who might make him feel inadequate or inferior. He preferred to meet his astrological, alchemical, and magical peers through their writings. His own contributions to the conversation among occultists were carefully written into his manuscripts where a few select readers might one day see them.

This chapter focuses on Forman's writings about astrology, magic, alchemy, and witchcraft. As I noted when discussing his medical education in chapter 2, astrology was interwoven with every aspect of Forman's life. He would do nothing without astrological consultation: "for astrologie is the booke and course of all naturalle things, the grounds of phisicke and mother of all artes what so ever. And without that thou canste doe nothing in phisicke nor magick."[8] Although magic and alchemy did not play much of a role in his practice, he had a strong personal interest in both. Believing himself especially gifted to practice astrology, he assumed that he was also destined to master the other occult sciences.

How several strands of occult practice came together naturally for Forman is demonstrated in the making of lamins, or sigils,[9] engraved amulets worn to ward off evil and illness and to attract good fortune. At the death of his mistress, the astrologer William Lilly inherited such a sigil, designed by Forman. It had been prepared originally to help the woman's first husband rid himself of a spirit who tempted him to cut his throat. Lilly told this story:

> She many times hear[d] him [her first husband] pronounce, *I defie thee* & she desired him to acquaint her with the Cause of his Distemper, which he then did. Away she went to Dr. *Simon Forman*, who having framed his *Sigil*, and hanged it about his Neck, he wearing it continually until he died was never more molested by the Spirit: I [Lilly] sold the sigil for 32 shillings.[10]

Though references to such sigils occur occasionally in the casebooks, one Forman manuscript has a section that focuses on the subject. In this volume, Forman gave detailed descriptions of a number of sigils, usually round disks engraved on both sides that could be hung around the neck as described in Lilly's account. In some cases, such as that of the lamin for Jean Shelly, begun on March 11, 1610, with the melting of the gold, Forman even drew an illustration of the finished product (figure 6). On March 16, the lamine for Mrs. Shelly aforsaid was finally ended. . . . This Lamin the making gould and all stode me in 4 pounds 13 shillings of the which he [the engraver] had 40 shillings for the workmanshipe and 53 shillings for gould and . . . the maid 12 pence and 12 to Barker.[11]

Such protection was not cheap. Forman did not expand on the financial details, and so we do not know what services "Barker" and "the maid" were paid for, nor how much Forman charged Mrs. Shelly when he finally turned the finished amulet over to her. We tend to dismiss such therapy as superstition. Yet this form of therapeutic magic was part of a serious intellectual framework in the early modern period, its rationale articulated most cogently by the Italian philosopher and physician, Marsilio Ficino.[12]

The seriousness with which Forman regarded such magic is made clear by another detailed account of a similar lamin engraved, not for a client, but for Forman himself.

> My gould Ringe with the corrall ston wherin ar Engrauen the caractes and sigill of [Jupiter] was mad. . . .

FIGURE 6: Forman's design for an engraved lamin or protective amulet made of gold, prepared for a patient. Sloane MS. 3822: 13v. Courtesy of the British Library.

The Corralle stone was as brod as a peace of 3d and was begon to be Engrauen with thes sigills of [Jupiter] folowinge the first of feb 1599 ante merid ad ortum Solis [A.M. at sunrise] wheron wer engrauen thes caracters Round about in a Cirkell. . . . [*An illustrative diagram appears in the manuscript here.*]

At this tyme the Ringe yt selfe was begon to be mad of puer gould, an he [the engraver] wrote till 8 of the clocke, and then at after none betwene 2 and 3. And so alwais in the howar artificiall and naturall of [Jupiter][13] till the Ring was Ended.

And the 22 of March folowinge ante mer [A.M.] at 45 p[ast] 5 he began to set the ston into the Ringe and yt was fully Ended 15 minutes post 6 ante merid, vnder the stone was put a bailif[14] and fine virgin parchment wherin was writen the name of the ass[cendants] of my birth & the caracte [astrological sign] & plannet thus. [Virgo Mercury] Simon Forman. This Ring most be worne on the littell finger on the lefte hand & yt preuaills againste witch[c]rafte diuels possession & to expell diuells. against thunder lightning storm & tempest & to giue fauour & credit & to mak on famouse in his profession & to overcom enimies.[15]

Forman's expensive sigils were not created as bait for gullible clients. In this account of his own ring, engraved over a period of five weeks with the utmost care for detail, we find Forman's own deep belief in the system he professed and the wares he sold. The ring, the astrological characters, even the virgin parchment that Jonson mentioned in the lines quoted in the epigraph to this chapter, are all present in Forman's narrative of the manufacture of his wonderful ring. What is missing, however, is Jonson's scorn. Forman was breathless with anticipation, not of cheating a client—as were Jonson's dramatic occultists—but of possessing the ring himself.

The integration, for Forman, of what we now see as separate occult disciplines—in the former example, astrology and magic—is obvious in his theoretical writing as well as in his practice. His treatise "Of Astronomy" begins with the following:

The Science of Astronomie is diuided into 5 partes. that is to saie, into Astronomy, Astrologia, Astromagia, Geomantia and Alchamya.

Astronomia is the knowledge of the heauens fixed stares, and plannetes, of their beinge motions natures and influences concordance and discordans, and takes his name of thes 2 wordes, Astra Nomos, which is to saie the knowledge of the starrs.

Astrologia is diriued of Astra & logos which is to saie the speach

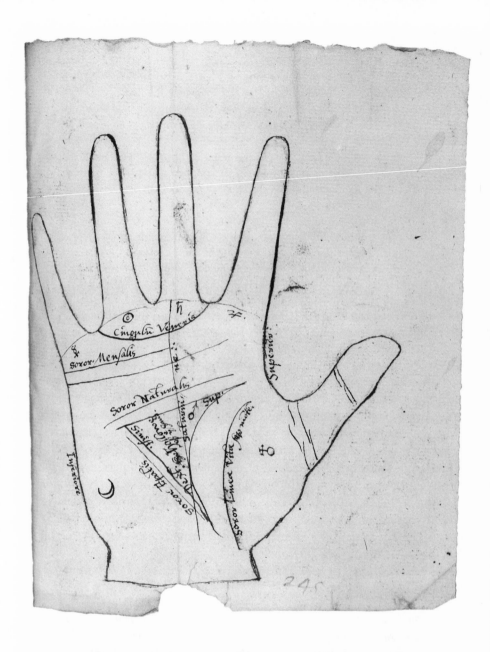

FIGURE 7: Forman's tracing of his own right hand, marked with the lines important for prognostication. This drawing shows not only the hand that wrote all the Forman documents but also Forman's obsessive interest in any sort of predictive scheme, here a version of palm reading. MS. Ashmole 205: 245r. Courtesy of the Bodleian Library, University of Oxford.

showinge signification & Iudgmente of the starrs and plannetes accordinge
to their motions places natures beinges and aspectes.

Forman's differentiation between astronomy and astrology is fairly clear. As
he continues with his definitions the language becomes less familiar:

> Astromagia is diriued of Astra & Magos, which signifieth the wisdom and
> subtiltie of the stares in doinge and effectinge thinges desiered and yt is
> called the third parte of astronomie and the operatiue parte or magicall
> parte therof. . . . Geomantia is called the lower astronomie and yt is deriued
> of geos which is a greke word and in lattin terra which is the Earth and of
> mantia also a greeke worde, which is said to be magosa which is said to
> be vaticinatio, which signifieth vaticination or fortellinge. . . . Alchimia or
> alchimagia whose science or nature is to teach the transmutation of mettalls
> and changinge them from on mettalle to another. . . . And thus Astronomie
> ys said to be of the Heauens and of the Earth, and is mixed of them bothe.[16]

Although modern scholars separate the various occult sciences, Forman envisioned them as parts of an elaborately interconnected system all subsumed
under "astronomy." So determined was he to make the system orderly that
he falsified the etymologies of his terms (alchemy = alchimagia) to force the
parallels. In his everyday life, Forman practiced this integration of occult
operations. He never attempted an alchemical experiment or prepared to
call spirits into a magic circle without first making an astrological cast to be
sure that the time for such a venture was propitious.

For the sake of clarity, I will discuss separately aspects of the occult that in
Forman's papers are interconnected: astrology, magic, alchemy—all of which
he embraced and found a place for in the system outlined above. Witchcraft,
which he feared and sought to prevent or to render ineffective, also played
a role in Forman's life, both in his own dreams and in the problems that his
clients brought to his door.

☞ Astrology

Astrology was the most important influence in Forman's life. He believed
in a God who had not only created the system described by astrology but who
had also given Forman special abilities to interpret it. He consulted the stars
both as part of his medical and advisory practice and for all kinds of decisions
in his private life, whether large or small. In 1598, for example, he cast to find
out whether it was "best to buy M. Havors rhubarb," an ingredient in some of
his medicines. The answer? "It is not good." Forman added, "ther came more

rhubarb presently."[17] Other personal casts asked whether to rent a particular room; which of two applicants to hire as a servant; who had stolen books from his study; whether to buy property; whether to loan money; whether his wife had really gone to her mother's; and whether she behaved honestly or not. Mixed in with these questions were those posed by friends and clients: was a woman pregnant? would the questioner meet again a woman encountered at Sturbridge Fair? (The astrological reply was yes, but warned that she was or would be a harlot and "she vseth sodomy.")[18]

Forman also asked questions about political and national issues. In 1597 he inquired of the stars whether the king of Spain would bring an army against England; in 1598, on October 18, he cast to find out "whether ther shalbe a peace concluded betwen England & Spain by the last of Feb nexte." In 1599 he wanted "to know how my L. Robert Deverex E of Essex shall speed in his voyadge into Ireland & whether he shall prevaill or no." A disastrous forecast followed.[19]

Forman's most consistent use of astrology was, of course, in the diagnosis of illness. Virtually all physicians of the period employed astrology in their practice to determine appropriate days for bloodletting and purging and to set a schedule for administering medications. Less common and more controversial was the use of astrology to assist in diagnosis and to predict the outcome of a case (judicial astrology). Clark notes, however, that "it was not because he was an astrologer that the College objected to Forman."[20] Their objection seems rather to have been that he was a bad astrologer. The *Annals* refer to Forman as a "Pretended Astrologer and great Imposter" and record that the College doctors examined him in the "principles of Astronomy as well as the Elements of Physick,"[21] finding him inadequately prepared in both areas.

Despite the College's scorn of Forman's astrological knowledge, he continued to use astrology constantly. He prepared a number of short treatises, both theoretical and practical, specific and general, of instruction in astrological practice. In "On Astronomy," quoted above, Forman explained and defined a host of astrological terms, rarely getting away from abstract astrological theory. This is quite different from his detailed practical volume entitled "The Astrological Judgmentes of Phisick and other Questions writen by Simon Forman DR of Astronomy and Physick 1606 . . . in which is comprised his experience for 20 years before."[22] Among the practical instructions this volume contains are how to set up a horoscope when a relative asks about a sick person and how to arrive at a diagnosis when a sick person has not consented to the consultation.

In this volume, organized according to the twelve astrological houses, Forman discussed how each was to be used for prognostication and judgment. The fifth house, for example, ruled the woman's matrix. Thus, for answers to questions about conception, menstrual periods, and pregnancy, the astrological physician should look to the signs affecting that house. In its description of the twelfth house, this text reveals the darker side of Forman's astrological knowledge:

> The 12 house is the house of witchcrafte, Enchauntmente, forspeakinge, overseynge,[23] harelynge [?], ill tongues, ill sprites and seacreate Enimies feiries and therfore by this house we knowe, whether on be possessed with an evill sprite, or whether any evill sprite doth followe on or haunte him, or whether he be blasted [blighted by a malignant planet] or feyrie strocke, or be wytched or enchaunted forspoken or overseen or in the handes of his secrete enimies or noe.

The problems enumerated above were regarded as medical because they were apt to produce "heauines thoughte mistruste ferfulnes . . . depe melancoly and madnes and possessing with diuills . . . causing dead palseyes consumptions lamnes [lameness] blastinge feyri strokes."[24]

Other of Forman's didactic astrological texts were less medical in nature. In one, he explains how to cast nativities (birth horoscopes).[25] In another, he gives rules for the astrological finding of lost objects and for determining the fate of an absent person.[26] Forman also offers instructions on how to deal with questions about going to sea—whether to go in a particular ship; how a ship at sea is faring; when an absent ship or an absent sailor will return.[27] In each of these how-to essays, Forman lavishly illustrated the general principles with examples drawn from his own experience. One manuscript in particular (MS. Ash. 366), a compilation of astrological tables written on stiff parchment, probably served Forman as an everyday reference book, ready at hand as he cast his clients' horoscopes.

Astrological topics dominate the only group of his personal letters known to survive, dated between 1599 and 1611 and addressed to Napier. In one, after complaining about the quality of a turkey pastry Napier had sent as a gift, Forman answered Napier's question about treating "parties that be trobled in minde."

> The wai to healp them is to purge the artiries for they ar spirituall diseases and procead from the hart & braine. Therfor after youe haue purged the bodi first of grosse humors with Jeralogodon 2 or 3 [times] then most youe purg the blod in the arteries when [the moon] is in [Libra, Gemini, Aquarius]

going to [Capricorn] and in as[cendance]. But thes parties in my opinion will haue no remedie till fornight after ester next or ther aboutes. They haue overpassed their tyme.[28]

The two professional friends apparently shared not only advice but also the tools of their trade. In another letter, Forman requested that Napier send him by the next messenger or trusty friend "the parchment book you gave me of astrology. . . . Bind it safe in something that it take not wet."[29] This may even have been the reference book of tables mentioned above.

In other passages Forman used astrology almost as an almanac maker might. Toward the end of his life, in 1610 or 1611, Forman gave instructions for when to plant particular trees, herbs, wheat, and beans:

> Beans most be set or sowen in Januari Februari or March in the full mone and they moste be steped in water 2 or 3 daies before youe set them. and they should be cut downe in June & July after the full moon in the third quarter of the moon & put in barnes.

To illustrate, Forman described his own bean-planting experience:

> I did set beans 1608 at the full moon in Februari and March. and those beans did blowe 4 tymes that yeare, and three tymes I had Codes [pods] gret store on them. I had gren beans to eat full and good the 27 of October after of them.[30]

Another manuscript contains Forman's record of the weather for each quarter or season of the year, quarter by quarter, for the mid-1580s.[31] Sometimes he predicted weather by astrological signs; at other times he demonstrated how actual weather conditions could have been predicted astrologically.

From such practical uses of astrology Forman shifted, in other texts, to more overtly manipulative uses of astrology, always concerned, as he was in the letter to Napier quoted above, with how to determine the propitious astrological time for a particular activity. In that letter, Forman explained that the time for treatment of Napier's mentally disturbed patients had passed and that it would not again be favorable until after Easter. Elsewhere, writing about the possibility of influencing love between two people, Forman again stressed the need to observe the astrological limits on time:

> But I haue found by Experience that all consisteth in the tyme of doinge yt for yf the tyme accordinge to the Reuolution of the heauens and aspectes of the plannetes agre not to his [the astrologer's] workinge all his workes shall be in vaine for all thinges ar done in tyme and bound for tyme and the

sprites them selues cannot fullfill any actes but they take and obserue the tyme, and because thou shalte the better knowe the tymes to obteine loue eyther by naturall causes, or vnnaturall, thou shalt here see what I in tymes haue proued my selfe. In the which times thou maiest make ringes lamines ymages caractes [magical symbols] candells or any other thing for loue and preuaille, and missing som of thes tymes, all thy Labor is in Vaine.[32]

Despite the very strict astrological timetable that governed the manufacture of such objects as love-promoting rings, images, and lamins—the activity with which this chapter began—their creation is most properly regarded as one of Forman's magical activities.

☞ Magic

Forman's interest in magic stretched back to his days in Salisbury, well before he established his London practice. He unabashedly, if cryptically, recorded his interest and experiments in his diary, beginning in 1579, the year of his long imprisonment when he wrote (oddly, in view of his incarceration): "This yere I did profecie the truth of many thinges which afterwardes cam to passe, and the very sprites wer subiecte vnto me, what I spake was done."[33] In 1583, what may be a reference to an empowering ring such as those mentioned above appeared in the diary: "the 17 of Decembre I had my ring mad with the egles stone."[34] In 1587, he first mentioned employing a scryer, John Goodridge: "and he sawe firste the 4 of November. . . . I practised magik."[35] Forman replaced Goodridge as scryer with his step-nephew, Steven Mitchell, in 1588: "In Aug. Steven cam to me first and did see first the 21 of Septembre."[36]

Forman and Goodridge worked together again in the 1590s, when Forman once more wrote of their attempts to call spirits. In one instance, on October 31, 1597,

> The said sprit did apeare and said that he walked ther for killing of his father. And he caste out moch fier and kepe a wonderfull a doe but we could not bringe him to humain form. but he was seen like a great black dog & trobled the folk of the house moch & fered them.[37]

In a series of attempts just after this All Hallow's Eve experience, Forman and Goodridge repeatedly made contact with spirits, but the spirits never completely materialized:

> This night [November 2] he [the spirit] cam according to his wont & raued moch & we bound him strongly, & kept him till almost 4 of the clok in the

morning. . . . This night [several nights later] he cam as he had wont & was very furious . . . & cast out moch fier.[38]

In September 1597, Forman had cast to know "whether ever I shall haue that powr in nigromantic that I desier or bring it to effect."[39] His experiments in spirit-calling a month or two later had only limited success, and mention of calling spirits ceases in the diary after this.

References to magic appear frequently in Forman's nonautobiographical writing. He read, and probably added to his library, magical texts that other occultists in the period cited frequently, including works by Albertus Magnus, Roger Bacon, Marsilio Ficino, Henry Cornelius Agrippa, Pico della Mirandola, and other authorities on both white and black magic. He wrote at some length about spirits and their nature. The following passage on the relative power of the four kinds of elemental spirits could well serve to gloss the magical debate between the English and German magicians in Robert Greene's comedy *Friar Bacon and Friar Bungay*:

> Thes earthy sprits ar the loweste of all sprites excepte infernalles . . . and thes sprites haue leste regiment of all sprits except the infernalls, and therfore ar inferior to all other. and ar verie stubborne & frowarde . . . and yt is beste to call them in wodes or old houses and in deserte places. The Sprites of the water ar next aboue the sprits of the Earth. . . . The Sprites of the ayer . . . appeare like angells or like men or women in humain forme and fair shapes, in fine cleare warme wether when the ayer is still and quiete and the heauens cleare & without cloudes and the wind still . . . and they appear sonest to one borne under [Jupiter, Gemini, Libra, or Aquarius] perfuming with swete odors & being well washed & clensed both in his appeirrelle and bodie with fair Intreaties prayers and gentell commaundes. The Sprites of the fierie region haue greateste Regimente and poware over all the sprits of the earth of the water and of the ayer & doe command them. . . . And thes thinges which I haue her writen and said ar the greteste seacretes of arte and ar not to be opened but to the wise.[40]

Forman's explanations of the spirits and their relative powers are very similar to those found in other magical works of the period, as was his claim to be one of the few initiates into the secrets of magic. By repeating these commonplaces, Forman was attempting to master the secrets of magic; he had used a similar technique when he copied the bloodletting diagram and recorded the steps of his first bloodletting when teaching himself medicine. He was learning the basics of magic, but he was not yet an adept magus.

He also wrote about Cabala, acknowledging the link—first forged by Pico della Mirandola—between it and Neo-Platonic magical theory. Like all forms of magical power, Cabala had its dangerous as well as its beneficent aspect:

> [Cabala] must be prepared through astronomi and influence of the stars, through which all wisedom is knowen from the beginninge or ground. . . . But nowe through the length of tyme, this arte hath been dyuided into 2 partes, the on is that which we haue nowe in hande [what Forman attempted to practice] and the other in apperance of great hollines, is joyning to the dyuille, as the mightie philosopher and great magus Artefius did set forth and write a bocke of it. In the which ther be superstitiouse wordes caracters and cerimonies, wherbye god is robbed of his omnipotence and power and is disshonored. Of which for breuities sake we will set downe heare 6 examples, to the end that every faithful harte may see what difference ther is betwene the true arte, and the diuelish falls arte.[41]

Forman worked hard at learning magic: he studied books, copied magical manuscripts, tried to set down in his own words what he had learned, and attempted—like John Dee—to put in practice the magical rituals that philosophers like Pico and Ficino had theorized about. Forman even dreamed about magic. On August 23, 1594, for example, he wrote: "I dremt I did see in a glas when I did call and that I did heare alsoe, & that yt was the first tim that euer I did heare or see & I was aunswered directly of all thinges."[42]

During the year 1597, Forman's spirit-calling activities seemed to reach their height. In a casebook note, he recorded an attempt to realize this dream of seeing in a magical glass:

> Item 1597 the 8 of August Monday am at 40 past 9 we began to mak our glase & to prai & Jhon fasted the Monday . . . Saturday before & the same daie & bought glas on the Saturday the 6 of Aug & we drue the circle in the virgin parchment.[43]

By choosing the proper time, gathering the proper equipment, and fasting (it is perhaps worth noting that "John"[44] did the fasting), Forman was attempting to follow the rules for summoning spirits, but he left no record of real success. He "saw" primarily in his dreams.

Forman never was secure in his command of spirits or of other aspects of white magic but, as a firm believer in learning through experience (a central tenet both of his medical practice and of his instructional books on astrology and medicine), he continued to try to control spirits. He felt blessed by God with occult talent and was certain that, if he could learn enough, he could attain the wonderful power that the authorities he trusted had promised would be granted to the wise and devoted man.

☞ Alchemy

With similar faith in his own abilities and the possibility of his success, Forman worked at alchemy throughout the latter half of his life. Forman's early papers contain few references to alchemy but, as he became more prosperous and had money to spend on the necessary supplies, his ambition to find the philosopher's stone, that substance that would turn base metal to gold and prolong life, mounted. A poem that introduces one of his manuscript books on alchemy emphasizes the time and money alchemy demanded:

> I Forman haue writen thes verses fewe
> The trouth of this art to thee to showe
> Crave wisdom of god the same to vnderstand
> Ells meddell not herwith nor tak it in hand
> For yt wil coste thee moch wordly [sic] pelfe
> But truste not others but doe yt thy self
> Learne therfore firste to cleanse purifie & sublime[45]
> To dissolue congelle distill and somtime
> To conioyne and sept and howe to doe all
> That when thou thinkeste to rise, thou doste not falle
> Truste to thy selfe and not to another
> I can say no more to thee yf thou were my brother.[46]

Just as he dreamed of calling spirits, Forman dreamed of alchemical success. He recorded a collection of dreams, dated from 1587 to 1594, which he entitled, "Of certain dremes and visions that I haue sene totching the philosophers stone."[47] A manuscript that Forman copied in 1592, "A dialogue of Egidius de Vadius betwene nature and the disciple of philosofie of the serching of the philosophers stone," suggests how he understood his command of the various medical and magical disciplines in which he was interested. Forman's copy concludes with these words: "1592 March the 23 writen out by me Simon Forman, practiser in phisiq chirurgery and astronomy and sercher of the secrets of nature for the philosophers stone."[48] The difference between "practiser" and "searcher," the first claiming mastery while the second implying a search for mastery, suggests that Forman regarded himself as still a student when it came to alchemy.

However, Forman continued his alchemical endeavors. A number of his manuscripts dated after 1600 are alchemical. Most appear to be copies from borrowed books or manuscripts that Forman made for his personal use rather than to instruct others. Ashmole manuscripts 1494 and 1491 are good examples. Together they form a two-volume alphabetical text titled "Of Appoticarie Druges." Despite its somewhat misleading title, the manuscript is primarily alchemical, defining terms such as "circulation," "cibation" ["a feeding and nourishing of the stone"], and "penetration" in an alchemical context. The volumes would have provided useful guidance for someone reading alchemical tracts or beginning to practice the art. Under "valis or vessells," for example, Forman diagrammed all sorts of vessels needed at various stages of the alchemical process, a helpful section for the would-be alchemist who was gathering his supplies (figure 8).[49]

Ashmole manuscript number 1472, another alchemical text, is also arranged alphabetically. Sprinkled through these volumes and found occasionally in other Forman manuscripts are formulas or instructions for various alchemical operations: "to gilde siluere," "to make gold water," "to make proiection [to transmute metals]." Forman regularly cited alchemical authorities from the medieval period such as George Ripley, Raymond Lull, and Thomas Norton, as well as contemporaries such as Edward Kelly, Dee's scryer. The standard nature of these sources is suggested by Elias Ashmole's inclusion of some of them (Ripley, Norton) in the middle of the seventeenth century in his *Theatrum chemicum Britannicum* (London, 1652), a book owned and annotated by no less an alchemical searcher than Isaac Newton.[50]

Forman went beyond mere study. Both his diary and his casebooks mention his attempts to create the philosopher's stone. As early as 1594, he tried to manufacture "the stone." In 1599, his alchemical activity increased; on March 27, he cast a figure to find out "whether my stone will prosper and com to good and whether I shall effecte yt & have good therof."[51] On August 8, he cast again "to knowe what wilbe com of my philosophers ston. Whether yt will proue profitable to me or noe & com to any good effect." This time, he added a note: "it was set on fier & spilt."[52] Three more times in 1599, Forman asked about his success in making the stone. Another failure must have occurred during this time, for in the third cast Forman asked whether to begin work once again.

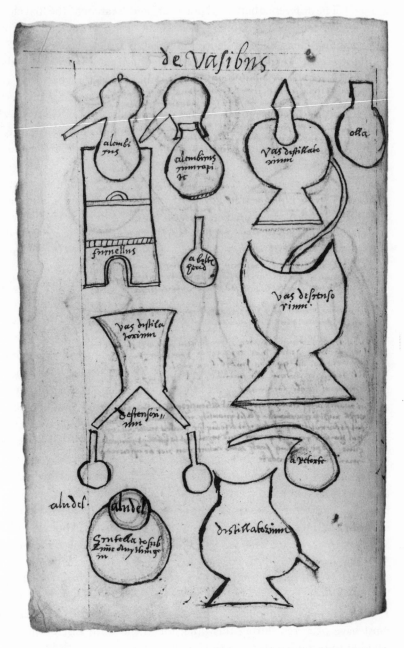

FIGURE 8: Forman's drawings of the various "vessels" needed for alchemical operations.

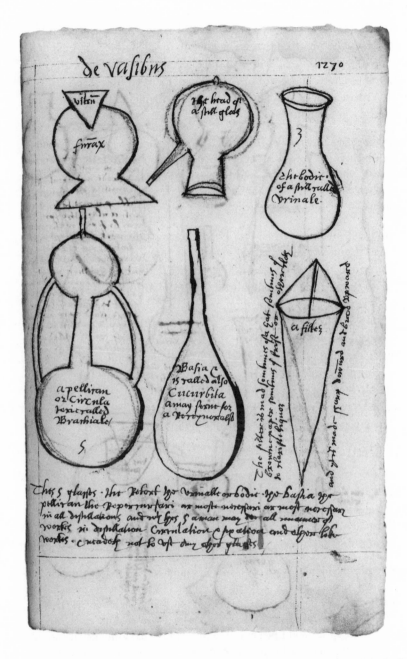

MS. Ashmole 1491: 1269–1270. The Bodleian Library, University of Oxford.

In yet another manuscript, Forman summarized these unsuccessful experiments. Here he reported that he had begun the alchemical process three times, and "it framed not." The fourth time he had used mercury with vitriol and saltpeter but, after more work, "by reason of many troubles I left it off for a time."[53] A recipe that Forman included in one of his alchemical manuscripts alludes to the rigors of alchemical distillation:

> In rispect and consideration of this my bocke that I haue her writen, wherin
> ar the conclusions of philosofie and other thinges hard to be obteyned, but
> with great labor Industrie and knowledge, and for because a man working
> moch aboughte the fier might wax feeble and fainte, to comforte him withall
> I haue set downe the making of jellye.

The ingredients include calves' feet boiled a long time in rose water and claret wine "if you will bestowe the coste," or in rosemary water and red wine if claret and rose water were too expensive. Boil until "a drop put on a thing doth stand and not rone abrod." The mixture was to be strained through a coarse cloth, and cinnamon, ginger, and sugar were to be added. The alchemist's restorative was nothing more or less than calves' foot jelly.[54]

Alchemical writings are among the last dated materials in Forman's manuscripts and suggest that his interest in finding the philosopher's stone continued until the end of his life. Alchemy's rewards may have seemed more tangible than the abstract knowledge that being able to contact spirits promised the practitioner of magic. In any case, after the 1590s, alchemy replaced magic as one of Forman's consuming interests.

☞ Witchcraft

The one aspect of the occult that Forman consistently shunned was witchcraft, although he certainly believed in its power. As usual, Forman's dreams revealed his concerns. In the following detailed description of a dream, Forman made the classic distinction between his white, magical, male enterprise and the black business of the female witch:[55]

> I drempt that I and Jhon Ward our clarke and another were in the chauncell
> of a church together and Jhon Ward was calling of sprites for me thought
> he had powar in calling of sprites, and [I] stod by loking on him to see the
> sprites but I could not see them but by glimpsinge and then me thoughte
> I sawe a white sprite. and I byd him aske the sprites what wold mak me to
> see and he determined to doe yt but we could not bring them to speake and
> talk to vs.

Here Forman in his dream experiences the same failure to persuade the spirits to talk that he recorded in his waking moments.

> I loked vp and sawe the church dore open, and I went to shut yt lest any body should com in and as I came to the dore, ther cam in a talle long old woman with exceading black hollowe eyes, and to daughters with her. And I asked them sayinge what ar youe and wherfore com youe heather. And the woman said I com heather to learne som of thy coninge for thou art calling of sprites heare, and my daughter here is a witch and she by her skille dyd knowe yt & brought me heather to haue som of this sprites. and she came that she might haue som also. And her daughter was the ugleste creature that ever I sawe & black with a long face yll fauored & she had mad contractes me thought with the dyuell, and me thought with that the body of the church was full of sprites flying vp and downe.

Forman offered in the dream the standard distinction between the work of the magician and the witch:

> And I sayd vnto the woman, doste thou and thy daughter thinke that my conninge and hers is like. I bind thes sprites by poware dyuine, and soe mak vse of them to godes glory and youe make contractes with the dyuell and giue him your soulles to worke mischef for youe. a waye you euill disposed creaturs god hath noe fellowship with the dyuell, and with that I waked.[56]

In this account, Forman carefully demarcated the sphere of his occult activity from that of the witch. He, John Ward, and another—three men—come to church where they call a "white sprite." Ward is the summoner, Forman—as always—is the careful observer and narrator. Drawn to them by the aura of magical power but desiring to leech off the men's power (witches had no power of their own, but received it only through a bargain with the devil), come three women, enough to suggest a coven but also the powerful number three. In fact, the second daughter, like the "other" with Forman and Ward, has no role in the narrative except to be one of three. These women are described as "black," "hollow," and "ill fauored"; the witch daughter is "the ugleste creature." The dream clearly marked off the territory Forman hoped to claim, white magic's difference from black witchcraft, representing the practice of the men as positive by contrasting it to the demonic plans and allegiances of the dark women. (Similarly in the occult drama of the period, white magic is often represented in direct opposition to black magic or witchcraft; Prospero's unstaged contest with the witchcraft of the ugly Sycorax is only one example of such opposition.) But Forman's dream also betrays his uneasiness about his proximity to the forbidden ground of witchcraft. His occult activity had, after all, attracted the three women who believed they could share his power.

Forman confronted witchcraft or suspected witchcraft not just in dreams but in his practice as well. Certain clients thought themselves victims of witches and came to Forman for verification.[57] In 1601, Nicholas Knight of Lambeth asked Forman whether "allis Baker of Lambeth or Alls Foote wyddowe of Stretham in Surrey haue bewitched his cattell."[58] Knight already believed himself to be the victim of witchcraft; he needed help only in identifying the witch. Sometimes a patient was troubled by apparitions or unusual occurrences, as was a woman "that dwells in the lyttle lane going into the felds beyond Holborn bridge. This woman is haunted at night with a goste, or sprite contynually and she heres yt often. . . . and ther is a sister of her husbandes that causeth her to be bewitched by an old woman."[59] In this case, the victim came with the symptoms, but it is unclear how much of the diagnosis was Forman's and how much her own. She must certainly have identified the in-law who wished her ill.

Cases involving witchcraft and forespeaking appear occasionally in Forman's casebooks, though he had many fewer than Napier.[60] In 1597, Barnard Tyrry, 23, complained of his head; he might faint; he was faint at heart, fearful, and trembling. Forman said that he seemed bewitched. The other cases in 1597 all involved older women, ranging in age from 43 to 65. Of these, one thought she was bewitched, but Forman decided that she had merely taken grief and cold. Mother Pace of Lemington, however, had trouble with her hip and sciatica, and was "blasted with an ille ayre or spirit"; Katherine Wild was bewitched and was in danger of death.

In the same year, Forman wrote about Joan Knight from Baldock at greater length. She complained of pain in the head and belly and suspected that she was forespoken by Katherine Bigrane. She and her five-year-old son had been seen by Forman on June 29 for medical problems. The boy pined and consumed [wasted] in his arms and legs and had terrible dreams. Forman had predicted eventual death. On her second visit on July 14, Knight wanted to know specifically whether she was a victim of Bigrane's witchcraft. Forman confirmed that she was "ouerseen" and added, "the first too potions that wer made for her [at the time of the last visit] wer burste, on by the wai homward & the other soe sone as yt cam home standing in the cobherd."[61] The unexplained destruction of the medicines helped confirm the presence of witchcraft.

Forman was quite willing to reject witchcraft as a diagnosis if the patient's condition so indicated. Compare the different diagnoses he gave two young children whose fathers came to ask for Forman's help; both children were sick in May 1601. Lancelot Bathhurste was twenty-nine weeks old, stuffed in his head and stomach, and "melancholy hath taken the brain." Forman said he was "forspoken & haunted with a sprite."[62] A few days later, Forman diagnosed Mary Tut, one and three-quarter years old, who was very cold and taken by fits, as having the "falling evil." He specifically found her to be "not bewitched nor enchanted."[63] Forman knew that bewitchment was a constant peril for his clients but did not always diagnose witchcraft when suspicious symptoms (such as fits) were present.

If a patient were bewitched, however, Forman was prepared with remedies:

> When any body is bewitched you shall do thus. Let one watch [when] the witch or partie suspected doe goe into her house and presently before any body goe in after her let on pull a handfull of the thatch over the door or take a tylle [tile] from over the doore of the witch, and put it in the fire and burne it settinge a paire of brandyrons [andirons] over it. . . . Or els take 2 horseshoes and heate them hote in the fiere and naile one of them at the threshold of the doore and quentch the other in the Vrine of the partie bewitched and set the Vrine over the fiere, and the horseshoe in it and set a trenate[64] over it, and make the Vrine boyle, till it consume, and so shall the witch be punished, but keepe her out, and let her not come in.
>
> Or ells take the smocke or the shirte of the partie bewitched and dipe him well in his Vrine, then put him [the urine-soaked clothing] in the fier and [the] witch undoubtely will come and be so tormented exceedingly.[65]

In one case, Forman prescribed for a patient a variation of the remedy recommended above. Katherine Brook, a widow of sixty, was faint with a fever and pain in her stomach and head. She vomited and scoured [had diarrhea], and her "order [ordure or excrement] coms vp at her mouth and she will die or scap hard 9 dais hence & hath marvaylouse fites and yt takes her about the navell first & soe workes vpward she seems to be bewitched." The treatment recommended was to "prepar 3 daies & purge & burne her water/ or mak a cake of ri [rye] flowr & her vrin."[66]

Such remedies, certainly not original to Forman, indicate that he took witchcraft seriously. Indeed, he criticized Reginald Scot's *Discoverie of Witchcraft*, one of the few books of the period to express doubts about witchcraft, as a foolish book "sold amonge the people to harden their hartes & make them carles [careless] of the thretes of godes Judgmentes."[67] From this remark, we can surmise that Forman believed that witchcraft was one way by which God punished those who misbehaved.

Like King James, another firm believer in witchcraft, Forman recognized that some claims of witchcraft were false:

> Many . . . persuade themselfes to [be] bewitched or forspoken or possesset with spirits, and . . . many . . . thinke themselues to be this or that through much melancholy oppressing the braine and hearte, as one sometimes in Magdalen Colledge in Oxford, that thought himselfe to be a glasse a Vrinall, and would not come nere the wale, for feare of burstinge,[68] another was in Cambridge, as I heard thought himself a cocke, and would croe like a coke and saye he was a cocke.[69]

Forman's choice of examples from the universities suggests his attitude toward the university-educated, such as his enemies the doctors. They could be as deluded as anyone else.

Though Forman was skeptical about certain individual claims of witchcraft, he firmly believed in the ability of occult spirits to intrude in the lives of men. An incident involving his step-nephew, Steven Mitchell, during the period when Forman was living in Sussex, bears witness to his belief in spirits.

> This boie was my sisters sonn and was my prentice, and I ryding to lowist left him at home and about on hower after I was gone he ran awaie and I comming hom at 7 at night my man told me of yt and I set this figure which wai he was gon & howe far, and I found he was gon som 4 mils almoste of to Chaly, and I toke my horse and rod awai erly in the morne and was at Chalie by 4 a cloke and I found him ther lodged in an alle house and was vp and redy to haue bin gone had I staied on halfe hower more he had bin gone and he wold not knowe me a great whill but said I was non of his unkell nor master & he wold not goe with me but of compulsion. so I caried him hom again, but did not beat him nor punish him for yt, because he went a wai by the prouokaent [provocation?] of the sprit as after he told me, howe the sprit caried him into the wod & ther lefte him.[70]

Forman's nephew clearly understood Uncle Simon's threshold of credulity with regard to the power of spirits to interfere with human beings. But this is not the only occasion on which Forman appears to a modern reader as oddly credulous. For example, symptoms that would today be read as unmistakable evidence of child abuse, Forman diagnosed as the mischief practiced by fairies and ill spirits. Thus his explanation for the physical condition of children like young Thomas Colford:

> This child was a bastard as his mother confessed and she confessed that both Philip Ho[l]mes and Leonard Holmes did both kepe her, and on of them was the father of yt but she knewe not which & they wer two brethren, & yt seams to be the sonn of Leonard [a judgment determined by astrological cast]. When yt was but 15 wickes old yt was most gryuously pinched with the feiries with black spotes on his breste sydes belly back arms & thighes & legs and on the buttockes & arms throat and cratched as yf yt were with pines.[71]

Physical damage done by spirits or by witches who ordered the spirits to perform mischief was a medical problem that practitioners attempted to treat when it occurred.

James Sharpe judiciously summarizes the period's response to witchcraft:

> Some people in Elizabethan and early Stuart England, as Richard Napier's case books show, were worried about witchcraft to the point of obsession and mental unbalance. Others . . . were able to reject belief in the power of witchcraft altogether. Most people, one suspects, were somewhere in between: willing to accept witchcraft as a possibility, able to recognize or suspect it when they thought it was harming them or people they knew, yet seeing it only as one of the many possible hazards that life might throw at them.[72]

Students of the early modern period often isolate its occult beliefs and practices as curiosities. In thus framing the occult, they follow those critics of Forman and John Dee who—because magic, astrology, and alchemy were part of Forman and Dee's intellectual interests and everyday activities— branded both men quacks or dupes and gave them little room in accounts of the intellectual life of the period. Yet consideration of the number and social range of Forman's clients—courtiers, clergy, tradesmen, laborers, servants— suggests that the norm for sixteenth-century London was closer to the occult sensibilities of a Forman or a Dee than to the skeptical perspective of a Ben Jonson or Reginald Scot. Certainly Forman and his clients saw a universe rife with occult powers. They were better off, they reasoned, if they took these powers seriously and did their best to control, to limit, or at least to be prepared for the occult's effects on their daily lives.

❧ S I X ❧

Forman and His Books

A MAJOR PART OF FORMAN's interaction with his culture and society involves his relationships with books. Books got him in trouble with the authorities; books were confiscated or stolen from him; he acquired, copied, and composed books; books taught him medicine; and books marked important milestones in his life. When Forman fashioned the story of his early life, his loss of schooling emerged as one of the major traumas of his childhood, coupled in his mind with the death of his father.

Forman's apprenticeship agreement with Matthew Commins called for three years of grammar school, which he never received.[1] When Forman asked to be released from his agreement, he explained that Commins "had not performed his covenantes according to promise, and therfore he [Forman] wold give of the trade and goe to his bocke againe."[2] Throughout his autobiography Forman expresses more love for books and education than he does for people. Had his schoolmaster not demanded high standards of him, Forman writes, he "wold have wepte and suobbed more than yf he had byne beaten." If the schoolmaster gave him permission to play intead of study, Forman would say, "play, play her is nothing but play I shall never be a good scoller." Even as a schoolboy, he remembers that he was set apart: "alwaies when his fellowes went to playe he [Forman] wold goe to his bocke."[3]

Though there is undoubtedly some exaggeration in Forman's recollection, a similar passion for books appears in the notes of the adult Forman. Whenever he moved from one house to another, Forman cast a horoscope on the day that he took possession of the new house. For one move, on April 10, 1593, Forman wrote, "I toke possession and caryed a bock into yt

and left him ther, but I cam not for good and all till the 14 dai of Aprill."[4]
Books meant home to Forman; leaving this book marked his possession of his
new house. When he lost or misplaced books, he grew extremely concerned.
On November 2, 1598, he cast "pro libro mea . . . bosone bock of ship"
[apparently a boatswain's record book or instructional book]. He added, "I
found yt in my own custody in Feb 1599—deo gratias."[5]

Much more serious was a theft of books on March 11, 1598, from
the study of a house he rented in Lambeth. Although Forman never said
exactly how many books were taken, he cast regularly through 1598 for their
whereabouts. Finally, in the 1599 casebook, he announced that the thieves
were three Cambridge men: Thomas Russell, William Grange, and George
Nicolas ("he is gon beyond sea & is becom a Seminary Prist").[6] At least two
of the men had tried to sell some of the stolen books to "mr. Coomy" and
had been caught. Forman listed half a dozen titles or authors (including a gilt
Geneva testament given him by his childhood friend and former mistress Ann
Young), but whether his list comprised the whole theft or only some of the
missing books is not clear. He must have retrieved the ones he listed because
in 1600 he began to translate one of them, an edition and commentary by
John of Saxony of a text of Alcabitius, into English.[7]

Forman had a history of books being taken from him. Matthew Commins had taken away his Latin books to prevent them from distracting his
apprentice from his work. Forman had begun to collect books at an early
age. He had enough in 1575 to excite the interest of "Cox" (no connection
to the "Cokkis" whose medical manuscript Forman owned) who brought
Parson Bref to examine them and enough to confiscate in 1579 when he
was sent to prison. The story of these confiscated books is very fragmentary,
traceable only through a few oblique references in Forman's diary. He did
not say how many were taken (he obviously managed to keep the Cokkis
manuscript), but when they were brought to John Penruddock's home in
1587, "many" were missing. The final reference to these books came in
1592 when Forman reported that he rejoiced finally to get them in his own
hands again.[8]

Whether or not it was these confiscated books that were responsible
for his imprisonment in 1579, he wrote that it was a book that led to his
thirty-six day jail stay in March, 1587: "taken in the church prainge & for
my bocke I was sente to prison." Above the entry he added "for a prayer
bocke."[9] Forman's books were still a source of danger in 1596 when he noted
in his diary on January 30: "Henry Pepper cam to me craftely to undercrop

[subvert] me and told me he sawe certain bockes of myn, as Picatrix, &c"; on March 1, he noted "strife with Pepper, about words."[10]

He even dreamed about his books. In one dream he is dead, and at his own wake he is given his books. He packs them up and moves them to another place. In another dream, he is in danger of being wrecked off the coast of Cornwall: "in thend landed safe . . . ther we lodged in an Inn & so I awaked & that night also a lyttle before I was troubled about hiding of my bockes of ppe [?] & I had strang bockes brought me writen in Karactes."[11] There is even evidence that Forman leased or bought a second property in order to keep his dangerous books away from his own living quarters (see chapter 7).

When Forman spoke of books, he might have meant either manuscript books or printed books; what part of his collection was printed and what part manuscript cannot be determined. Forman was an avid copier of texts. I have noted his laborious copying of Boorde's text into his Cokkis manuscript (which turned a printed book into a manuscript book) and his copying of seven books of Paracelsus that he borrowed from William Falowfild. In his diary for 1600, he recorded that he "wrote out the 2 bockes of De arte memoratu of Appolonius Niger. . . . I copied out also the 4 bockes of Stegannographia and diuers other bockes."[12] He was on the lookout for books he wanted, probably to borrow and copy. In the 1601 casebook, he jotted a note about "Mr. Horner in Croked Lane at the corner house a victeling house he hath Mr. Lines profecies in parchemente."[13]

Oddly, there are no references in all of Forman's papers to buying books, either in manuscript or in print. He seems to have preferred to borrow texts and to make his own copies. In his early years when finances were very tight, this preference might have been explained as a way of saving money, but by the late 1590s, when Forman bought armor, household goods, real estate, good clothes, and art, money can no longer have been the dominant concern. Perhaps book buying was something he did not record—surely he must have bought some books—but if so, his silence is odd considering all the purchases he did mention. This question makes Napier's "acquittance" for Forman's books sixteen years after his death all the more important to understand (see Introduction). If Napier sent books back to Clement so that Clement could sell them, then Forman must have had a collection of books not in his own hand, books that he had presumably bought, since Napier clearly retained Forman's own manuscripts. (The reference in Napier's note to "mathematical bookes"[14] supports this reading of the note since Forman's Ashmole manuscripts are unlikely to have been described as mathematical.)

If Napier bought the books he had been housing for sixteen years, however, then Forman's books were probably largely those that he had copied.

Forman had no qualms about "improving" the texts he copied or translated. We have seen earlier the way he wove various sources into the Cokkis manuscript. In a manuscript of Artephius that he translated, "The Kaye of the greater wisdom," he concluded the text with the following note:

> Explicit clauis sapientiae majoris Artifio translated into Englishe 1609 23 of May by Symon Forman. The Astrologicall phisition of Lambeth.
>
> But in the Lattin coppi was moch false Latten and in mani places wordes and sentences lefte out. The which accordinge to our vnderstandinge sence and knowledge we haue Repaired & made more perfecte and playner to the Reder in many places. Wher we could make reason or sence therof. The reste we translated as we found yt without sence or reason in many other places.[15]

Far from being apologetic about deviating from his originals in transcriptions and translations of texts, Forman was proud that he could make them "more perfect and plainer to the Reader" whenever possible.

☞ Print Publication

Though he composed a number of "books," Forman saw only one into print, a seven-leaf quarto entitled *The Groundes of the Longitude: With an Admonition to all those that are Incredulous and believe not the Truth of the same. Written by Simon Forman student in Astronomie and Phisique, 1591.*[16] Many of his manuscript books seem ready for a printer, neatly copied, ruled, and sometimes even marginally referenced,[17] but Forman never returned to print after this one early pamphlet publication. He claimed, in a letter to Napier, to be working on

> the bocke that I told youe I mente to put in presse. I haue halfe done. therfore I pray forget not your promise, for the aunsweringe of all Invectiues againste our profession, that youe may haue yt redy with expedition in the English tongue for all the wordle to vewe.[18]

Though Forman here urged Napier to fulfill a promise to write a vernacular defense of astrological medicine,[19] he gave no indication of his own book project. He "mente" to put his own new book in press, but elsewhere he expressed scorn of printing. In an enigmatic little list entitled "Thes thinges ar against a common wealth," Forman began:

yron mills. for spoil of wood
glasse houses for spoil of wood
sugar houses for spoil of wood & egges
printing of bockes. because yt hindereth scollars and writing & maintayneth
vice.[20]

Other negative references to printed books appear among his papers, though in *The Groundes of the Longitude* Forman listed, among examples of important discoveries made by individual men (in defense of his own claim to have single-handedly discovered how to figure longitudes), "the arte of Printing."[21] At the end of the tiny quarto Forman promised that

> The Tables hereto belonging shall follow, and be printed shortly, with certaine other Bookes of Astronomie and Astrologie, as the Booke of the three sortes of houres, Naturall, Artificiall, and Magicall, with all the doubtes of Astronomie, and alterations and significations of the Planets, the moouing of the eight Sphere, and the way to erect a figure both by the Eccliptike line, as also by the oblique ascention, wherein the misterie of Arte lieth hid, with diuers other Bookes God willing if they may be permitted.[22]

In 1591, Forman planned to print other books, but none ever appeared.

The Groundes of the Longitude is one of Forman's most peculiar works, for it tells almost nothing about longitude and contains none of the practical detail with which most of Forman's manuscript books are filled. Instead it is, primarily, an elaborate defense of the proposition that an unknown like Forman could discover how to determine longitude and, second, an advertisement for his services as a tutor in the subject:

> Any man that is desirous of the knowledge thereof may learne the truth thereof at the Authors handes if he repayre vnto him, or else if he or they repaire to *Master Robart Parkes* [the text mentions "Robert Parker marchant of London," presumably the same person, several lines earlier] in pudding lane.[23]

Forman was trying to drum up business with this publication, though he may also have believed his method was too secret or complex for the general reader. He clearly had no intention of printing real information: "they that doe know it are sworne by a sacred othe not to manifest or teach the same to any without leaue before hand of the Author."[24] It is unclear whether his caution was based solely on his concern that his sale of information would be jeopardized if he put details in print or whether he genuinely believed that his information was for the restricted few. Forman's pamphlet claimed to offer fifteen grounds for determining longitude, most drawn from Genesis, Ptolemy, and Sacrobosco, all standard Christianized Ptolemaic cosmologies. For example, one ground states: "the Earth is quiet and vnmoveable, and is accounted the Center of the worlde."[25] But at the end of the list of grounds (which explains nothing about longitude except that it is measured from east to west, in contrast to the north to south measure of latitude), he again reverts to secrecy: "Too Groundes more I haue left out, because they are most true, so they giue too plain evidence, and too much vnderstanding to a subtill witte."[26] Forman insisted that he had knowledge to offer, but he would not divulge it in print.

Though Forman's treatise seems perfectly innocuous in its bland emptiness, Thomas Hood, a teacher of navigation and designer of navigational instruments, took offense. Forman began his pamphlet by mentioning various navigational instruments—the compass, the astrolabe, the "Crosse staffe and Ballestile." Hood had published the previous year a work entitled *The Use of two Mathematicall Instrumentes, the Crosse Staffe . . . and the Jacob's Staffe*. Hood's cross-staff modified an already existing instrument called the balestilha. Forman had obviously been referring to Hood's new instrument in his opening paragraph in what seems to the modern reader a rather complimentary way, classifying it with two venerable and indispensable navigational tools. Nevertheless, Hood interpreted Forman's reference as an attack, and in *The Use of both the Globes, Celestiall and Terrestrial* (1592), he complained in the preface that "one (how profoundly soeuer he thinketh of his learning) not being hable ether to wright true English, or Latine, hath gone about to *form an* outrageous and most impudent Pamphlet to my disgrace, & to commit it to the presse" [italics in the original].[27]

Like Forman's, Hood's pamphlet invited prospective pupils to come to his residence for instruction. Forman's commercial bid for pupils must have seemed to Hood, who had studied both medicine and mathematics at Cambridge, an attempt by an uneducated upstart to draw away his own clientele.[28] Forman was aware of Hood's attack; in the 1591 diary entry he noted: "the 22 of Novembre Mr Hoodes bock came out against me."[29] There is some evidence for an intervening publication by Hood, now lost, which responded directly to Forman's pamphlet. Johnston quotes a reference by Thomas Harriot to "Forman's book of the longitudes . . . [and] Hood's Answer to the same" and points out that though Forman refers to Hood's attack on him as already published in November 1591, the Hood text on the globes, which mentions Forman obliquely in the preface, was not published until 1592.[30]

Whatever the exact details of Hood's attack, his printed rebuke may have persuaded Forman that print publication left him more vulnerable to public attack than if he published in manuscript, where he could more readily control the circulation of his text. In any case, Forman's 1591 pamphlet said less about its ostensible subject than any of his later manuscript texts did about theirs. There is no further reference in his papers to his great discoveries about longitude. Despite his noises about publication in the Napier letter, he left no evidence that he intended any of his later manuscript books for the press.

☞ Forman's Book Collection

Unlike John Dee, Forman left no catalog or list of his books. Titles that he mentioned owning or copying were usually present as well in Dee's library. Both men also recorded dreams about threats to their books. Nonetheless, in almost every other respect Forman's attitude toward his collection of books seems different from Dee's.

William Sherman has argued persuasively that Dee's library should be seen as a "privy library," restricted in its use but nevertheless open to certain people who interacted with Dee. Members of the court, foreign scholars, even the queen, came to work in the collection or to look at it. Sherman suggests that Dee may have even kept duplicate copies of some of his books so that he could lend or sell them to scholars or those who came to study with him at Mortlake.[31] Moreover, Dee's library was not confined to a single room in his home but spilled out into several rooms. Sherman writes, "Dee's base of operations was his own household, and his textual activities were carried out alongside his domestic and communal duties. . . . [Dee's library] represented a place where court, city, and university could meet."[32]

By contrast, Forman's books were for the most part segregated from his domestic space; during many of the years he lived in London, he rented a separate property in which to house them. Sherman sees Dee's library as a meeting place for a select group of nobles and intellectuals, but I find it more credible to think of Forman's "study" as a locked room to which only he had access and which others might enter only at his express invitation. The constant arrival of patients and clients at his consulting room made such a private place more necessary for Forman than for someone to whom the public had less resort: one more difference between a person who, like Dee, benefited from the support of patrons, and someone who, like Forman, found financial support by working in a far less exclusive milieu.

The book-filled study was Forman's refuge not only from patients, however, but from his domestic life as well. In Dee's various records, his wife figures prominently. She is the witness before whom Richard Cavendish swore to return a borrowed book; someone about whose health Dee worries in his diary; a central figure in the household space which was also Dee's library and place of business.[33] By contrast, Forman's young wife is rarely mentioned, except as his most regular sexual partner and as the object of his jealousy and suspicion. Her sphere of activity and of imaginative resonance both seem almost completely separate from the arenas where Forman's intellectual life and work took place. Dee made his collection of books one of the chief means by which he communicated with the world at large. Very differently, Forman made the room he filled with his books a place to burrow, to hide from a world he interpreted as often unfriendly.

Lacking a catalog, any reconstruction of what Forman kept locked in his study must at best be tentative. Although he mentions a number of specific texts in his various manuscripts, in only a few cases is his ownership of those books certain. The library was predictably richest in medical and occult works, a number of which he probably acquired by making his own copies of texts that he had borrowed. He reported copying a Paracelsian text, Apollonius's *De Arte Memoratu*, and *Steganographia* by John Trithemius. Bound into manuscript volumes along with Forman papers are a copy of Chaucer's *Treatise on the Astrolabe*[34] and a text by Sacrobosco[35] as well as fragments attributed by Forman to Avicenna, Roger Bacon, George Ripley, Raymond Lull, and Thomas Norton.[36]

Forman probably owned some travel and reference books. He repeatedly cites *Mandeville's Travels*, for example, and mentions Maplet's *A Green Forest, or a Natural History* as well as Thomas Elyot's dictionary, cited for evidence of a giant's skull found near Salisbury.[37] He frequently referred to Chaucer with great admiration. But he attacked Reginald Scot's *The Discoverie of Witchcraft* and John Harvey's *A Discoursive Problem concerning Prophesies* as "folish bockes . . . sold amonge the people to harden their hartes & make them carles [careless] of the thretes of godes Judgmentes."[38] He had evidently read both books, but he may not have owned copies. He transcribed a poem praising the explorer Martin Frobisher and referred to John Lyly's fictional creation Euphues in his autobiography.[39]

Though Forman probably owned, in printed texts or manuscript copies, many of the texts he mentions, my conclusion that he owned a sizeable book collection is based chiefly on the way in which he (and later Napier) talked about "the books" and on the arrangements Forman made to house them. We know that he had a "study" where he kept his books as early as 1598, because the study door was broken open when the Cambridge men stole his books. Whatever the makeup of the library which his father left at his death, Clement Forman clearly believed the books numerous and valuable enough to be the nest egg that would pay for his legal training.

Why did Forman gather a book collection? He clearly wanted books for the practical information they gave him about medical and occult subjects. He was willing to copy, to edit, and to "correct" books to get this information. Forman also used his books as authorities, as backup for his own observations. In his poem on "Anti-Christ," the margins are sprinkled with citations to authorities. He wrote of the serpent that would rise from the tribe of Dan:

Yt is thus said in holly write
Ex babilonia exibit
A serpent foulle that shall devoure
The whole wordle in an howare.[40]

In the margins of this verse, he cited both Augustine and Mandeville (I cannot find the corresponding reference in Mandeville, which raises the possibility that he may have faked some of his marginal notes in order to appear to cite impressive authorities).

As we have seen, Forman had no reservations about altering a text he was copying or translating to make it "more perfect." He treated his own medical and occult writings in much the same way, adding additional information to them, occasionally crossing out material that he no longer wanted to include, and generally treating text as organic and flexible rather than as fixed. It will come as no surprise, then, that in his more "literary" compositions, Forman's interest in reworking and revising text continues.

☞ Nonscientific Texts

Forman had ambitions as a writer: he composed a series of short poems, most autobiographical and narrative, longer poems on Queen Elizabeth and her father, and on the coming of the Antichrist. He also wrote a narrative list of the giants who descended from Noah's family after the flood, an account of the creation of Adam and Eve and of their postlapsarian life, and a descriptive list of Arthurian characters, as well as the autobiographical pieces discussed earlier.

As a poet, Forman had no consistent ear for how poetry should flow or for felicitous language. Sometimes his verse scans fairly well:

And when I was in greate dispair
Then god did comforte send
Confounding all my dedly foes
That mischeife did pretend.
For this and for all other thinges
Which god hath done for me
I doe give thankes vnto the Lord
And praise him hartily.

But another stanza from the same poem is metrically irregular:

They Joyed in my Restles woe
And nod their heades at me
And made my frindes for to exclaim
And crie out, fie on thee.
And spite on me as they wente by
Speakinge reprochfully
Behould the man whom god forsakes
Take him and let him die.[41]

Several of the poems, including the one just quoted, acknowledge by their titles the personal nature of their subject. Forman wrote poetry, just as he wrote prose, about the drama of his own life. Some poems seem, by title, to have nonautobiographical subjects, such as the six-leaf poem "Psalme per formann of the wickednes of the Tyme." In this poem, God threatens vengeance for the evils commited by men, especially evils against the poor:

Such ar the fruites of eville trees
Which moste be rooted vp
And when my Vengeance I [God] powr forth
They shall drinke of the cupp
For in the depth of Synne they dwelle
And wallowe to and fro
The poore they swallowe vp as bred
And doe no mercie showe.
Of Justice they haue noe regard
Nor of the Righteouse cause
For money and for money worth

They doe perverte my Lawes.
They doe respecte in Judgment ofte
The greatnes of the man
And not the rightnes of the cause
Which makes men curse and ban [utter maledictions].[42]

The sentiments are familiar—"Plate sin with gold, / And the strong lance of justice hurtless breaks; / Arm it in rags, a pigmy's straw does pierce it"[43]—though the style is quite different from Shakespeare's iambic eloquence. Even in such a poem, which is ostensibly social criticism, Forman's sense of personal injustice rings out, along with an almost bloodthirsty desire for vengeance. In the lines below, Forman becomes the first-person narrator who addresses God:

And let myne enimies feele thy force
And those that me withstand
Find out thy force and let them feelle
The poware of thy Righte hand
And like an oven burne them Lord
With firie flame and fum
Thyn anger let destroie them all
And fier let them consume.[44]

The poem retells Forman's own story about staying in London during the plague, about the doctors, about receiving his Cambridge degree. The wickedness of the time has been transformed to wickedness against Simon Forman, and only God's mercy to him (and Forman's skill) has kept him safe from his enemies.

In his long poem "Of Antichrist," Forman manages to keep his own story out of the text.[45] This poem is a prophecy about the coming of the Antichrist as a necessary forerunner to the Last Judgment. Summarizing scriptural prophecies, Forman elaborates on the signs by which the new Antichrist will be known and on his considerable powers. The child will be born in a Lord's palace of a "lewd lasse" of high degree, and at his birth marvels will appear: a rain of pearls and serpents flying in the air. The boy will be taught witchcraft and magic so that he can seem to make the dead rise (an illusion).[46] He will deceive the people by his crafty talk, his magic, and the gifts that he will give. If these tactics don't result in allegiance to him, he will torment those who withhold their worship. Eventually the tide will turn against the cruel Antichrist, and he will withdraw to a tent on Mount Olivet where the angel Michael will slay him.

> Then shall be such persecution
> And of people such destruction
> As never was before that daie
> Nor after wardes shalbe per say
> For some shal sai he was true Christe
> And som shal sai yt was not soe
> And soe: together by the ears they shall goe
> But the Jewes shall then belyue
> For grace that god shall to them giue
> And in true faith shall then enduer
> As yt is said in the scripture
> And the Church shall rest in peace
> That godes grace may then encrease.[47]

The poem concludes with six leaves detailing the omens and events of the Last Judgment. Forman dated this piece 1603, which suggests that the plague then raging in London may have prompted him to think apocalyptically. In prose notes in Latin and English that follow the poem, he recorded other details that may have influenced him to examine the subject of the Antichrist:

> anno domini 1602 in Januari yt was reported that ther was in persia such an antichrist then of some 12 or 14 years of age, that did many wonderfull thinges, as to rais the ded, cuer all diseases, by laying his handes only on them. he could walke vpon the water and doe many other miracles, as yt was by diuers reported. . . . The third Antichriste is that which is yet to com of which I haue before writen, but he is not yet borne nor shall not be, but he shall rain in Jerusalem about the year of Christe 1666.[48]

Forman here displays the same caution that prompted him in a prognosis to say "will die or scape hard." The date of the Antichrist will be "about" 1666, and he constructed the third digit of the date so that it was simultaneously a nine and a six. Thus the date became "about 1666" *or* "about 1696."[49]

What prompted Forman to write poetry about such a subject—often dull, repetitive, and quite bad poetry? In part, he desired to imitate, to do the fashionable thing, and to demonstrate his intellectual seriousness. For seriousness is the watchword of Forman's poetry, filled as it is with doom and gloom, cries and threats of vengeance. A single love lyric and a poem of praise to the queen (discussed in chapters 7 and 8) are the only exceptions. He seems to have felt that by scripting his complaints and prophecies he had a chance, even posthumously, for an "I told you so."

> Thus did I write of antichriste
> . . . .
> That youe mighte knowe my wholle entent
> That when my head is laid full lowe
> My writinge may youe all then showe.[50]

That Forman's writings exist only in manuscript, however, with no evidence of any attempt to put them into print, may seem to call into question his expectations for their preservation and later revelation as truth. In his creation account, Forman recorded how Abel, the son of Adam and Eve,

> made a boocke of all the vertues and properties of the plannetes which forknowing that the wordle should perishe throughe the generalle flod, he enclosed yt so coningly in a stone that the waters could not com to corrupte or destroie the same. wherby it might be preserued and after mad knowen to all people.[51]

The individual who found Abel's book enclosed in the stone was Hermes Trismegistus who "profited wonderfully by applyinge the contentes therof to his use."[52] Perhaps Forman had ideas of a similarly miraculous preservation and recovery of his own prophetic words. After all, until the late fifteenth century, wisdom had been preserved solely in manuscripts. Forman's planning for the future of his compositions took place within a culture not yet fully dependent on printed text.

Forman's account of the creation of the world, part of his commentary on Genesis, is marked by homely didacticism. Almost every detail of the creation Forman narrated was a commonplace; his account could, in fact, be useful today to instruct modern undergraduates in the rudiments of Ptolemaic cosmology and the sixteenth-century survival of a pre-Copernican view of the heavens. For Forman, "new philosophy" did *not* call all in doubt. He outlined the ten spheres, beginning with the outermost, the primum mobile, and continuing to the ninth, the "glassen sea" of waters above the firmament, the eighth, the firmament itself where are located all the fixed stars, and concluding with the spheres of the seven planets. The originality in his narration appears in his explanatory analogies, which derive from his own areas of interest. His explanation of the nature of the original chaos from which God created the world demonstrates this characteristic:

> Then was the sprite of the Lord borne vpon the face of the waters which was the Liquides forme of thinges and the most apteste to make moste formes shapes and creatures of. As for example, A man taketh a great pote & filles yt with water, honni oylle wine verjuce [juice of unripe grapes] milke and such lyke lyquid thinges. and he setes yt on a fier to distill. Howe many sortes of water may he drawe out of this smalle chaos. & euery on better then other. and yet in thend ther is dreges lefte. which may be congealed into a thicker or harder masse, out of which again also, a man may drawe or make diuers other thinges and forms.
>
> Soe was yt with God in his huge Chaos.[53]

In his account of creation, Forman repeatedly resorted to analogies to explain what happened at the beginning of the world. His discussion of the creation of the heavens breaks off abruptly in the middle of an explanation of how the sun lights the other planets and resumes again with Adam and Eve's creation. This part of the creation story Forman copied from an apocryphal text written around the second century A.D. and circulated in many versions during the medieval period.[54] As he nearly always did, Forman embellished his source. In their story, another of Forman's analogies appears in a marginal note to explain exactly what happened after Adam and Eve had eaten the apple:

> So adam & Eva did eat good fruite in which was noe poison nor evil to troble their bodies as men vse to eat good and holsom meates & never feell sicknes nor diseas, nor distening [distending] of their bodies but yf they eat the appell colloquintida or som rubarb ellebor agarick or som such thinge wherin ther is a poisoned substance (although yt show well) then theyr stomakes bowells and whole bodi is sick & sore trobled by which they presently knowe they haue eaten som poysened & evill thinge, wherby they presently knowe that ther ar bad meates as well as good & will evermore take heed howe they eat therof. but yf on had told them before saying take heed and eat not this apple of colloquintida or this hemlock for yt will poison thee, they will not beliue till they haue proued yt. And when they haue eaton as Adam did (and be poysoned) then they cry out and say O I wold I had not don yt, but then yt is to late, the poison & venom hath taken hould and root in them and they most die, or be deformed or becom monsters. for then their bodies swell

and becom full of sores botches and blaines and soe they ar altered presently from their first form & shape. as Adam was . . . for his bodie being poisoned with sinne he becam monstrouse and lost his first form and shape divine & heauenly and becam earthy full of sores and sicknes for evermore. And soe as a leprose man is chased or expelld out of the company of good hole and sound men leste they should be infected by him, even soe was Adam cast out of paradice from god & his angells to wander in the wordle with care and sorowe because he was infected with sinn against god.[55]

Forman's purpose was to understand the mysteries of God's acts by finding a comprehensible analogy from within his own experience. In fact, he was unbothered that he had to combine two different medical analogies—eating of poisoned fruit, which deforms the body (according to Forman) but which is not contagious, and leprosy, which he thought to be contagious—in order to explain the experience that resulted in the fall and expulsion from Paradise.

The creation essay is neatly copied within large ruled borders; on several leaves Forman filled the margins with more carelessly written notes, thus annotating the manuscript he had copied. Other evidence of careful editing appears in two pages, which repeat almost the same information about the fall of Lucifer. One is obviously an edited version of the other; the draft copy was bound in by mistake. The more carefully written copy is didactic: Lucifer was shut up in Hell for 4504 angelic years. The earlier draft is uncertain: was the imprisonment to be reckoned in angelic or natural years? "I knowe not." It also has an unfinished sentence with blank space, "the angelical year conteyneth of our yeares _____."[56] In the finished version, Forman eliminated the questions and uncertainties that his draft betrayed.

Despite the creation text's intrinsic interest, the reader must ask why Forman chose this particular treatise for one of his most carefully prepared "books." One answer lies in the way Forman made the creation and history of Adam and Eve incorporate his own medical and occult interests. (Perhaps this was a way once again to write indirectly about himself.) I have mentioned the use of medical or alchemical analogies to gloss the creation story; the relevance of the creation and its immediate aftermath to Forman is even more apparent in the anecdote of Abel's book, later found and used by Hermes Trismegistus, and an analogous account of an astronomy text, composed by God and carried to Adam by Raziel, the angel who taught Adam astronomy. Solomon eventually found this book, along with Moses' "rod and square tables of gold containing the most holy names of God." Forman was repeating genealogies for his occult texts and traditions, much as he created genealogies for his own family. To link the study of astrology and astronomy to the creation and to Adam was to give these intellectual pursuits respectable pedigrees. In the same way, Forman sanctioned prophecy by having Adam, on his deathbed, explain to his son Seth the future he had glimpsed when he had eaten of the forbidden tree.

Medicine was also given its foundation and rationale when the text explained that, to punish Adam, God gave him seventy "wounds" (he seems to vacillate between seventy and seventy-two; with creative counting I find he lists seventy). These wounds, which Forman lists under categories such as "general both to man & woman," "in the throat of men & women," and "in the Reines," comprise most of the diseases and abnormal medical conditions identified by sixteenth-century practitioners.[57]

Another group of thirteen "wounds" falls outside the original seventy:

Thes diseases com only in women and not in men and ar moe then the number of 70, that god imposed soe mani moe vpon women then vpon men because she harkened to the serpent.
The mother
The mole [a false conception] of the matrix
The precipitation of the matrix
barrennes
fals conceptions
turninge of the matrix
the wolfe [malignant growth] in the breaste
Sorenes of their brestes
Agues in their breastes
Stoppinge of their menstrues
A flux of their menstrues
The whites
The grene sicknes.[58]

Here Forman answered for himself a question that arose from the casebook records: why were female patients more numerous than male patients? Forman's straightforward explanation was that illness is part of God's postlapsarian curse, and since woman was *more* guilty than man because she listened to the serpent, she received more diseases.

I have suggested that Forman's purpose in copying the creation text was to provide the frame within which his own interests in the occult sciences and medicine might find legitimation, but such a rationale does not seem to explain his interest in giants.[59] To be sure, he connected his brief accounts and descriptions of giants with the creation account by relating the giants genealogically to the sons of Noah, and in two or three cases Forman included occult abilities in his giants' biographical sketches, as with those of Multan and Radus. His account of these two giants is typical of all his portraits of individual giants:

> Multan sonn of Sem was a man of great knowledg in magike astronomy and nigromancy. and ther was moch controversy in arte betwen Radus the sonn of Cham and Multan who confounded the magicall house that Radus builte. This Multan was 900 foote longe he was begotten by Sem on Marrades a sprite of the ayer. he lyued 900 years and died without issue.
>
> Radus sonn of Cham the sonn of Noah was 900 foote longe. he was verie stronge and was greatly seen in magick astronomie & nigromancie and in all other artes then vsed and was more skillfull then Cham his father for the sprites taught him. he could make the philosophers stone and had more therof then ever any man had and he did yt in a dai. and he did vse to eate & drinke therof often wherby he lyued 980 yers. he slue 12 giantes in on dai that made a battaill against him. This Radus raised by magike a great and a fair house or buldinge of stone 6 cornered. and at every cornar a dragon & a lyon. The which house was destroied by the arte of Multan the sonn of Sem. This Radus had 2 sonnes vz Valda and Varus.[60]

This genealogy of giants continues through roughly forty-nine individuals. (Counting is difficult because of repetition and an occasional female, who did not count in the genealogy.)

Though giantology was a popular subject in sixteenth-century Europe and several ingenious explanations had been advanced to explain the references to giants in Genesis,[61] Forman's account matches no others I have found. The most common explanation for Genesis's giants was that they were antediluvian creatures, monstrous both in form and behavior, and that God sent the great flood to eradicate them from the earth; indeed, the floodwaters were extraordinarily deep so that even the tallest giants would drown.

Forman's giants are all postdiluvian, however, direct descendants of Noah and thus not demonized as "other"—"what cultures fear and loathe"[62]—but rather presented as a natural stage in the history of God's creation. This conception is close to the revisionist view of Joannes Annius Viterbensis who, in his *Antiquities*, created a set of fake texts accompanied by commentaries that presented giants as intellectually superior descendants of Noah, himself a giant: "In the early postdiluvian world invented by Annius, the arts, the sciences, and monotheistic religion became the exclusive property of barbarian

Giants."[63] As we have seen in Forman's references to the giants' possession of occult arts and the philosopher's stone, his account incorporated elements of Annius's revisionist view.

Annius perpetrated his enormous textual hoax in the interests of establishing a direct genealogical link between the patriarch Noah and the Italian papacy; his purpose was nationalistic. Similarly, Jean Lemaire, a French author, used Annius's work extensively in his own *Illustrations de Gaule* but, by repressing much of Annius's commentary, refocused the genealogies to elevate French claims of superiority of descent and to downplay the Italian. Thus, revisionist work on giants in the period seems primarily motivated by nationalism. Forman's text is no exception. He neglected no opportunity to stress the giants' connections to England[64]: Vander, eight generations from Noah's son Japhet, "lived somtimes in England in Sussex. he was 240 of our yeardes longe. . . . When he was 20 yeares old he cam into England before Brutus cam into Ingland. and he came out of the West Indians."[65] The land was called Albion, according to Forman, because of Albina, a king's daughter who came to England with her sisters: "the sprites of the ayer did lie with them and had copulation with them and did engender on them many mightie giantes."[66]

He wrote of the giants Momdid and Momdidla who brought the Stonehenge stones from Africa to Ireland. (Forman alluded to Geoffrey of Monmouth's account of Merlin's movement of the stones to Salisbury, but offered much more detail about the giants' end of the operation.[67]) Finally, he retold Geoffrey's story of the struggle between Corineus, Brutus's companion and resident giant slayer, and Gogmagog, an English giant descended from Cham.[68]

Despite Forman's nationalistic details, however, his interest in giants seems to have had a motivation that reached even beyond national interests. Throughout his account, Forman depicted the giants as a natural step in the history of mankind's descent from Adam and Eve. On leaf 87r of Ashmole manuscript number 802, Forman drew a diagram (figure 9) to illustrate three major cycles of time (and within each major cycle three minor cycles) during which the maximum life span of mankind had gradually diminished. In the first cycle, "circulus major," men might have lived as long as 1,200 years; in the minor phases this span diminished to 1,050 years, 900 years, and 750 years. By the time the second grand cycle began 600 years was the maximum life span; when the cycle which was in progress in the late sixteenth century, "circulo minor," had begun, mankind had had a potential life span of 300 years, but by Forman's own day the life span was about to become 75 years,

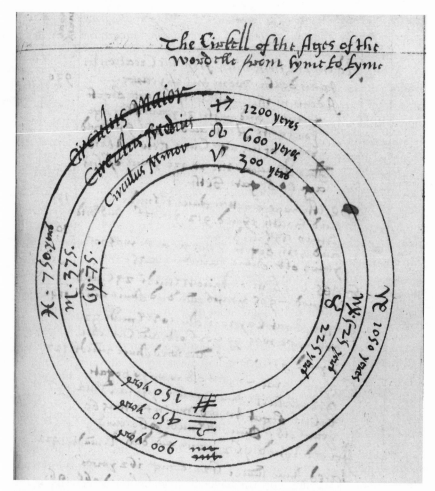

FIGURE 9: Forman's design of "The Cirkell of the Ages of the wordelle from tyme to tyme." By his calculations, his own time was represented on the inner circle on the left where the age of a man had become seventy-five years. Soon, he believed, both time and the world itself would end. MS. Ashmole 802: 87r. Courtesy of the Bodleian Library, University of Oxford.

just entering the final minor phase of the final cycle. This may explain why, in preparing his own genealogies, Forman created very long-lived and vigorous forebears. As the poem on the Antichrist demonstrated, Forman was prepared for the end of the world; man was about to be snuffed out.

Within such a comprehensive view of time since creation, Forman's assumption that the giants were distant, long-lived ancestors has a certain logic. He saw the gradual diminution of man's longevity and his physical size as part of a pattern of general shrinkage that would end with the Apocalypse and Judgment Day. John Donne uses a similar idea in "The First Anniversary."

Perhaps it should come as no surprise, then, to discover, following the list of giants in Ashmole 802, a similar list of Arthurian characters, shrunk markedly in both physical size and life span from the giants, but still larger than sixteenth-century life. For example, Forman writes that King Mark of Cornwall was twelve feet tall and lived 103 years, making him a match in height for Queen Guinevere, who was also twelve feet tall.

Forman's cameo descriptions of the Round Table characters are characterized by more specific physical detail than those of the individual giants. So particular are they that a colleague looking over my shoulder remarked that Forman's descriptions belong on a modern police blotter. As examples, I quote Forman's description of Arthur himself and of his villainous bastard son, Mordred:

> *King Arthur* was 15 foote longe in the prime of his yers. his berd was somwhat flaxen, but gray in his age and longe and very brod. his hair gray and longe & a brod full face somewhat ruddy. a gren Iuell [jewel] in his right eare. a thick body well made & a full breste. a ringe on the lytell finger on his right hand set with rubies. he slue 50 knightes with his own handes that dai he was slain. he had 5000 and more men in his last battell and murdred [Mordred] had 4000 and all were slainte, ner glassonbury & he was buried by morgan le fay in the valle of Avalon. he was buried 15 foote depe. . . .
>
> *Sir Mordred* was 14 foote long. . . . he was croked backed in the midst of his back & lefte shoulder. the hair of his hed was blackesh longe and a long red berd plotted vp lik a horsetaill. of a swarte fauour & complection and blered on both eyes. the teath of his vpper Jawe hung out over his lower lip. and he drawed in his lowar lip with all. a great thick & long nose ridged a peace of his cheke on the lefte syd of his nose cut a waie. blackesh eyes. and a peace of flesh cut also from the balle of his right cheke. The hair of his eybrowes was blacker then the hair of his head & very longe a great long mouth. he was cr[u]ke legged for his knes went outward & his toes & his heells went inward.[69]

Forman said nothing of Mordred's bastardy (a subject on which Forman himself may have been sensitive) but, by physical description, he managed to demonize him as a crooked, facially scarred, black-haired, red-bearded character. By contrast to Mordred, Arthur was blond and graying, "well made," and adorned with precious stones. His heroic battle record merits mention; Mordred's is ignored. Mordred sounds much like Shakespeare's Richard III. Like Richard, Mordred is physically marked as a villain and compared with animals (his beard was plaited like a horse's tail). Forman understood, at least in a general way, how to make language work without being authorially intrusive (although he infrequently practiced such self-erasure).

Forman made no attempt, in either the list of giants or that of the Round Table knights, to create a coherent framing narrative, although he was certainly familiar with narratives of the Round Table. Following the lists of giants and knights and before the diagram of the cycles of time mentioned above, Ashmole 802 contains Forman's version of the first chapter of the English prose *Merlin*, which had been translated from the French around 1450–60. If Forman was copying the English translation, however, he was remarkably free—even for him—in substituting his own language for that of the original translator. For example, the original translation explains Merlin's free will to choose between God and the devil thus:

> And ther the deuell was disseyued of his purpos, that he hadde ordeyned that childe to haue his arte and witte to knowe alle thynges don, and seide, bothe that were paste and that were to come. And our lorde, that alle thynges knoweth, sye the repentaunce of the moder, and that it was not her will that was so be-fellen, he wolde haue hym on his parte; neuertheles, he yaf hym fre choys to do what he wolde, for yef he wolde he myght yelde god his parte, en to the feende his also.[70]

In Forman's version, God, rather than the devil, gives Merlin power to see the future. Not the mother but the child is blameless, and the free choice issue is put more forcefully:

> Our Lord wold not that the soulle of the child should suffer for the offence of the mother, but gaue him powar from him selfe to knowe thinges to com as from the dyuell he had receyued knowledge of thynges paste.
>
> Bie this meanes did the child knowe all thinges paste presente and to com, which is to say, thinges present and paste thorowe the poware of the dyuell, and thinges to com by the will of al mighti god, so that he had free will to chuse wher he wold goe to god in doinge good or to the dyuell in doinge evill & in folowinge his preseptes.[71]

Forman's characteristic repetition and amplification appear in this text, but whether he was copying from another translation of the same French source, freely interpreting a copy of the extant fifteenth-century English translation, or doing his own translation is unclear. His usual freedom with copied text is apparent in some of the details. In a section he labeled "Cap. 32," Forman begins "now the story saith," but he cannot resist interpolating a medical aside while relating how one character, upon hearing that a damning secret from his past is now public knowledge, slinks off alone and, influenced by the devil, drowns himself in a river. "This may be a warning to all angri and melancoly persons," Forman interjects, departing briefly from the story, "not to fly companie in distres & grife. for the dyvell doth mor often frequent a man or woman in solitarines then he doth when they ar in company."[72]

Also characteristically, Forman did not complete his version of the Merlin narrative, breaking off just as Merlin has convinced Blase the hermit to write a book. But the section he did copy (not present in Malory's *Morte* or in several other versions of the Arthurian legend) begins with the devils mourning the loss of Adam and Eve, whom Christ has liberated from Hell, and vowing to create in the body of an earthly woman a son begotten by a devil who will rival Christ. Once again, as in his accounts of giants and Round Table knights, Forman telescopes time. Upon the loss of Adam and Eve, devils create Merlin who interacts with Arthur and is thus linked with the story of Britain in which Forman and his contemporaries are now playing their part. Merlin's handiwork, the circle of stones at Stonehenge, was still visible for Englishmen to see, and all history became part of a single gigantic narrative that stretched coherently from creation to the imminent day of Judgment. As Clark points out, "Most obviously . . . [apocalyptic thought] has very great explanatory power in revealing the general unity of history and in placing individual events in a planned and inexorable process which is about to be completed."[73]

The existence of Biblical patriarchs, giants, knights, Merlin, Forman's own long-lived ancestors, and of Forman himself—inserter of medical analogies—within the cycles of human time was affirmed and then dropped without further comment. Time itself provided the unwritten frame that held all these scattered accounts together and ordered original chaos. In imitation of the Creator, Forman had made his own stew and then, one by one, pulled item after item out of the narrative mixture.

At the very end of the section on giants, as he did with many of his other texts, Forman appended notes, this time contemporary evidence of giants in

England. Sir Thomas Elyot had mentioned a giant's skull in his dictionary, and Forman himself owned the tooth of a man found buried standing upright, wearing complete armor, a mighty battle axe beside him (perhaps one of the giants who fought Brutus and Corineus). The eyetooth was as broad as two fingers and three and a half inches long. Forman knew details of the find because his wife's stepfather, John Russell, a surgeon of Canterbury, had been present when the discovery was made and with his own hands had pulled out the tooth, which he later gave to Forman. Thus far the story is compelling in its circumstantial detail, but Forman continues: "on the vpper parte or end of the toth that he ded chewe withall wer caractrized the hebrue charactes certain of them the which I drewe out into a bocke. This was found about the year 1596."[74] This detail, Hebrew characters on the huge tooth, may discredit Forman's account for modern readers, though clearly not for Forman who copied the letters into one of his ever-present books.

Forman offered one last note on giants:

> Myself being in cambridge about the year 1603 I did see the chek toth of a giant in a poticaries shop against Doctor Butlers lodginge that did way 8 pound waight & ther was a nother as they said that did way 8 pound and a halfe but I sawe not that. Thes was both found ner Cambridge in digginge a gravell pit.[75]

Forman knew precisely when he had been in Cambridge—June, 1603, to receive his medical license from the University—but he loosened his hold on that date "about the year 1603" to emphasize the less credible details—the weight of the tooth, its exact location in Cambridge—and by denying personal knowledge of the second tooth, he refocused his reader's attention on the credibility of his account of what he *did* see, the eight-pound tooth in the apothecary's shop.

Whether or not Forman actually encountered the giant teeth he described is not the issue. His ability to be detailed and circumstantial both about what he has seen and what he cannot have seen (i.e., the crooked back and plaited red beard of Mordred) is important for our understanding of how Forman created text. The lines modern culture has traditionally drawn between fact and fiction, history and creative narratives, have been called into question in our own day by postmodern literary theory. For Forman those lines never existed and would have been unthinkable. Adam and Eve, Vander and Gogmagog, Arthur and Mordred had just as much physical reality to Forman as the doctors with whom he feuded or the queen about whom he dreamed. Those characters whom he had not met, but about whom he wrote, had simply been placed at a different point within the cycle of time that coiled unbroken from God's creation to his judgment.

I have treated Forman's accounts of giants and of the knights of the Round Table as his own, although I suspect that sources for them exist or once existed, just as sources for the Merlin story and the life of Adam and Eve exist. Borrowing freely, Forman wove his sources and details together until he created a narrative that he could use to understand his place as Englishman and astrological physician within the created universe.

An account of both the books Forman owned and those he wrote appears in this single chapter because the distinction between these categories was not as clear for Forman and his contemporaries as it is for modern readers and authors. This is because he was still largely influenced by a manuscript tradition, in which an author's name might or might not have appeared on a text, where the copyist felt free to abridge, alter, perfect, or add to the text he copied. Forman—the "scriptor non factor" label he occasionally placed at the end of a copied manuscript notwithstanding—would have been hard-pressed to say which books were "his."[76]

Despite the difficulty of making this distinction, however, a few characteristics of Forman as writer do emerge. His strength as a writer of prose lay in his observational skill (which must have served him well in his astrological and medical practice) and his eye for detail. He depended heavily on repetition as an organizational device, breaking whatever subject he wrote about into parts and reiterating those parts as a means of keeping himself on track. He was conscious of the need for organization and singleness of purpose. In an alphabet book, he wrote:

> Nota of writing or setting forth any bocke.
>
> In setting forth of an arte, or in writing of any matter, youe ought to gather together that only that apperteins to the matter youe writ or entret of and to hould youe to that only, leving to all other artes and matters that which apperteins to them, the which doing may be called the rulle of Justice/ as for Example yf youe will writ of phisicke youe mai not meddelle with dyuine matters or logik or arethmatick, but leaue that to dyuins, to logitions & arethmetitians every arte to yt self, and hould youe only to your matter.[77]

Forman was notably unsuccessful in most of his texts in following this advice to focus, but the note is evidence that he had thought, at least a bit, about *how* to write books, not just about the information which they would contain.

Most important, however, is that Forman wrote constantly. He used his books to hold information, to convey information, to shape and present himself, and to make orderly and comprehensible a world that might otherwise have seemed merely chaotic and diseased. Books offered him a way to manage the past, present, and future from within the confines of his study.

Forman in Society

FORMAN'S PROFESSIONAL LIFE is a history of challenge and dispute; he por-
trays himself as alone against the fraternity of licensed, university-educated
College physicians. Even his professional friend, Richard Napier, in distant
Buckinghamshire far beyond the College's jurisdiction, is usually little more
than a distant audience for the recital of Forman's troubles. Forman's personal
life, as revealed in his manuscripts, is almost as lonely as his professional isolation. Though he makes repeated references to particular male acquaintances
throughout his papers, only Napier emerges as someone who might be called
a friend. The men who appear most frequently in Forman's personal papers
are those, like Peter Sefton, with whom he had protracted legal disputes. His
primary personal relationships were with women, with relatives, and with the
servants whom he hired for domestic service or to help with his astrological
and medical practice. Even these relationships were frequently stormy.

How representative of his culture in his everyday personal life the
idiosyncratic Forman was cannot be determined,[1] but his manuscript notes
surely give some flavor of social and domestic life in London at the close of
the sixteenth century. I focus on those details that illuminate his relationships
with women, his children, and his servants, and on the details of his growing
consumerism as he moved his place of residence and acquired property and
moveable goods.

☞ Women

Although Forman became something of a specialist in women's health
care, his relationships with individual women were generally not happy.
Beginning with his mother, who he thought hated him and who refused

to pay for his schooling, Forman recorded a series of troubled and troubling encounters with women.

During his apprenticeship, Forman felt positively toward his master, Matthew Commins, despite Commins's refusal to allow him to attend school, but he recorded quarrels with Mrs. Commins and their woman servant, quarrels that culminated in violence. Having been knocked about for some time by Mary Robartes, the Commins's kitchen maid, until "blod should rone about his eares," Simon[2] repaid Mary in kind one day after she refused to help him serve customers in Commins's shop:

> Simon put vp all and said lyttle, but made the beste shift he could and ryd them all awaie, and shut the shop dore, and toke a yerd[3] and wente into Mary, who so sone as she sawe him was redy to have him by the eares, but Simon stroke her on the handes with his yerd, and belabored her soe or [before] he wente that he made her black and blue all over & burst her head & handes that he laid her alonge crying and roringe lik a bulle for he beat her thorowly for all her knauery before to him done.[4]

When Commins heard the story he supported Simon, telling him to beat her again should she be obstinate. Triumphantly, Forman recorded that from that day forward "Simon and Marie agreed soe well that they never were at square after, and Mary wold doe for him all that she could."[5] From his perspective, physical violence had been the appropriate and effective way to tame the shrew.

When Simon tried a similar approach with Mrs. Commins, however, the outcome was different. She was about to beat Simon for losing some flax (which Forman said he had not done): "when she wold haue beaten Simon, as she had wonte to doe, with a yeard, Simon toke the yearde from his mistres and thruste her vp behind a dore and put the dore on her whervpon she durste not meddle with Simon again."[6] In this instance, the mistress had the status advantage,[7] and when she complained to her husband he beat Simon, though Forman asserted that the beating was against Commins's will:

> but he knewe his wife to be a wicked, hedstronge, and proud fantasticalle woman, a consumer and spender of his wealth and often tymes they too were also at square insomoch that twise he had like to haue killed hir by casting a peir of tailors shers at her for once they went so nere her, that as she was going in at a dore, he nailled her clothes and smock at her buttockes to the dore and the points of the shers wente clean throughe the dore and she honge faste by the taille.[8]

Forman believed that women needed to be controlled physically if other means proved ineffective. In Forman's narrative, master and man join in their denunciation of the woman:

> When Simon and his master wente to his farme together . . . they wold on complain to another of his mistress & her pride. And his master wold say to him Simon thou moste suffer as well as I my selfe. Thou seeste we cannote remadie yt as yet, but God will send a remadie on daie.[9]

Despite such bonding with his master, Forman asked to be released from his apprenticeship partly as a result of his physical confrontation with Mrs. Commins.

Another early relationship with a woman, notable mostly because of its renewal a decade later, arose from the hero-worship of a young girl, Ann Young, for the somewhat older Simon. As always Forman's first interest was in pedigree:

> Ther was a man of good reputation and wealth that dwelte not far from Simons master, that had a proper fine maiden to his only daughter, the which being but yonge of yeares and yonger then Simon, that loved Simon wonderfull well, and wold suerly see him once a daie, or ells she wold be sicke.[10]

After offering some instances of "A.Y.'s" obsession with "Simon," Forman summed up his view of their relationship:

> As for Simon, he loved her not but in kindness, but because she was soe kind to Simon, he wold doe any thinge he could doe for her. And this love on her syde lasted longe as herafter shalbe showed.[11]

Years later, Forman met Ann Young again: "1582 . . . in June I first cam acquainted with A.Y. aboute the 12th dai." By 1584, their relationship had deepened—"the 29 of February was the first tyme that ever I halikekeros harescum tauro with A.Y."[12] In this period of their relationship, Forman seemed genuinely attached to Young, though the attachment is expressed in terms of economic success in 1584: "This yere I had many thinges giuen me and many newe friends, & moch good of the woman whom I loued, & I thriued resonable well." By the next year, the couple had produced a child, Forman's bastard son Joshua Walworth.[13] As the diary continued, Forman made occasional laconic references to Young by which we can trace the course of their relationship. In 1587, "A.Y. and I wer like to have bine betraid. . . .

1588, the 30 of Jun A.Y. and I fell out." That same year, Forman recorded that Young was taken away by the constable. Not until seven years later did her name resurface in the diary; in 1595, she sent a messenger to Forman. By this time he was immersed in his London practice, deeply involved in an adulterous affair, and not very responsive to his childhood sweetheart back in Salisbury.[14]

However, in June, 1595, having just patched up one of his recurring quarrels with Avis Allen, his London mistress, Forman rode to Salisbury: "the 30 dai of June was a finall conclusion & end of all our frindship betwen A.Y. and I, and I rec[eived] my ringes and jewels againe from her." A final diary entry recorded Young's death in 1600: "thes yere the 8 of May, An Yonge died of a dropsy."[15] Forman recorded less struggle and unhappiness with Ann Young than with any of the other women with whom he was deeply involved. Between them he reported few quarrels and no physical violence.

His casebooks reveal more emotional involvement with Ann than the terse diary entries indicate. In the late 1590s, Forman dreamed about Ann Young.[16] By that time she was married to Ralph Walworth and had three children. In one of Forman's dreams she appeared with her three sons, "and Joshu stode betwen my leges et videtur me esse prim filius [and seemed to be my first son]." In the dream, each of the two younger boys was paired with his own father, neither of whom was Ralph Walworth. This dream occurred in May 1597, when Forman had again ridden to Salisbury to visit Young. At its end he noted "that night folowing I spake with her & sawe her 3 sonnes."[17]

Forman used Young and her husband as an example when he explained how to tell whether an expected baby will be a boy or a girl: count the letters of the parents' names plus the names of any previous children. If the number is odd, the child will be male; if even, the child will be female. Given Forman's (and the period's) erratic spelling, this method could nearly always be made to turn out as desired, as the Walworths' case demonstrates. Note how the fictitious names dissolve into the real ones as Forman's account progresses:

> Agneta.6.[six letters] she was maried to Radulfus.8. the number of thes too names is 14, and yt chaunced that Agnis was with child. Nowe by the number of their too names the first child of Agnis should be a maid, but it fell out otherwise for yt was a boy. By this we knowe that Rafe was not the father of that boy but som other body. And yt was proued that Agnis loued on Simon, who had layen with her often, and therfore we take the number of Simon & agnis [Agneta] and yt is xi which showeth her firste child by Simon should be a boy and yt was soe and he was named Joshua.[18]

Forman avoids spelling Young's husband's name "Ralph" because that would yield the same number of letters as "Simon" and destroy Forman's demonstration. One doubts that this method was widely used to allay the anxiety of the patriarchy about whether children their wives bore were their own, but it allowed Forman to demonstrate that his methods "worked."

From 1597 until her death in 1600, Forman occasionally received messages from Ann Young. He cast several times to see "what state she is in" or "beste to go or send to her to helpe her." He retained a bond of concern and affection for her and for their child. Forman even had some thoughts about marrying Young in the period between the death of his mistress, Avis Allen, and his marriage to Jean Baker. He cast to see whether Ann's husband Ralph, who he had heard was ill, would die. In her final illness, Young sent for Forman's medical advice. John Evans of Wilton on February 20, 1600, brought a letter asking "life or death." Forman wrote "dropsy and swollen with water most grievously" and dispatched a remedy of herbs and berries to be mixed with four gallons of new ale. In May, however, she died. After an interval, Forman took their son Joshua into his own household.

Forman usually reported encounters with women neutrally or negatively, often within economic contexts. In 1582, two years before his sexual relationship with Young began, for example, Forman wrote that, for the first time, he "did halek cum muher [had sexual relations with a woman]."[19] Thirty was late for a man to begin sexual activity (I find no indication in the manuscripts of any interest in men as sexual partners). In 1583, "I did halek cum two muher [with two women]. . . . We went to London & lay ther till we had spent all."[20]

By 1590, Forman's friends—if not Forman himself—had begun to think about his marriage prospects. In Forman's manuscripts his potential marriage is always presented as a business transaction. In 1590, he writes that "I was offred a wife mani tymes . . . & had the sight & choise of 4 or 5, maids and wydowes."[21] However, Forman was still struggling financially and in no position to set up a family. By 1592, he had become interested in the marriage market, though his financial situation had only marginally improved. That year in "the begininge of Aprill I borowed moch mony again of Hugo, and the 7. of Aprill I went first a woing to An Nok. And I bought me moch aparelle & began to com to credit but yt was but a bare yere with me."[22] Wooing for Forman, as for Bassanio in *The Merchant of Venice*, was associated with making the right impression: both men needed new clothes.

Two months later, however, he began his twenty-two week struggle with the plague, and he recorded no more thoughts of marriage until October

1593, when he went wooing a widow, Mrs. Lodcaster. It was in the year 1593 that he first met and treated Avis Allen, a married Catholic who became his mistress until her death in 1597. All talk of marriage dropped out of the diary while the affair continued, although Forman continued to have sexual relations with a number of women besides Avis Allen during their relationship.

The casebooks, several of which were written during the Avis Allen years, leave no doubt that his relationship with her was the most passionate of his life. Rowse recounts the stormy details of their intimacy in a chapter he entitles "A Love Story and a Dream Life."[23] There was jealousy on both sides: she grew upset when she found another woman's apron in his house, when she found sex-stained sheets on his bed, and when she met a woman of whom she was suspicious at Forman's garden gate.[24] He suspected that she might be interested in his servant and that she lied about where she had been. They quarreled constantly, sometimes to the point of violence, although Forman recorded only her violence toward him: "A. Al. hit me in the mouth with her hand. . . . A. Al scratched me by the face that I bled."[25] Again and again, Avis Allen attempted to call a halt to the affair. She tried to forbid sexual relations, but inevitably their quarrel would be made up with lovemaking, only to break out again with renewed violence. Forman described one of these quarrels with Allen using battle imagery, recalling how he went to the house where she lived with her husband, quarreled with her, left her, and then

> I toke occasion to goe vp again to spek with her & seaming strange at firste
> I gaue the onset and wone the fild et halek harescum tauro. . . . & soe we
> becam frindes againe. but yf I had let [Mars] passe out of my handes I had
> loste the victory.[26]

Forman's casebooks for this period are filled with personal casts about Avis Allen: was she at home? would it be all right to visit her? when would she come to him? who was visiting her? was she well? was she pregnant? was she thinking of him? should he send her a letter? Forman had always kept his emotional distance from women, at least on the evidence of the cool tone of his remarks about them in the manuscripts, but he clearly had no control as he struggled with this passion.

In June 1597, while Forman made one of his periodic trips to Salisbury to check on Ann Young, Avis Allen lay sick with what was to be her last illness. When Forman returned, Mrs. Allen sent to request an astrological cast about her illness; four days later her husband came to consult Forman about Avis "without her consent" (both husband and wife were regular patients of Forman). Mrs. Allen was bled and given a Forman "dram" on June 11 but, on June 13, she died. Told of her death, Forman wrote, "Est mortua. Est mortua. She died this 13 dai in morning."[27] His diary entry for 1597 was very brief, beginning simply, "1597. Avis Allen died 13 of June."[28] Forman continued to think and write occasionally of Avis Allen. One of his patients looked like Avis, having "a mole vnder the nose abov the lip lik her,"[29] and he wrote a biographical note about her in his book of nativities:

Her mother said she was begotten about 4 at after none againste a birch the friday after Saint Ieorges dai. She staied in her mothers womb 270 dais. 1 howare & a half. . . . She was maried to a merchant. She was a catholik & wold not goe to church. she died of a catarrhus [apoplexy] not being harte sick. 1597 the 13 of June about 7 of the clok in the morninge and was buried out of Christen burialle. her mother did never love her well. she was moch trobled about her religion/ she had 2 children. a maid & a boie and a 11 or 12 scapes [miscarriages] besides. her children died before her/ she was a woman somwhat talle. a good motherly face fair and of a good nature and disposition.[30]

This brief sketch suggests the difficult life Forman's mistress must have led. A bastard (she bore her mother's name, not her father's), thinking herself unloved by her mother, troubled about her religion, pregnant thirteen or fourteen times by the time she died at thirty-six, but with no living children, she apparently clung to her Roman Catholicism, would not go to church, and was buried without religious ceremony. In another manuscript, Forman wrote ruefully: "She was friendlie faithful to thend but ther was mani brackes [quarrels] betwen vs."[31]

At times, Forman's anger at her death surfaced. In her nativity, Forman claimed that she was "not harte sick," meaning that her illness need not have been mortal. In his book of "Astrological Judgements of Phisick," Forman used Mr. Allen's question for his wife in the last days of her life as an example of the husband who inquires about a wife without her consent, commenting that

this womanes dizease was caused . . . of moch burnt melancholy and blod. and yt did rise vp in her throte like catarr and soe stopte her wind, for certain docters gaue her 2 glisters [clysters or enemas] & kild her with the third. and I had alwaies forbydden her to tak any glister. Yet she wold not doe by my counselle, but folowed others aduise and died not being harte sicke. thorow foly of her phisisions.[32]

Here was one more charge that Forman could lay to the account of his rival physicians.

Compared with Forman's complex relations with Young and Allen, his comments about his 1599 marriage to Jean Baker seem rather bland and emotionally cold. Once he had absorbed the loss of Avis Allen, Forman actively re-entered the marriage market. On January 1, 1599, he cast a horoscope to find out whether he would be successful in love and on the page adjoining wrote a love poem. Titled simply with Forman's name, the poem appears to be a dialogue between a timorous lover and someone who advises the lover to take the risk of declaring his love.

> [Lover]: She is a pug of perles price
> [Advisor]: Then loue her nowe yf thou be wise
> [Lover]: But yf I loue, and not attaine
> [Advisor]: Then hast thou loste thy louing paine
> [Lover]: I dare not loue to loose the price
> [Advisor]: Attempte and saye yf thou be wise
> [Lover]: My hart misgiues she will disdain
> To lesse my loue and breed my paine.[33]

The debate continues for another twenty-eight lines until the lover is convinced to pursue love and thanks his advisor.

At forty-seven, Forman was determined, after numerous sexual relationships, to become a wooer. Like many young male stage lovers—Orlando in *As You Like It* and Benedick in *Much Ado about Nothing* come first to mind—he associated wooing with writing love poetry. Because he as yet had no particular woman in hand, the poem reflects his own uncertainty about whether he can successfully play the role required. He learns through writing how to act, and then turns his real life back into text as he records events from his experience as examples in his didactic manuscripts. (His analysis of Mr. Allen's question about Avis, his dying wife and Forman's mistress, is just one small example of this practice.)

As usual, Forman expressed caution about "the price," even of wooing. He worries in his love poem that wooing might cost him time, respect, and dignity. Not to worry, his counsellor assures him later in the poem, "aduentures in such lovinge thinges / belonges to beggars knightes and kinges." This is the only amatory poem among Forman's papers but, like most of his other poems, the love poem is about himself, not about the unknown woman of "perles price."

Once his mind was made up, Forman vigorously pursued his quest for a wife. Soon he was interested in Sarah Archdall, questioning the stars about what she thought of him and when they would meet again. He met her twice at the Curtain theater and negotiated with her uncle. He cast at least five more times to ask about her, but then her name disappeared from his notes. Within a week after his last question about Archdall, he was asking the stars whether Ann Soror would make a good wife, but after speaking with her he did not care to pursue her further. On July 3 and again on July 12, he cast to know whether to marry Jean Baker.[34] After the July 3 cast, he added, "I maried her. She had nothing in respect to take to, and she was som what collarik of nature & self-willed yet quickly rebuked at last."[35] A more neutral description of one's new bride would be hard to find, although Forman eventually became somewhat more affectionate toward her, giving her the nickname "Tronco." The 1607 diary recorded the Formans travelling together to Greenwich and London, having dinner at friends' homes, and entertaining friends, clients, and the ever-present relatives at their Lambeth home, so the marriage eventually became quite companionate in social settings.[36] Nothing suggests that Forman ever involved his wife in any way with his work.

Jean (or An, as Forman sometimes wrote) was sixteen at the time of her marriage. Her most attractive asset for Forman was her family (he mentioned no dowry or money). She was "Sir Edward Monninges sisters daughter," a pedigree that Forman recorded at least half a dozen times in his various jottings. When Forman wrote "the issue of Simon Forman" a decade after his marriage, he was remarkably unenthusiastic about his step into matrimony: "he [Simon] maried her at Lambeth by chance asking her a question in that behalf. the which she toke advantage of, and he wold not goe from his worde."[37]

In the early years of his marriage (about which much daily minutiae are captured in the extant casebooks), Forman demonstrated stereotypical anxiety about his wife's fidelity. As early as six weeks after their marriage, Forman cast to know whether his wife had another lover and was false to him, and by 1600 these fears had escalated. He noted that his wife had lied about where she had been, and later he reported that "Ledsom" had gone up "priuily" to his privy. He suspected that this trespasser was having an affair with his wife since the two had had a conversation four days before.[38] On April 9, 1600, finding that his wife had lied about her whereabouts, Forman provoked a quarrel that ended with violence:

Because I liked not her lies and excuses she begane to talk peremptory vnto me with howlinge and weepinge, and wold not be quiet till I gaue her 2 or 3 boxes.

Forman then checked with the stars about his wife's behavior and continued: "she wilbe meritrix [a whore] for yt seames pollici . . . and that she went to som other intente, but as yet ther is noe facte done."[39] Thus Forman continued to expect his wife's infidelity even though the stars assured him she had not yet cuckolded him.

Despite their quarrels, the newly married couple carried on an active sex life, which Forman was careful to record in case a conception should occur. Conception was not likely, however, until young Jean had had her first menstrual period, an event that Forman happily noted on October 3, 1600, fifteen months after their marriage.[40] Forman was convinced that his wife enjoyed sex and frequently reached orgasm ("et eo tempe fuit illa valde cupida de hallek et matrix sugit virgam"); after this note he immediately cast to see if she had conceived. Sometimes he did not even bother to record the sexual act, but merely noted the satisfactory response of his wife's womb: "Anno 1599 the 30 Septem am at 4. matrix uxoris sugit virgam." Her sexual responsiveness could be seen as something of a mixed blessing, however. It meant that she was likely to conceive easily, for according to contemporary medical theories about conception, the woman had to achieve orgasm so that the "seed" from both sexes could join. But it also meant that she was "warm" and lusty. She might well look beyond her husband to satisfy her sexual "cupiditas."[41]

In his manuscripts, Forman offered several astrological methods for determining whether a child belonged to its supposed father. In lines reminiscent of Edmund's, in *King Lear*, about the difference between the vigor of an illicit sexual liaison and the coldness of the marriage bed, Forman admitted that if a woman was adulterous, a child was more likely to come from the lover than from the husband:

Yf thou woldeste knowe wher [whether] the child that is borne be the child of the supposed father or noe, or wher he be a bastard or child of som other man, because ther is lyttle faith and credite to be giuen to women. for women be many tymes giuen to Luste, and desier to lie with diuers men and *in the appetite of Luste they often conceyue wher ells they wold not many times conceyue*, yet thoughe they lie with never soe many men they will say they lie with none but their husbandes, and that their husband is father of the child [my emphasis].[42]

Even as he fretted about his wife's possible infidelity, Forman continued his own sexual encounters with a variety of women, sometimes recording several partners in a single day. On January 15, 1601, he noted "am at 9 halek An Condwel et mer. at 12 [noon] Francisco Hill" and in the 1607 diary fragment, his conduct (and vigor) remained unchanged: "the 9 dai [of June] am at 8 halek hester sharpe, et halk pm at 3 An docoman. et ad 9 pm halk Tronco [his wife]."[43] The diary fragment from 1607 recorded regular and frequent sexual relations between husband and wife, with Forman still making notes about Tronco's sexual avidity.

Forman's receipt of personal confidences from women patients and his own sexual experiences with many, apparently willing, women had made him deeply cynical about female behavior. He never reflected in his papers on his own lifestyle or morals. The apparent ease with which he found sexual partners served only to convince him more profoundly of the untrustworthiness and general duplicity of women. In his 1593 treatise on the plague, an attack on the corruption of many segments of society, he was especially detailed and virulent about the hypocrisy of women:

> O it is a wonder to see, howe demurely mani fine & proper women will goe in the streates, how solemply they syt at tables, howe deuoutly they com to the church, as thoughe they were religious, and yet verie strumpets, and those that a mane wold thinke of great honestie & credite, and yet moste common in silence of their bodies, they paint theire faces, and set out their broidred heare with periwiges and get them a gowne with a great hope [hoop] on their taille, lyke on makinge a hobby hors in a morrish daunce, moste filthie to loke vpon and hatefull before god and man. They flatter men with faire speaches and entise them with sweate wordes as Sallomon saith, Even as the fouler whistling merilie deceyueth the simple birdes, to drawe them to helle & to the way of perdition, drowninge them in the sincke of sinne and sendinge their soulles hedlonge to everlastinge paine.[44]

In Forman's view, women were always the enticers and men, like simple, silly birds, were taken in by their wiles. Forman never shows any guilt for his own far-flung fornications or, after marriage, his repeated adultery. I suspect that some of the sexual acts he records with women patients may be barter arrangements in which he receives payment for consultations and medicines in the form of sexual favors. However, my only evidence is the obvious fact that many of these acts take place during his workday and with his patients. From childhood until his death, Forman never trusted members of the female sex, though he clearly took much physical pleasure from them.

☞ Forman's Children

Toward his children, both legitimate and illegitimate, Forman's attitude was somewhat warmer. I mentioned earlier his delight when his wife bore him children, especially his son Clement, that remarkably precocious child who was "all ayer." Forman also felt some duty and concern for his bastard children. His first son was Joshua Walworth, Ann Young's oldest boy. When his mother died in 1600, Joshua was fifteen. In his book of nativities Forman recorded one for Joshua Walworth, a bastard, whose mother died May 4, 1600, and whose father "will com to gret credit and fame":

> Joshu came to dwell with me 1602, about midsommer and he died the 8 of Octob 1603 . . . of an impostum in his stomake and he had the plague alsoe & had godes tokens on him before & after he died. he liued 18 years 7 monethes and 12 daies and 6 howars. . . . we sai the father of the child is som phisision or professor of phisicke.[45]

In another account of his son's death, Forman gave more detail.

> The Tuesdai morninge . . . [Joshua] went to London [from Lambeth] and toke the plague and the Saturdai folowinge, in the morninge about 8 of the cloke he was vp, And sate by the fier with other Company talkinge and in laughing the Impostume brake and he vomited a gret bole fulle of black substanc and the bag[46] wente backe again. And a lytell before 2 after none he begain to vomit again and the bag cam vp into his throte and he thrust his fingeres into his throte to pull out the Bag and died with his fingers in his mouth, and was worshipfully buried at Lambeth. 72 milles est from the place he was borne.[47]

Forman did not break his emotional control in this passage, but the details he recorded and his repeated return in his notebooks to Joshua (as he returned to Ann Young and Avis Allen) suggest an emotional attachment to this first son.

Forman was less certain about, and less attached to, his other bastard children. A mysterious child "An" appeared in Forman's diary in 1594–95, but no casebook exists for that period to provide specific details. On March 11, Alice Barker "peperit" [delivered] and the next day she sent a message to Forman. Soon the authorities were involved. "The 21 dai I was afore the bench of Aldermen for Alls Barker." Apparently a bastard had been born, and Forman was being forced to pay up. He noted in his diary that 1594 was a quiet year, but that "the discourtasi of A[vis] All[en] trobled me often, and the baster." Was "the baster" Alice Barker's child? "The 20 Apr. An was christned. Then begane the variance betwen Kate Nicolls and me & Nurse Dandly."[48] The note apparently refers to a dispute over care arrangements for baby Ann.

In June 1595, when this child would have been about fourteen months old, Forman noted: "The 11 dai, am at 8, I put An to a newe nurse, to Clemense ye Taillers wife of Gret Bowcome, in Surrey."[49] If Forman had been given, or had taken, responsibility for the child's nursing care, as these notes suggest, he apparently had discharged his duty, for Ann was not mentioned again.[50]

Forman suspected that Alexander Allen, the boy whom Avis Allen bore during their affair, was his. But the child died at nine months. According to Forman's diagnosis, "the nurse had over put the mould of [his] head with striking yt vp to hard,"[51] and so Alexander received only passing mention in the diary.

Just before Forman's marriage in 1599, Bess Parker, a former servant with whom he had had repeated sexual relations, gave birth to a girl named Fenema. Forman had long disapproved of Bess's conduct and had, for the time she was in his household, from Easter until Christmas, 1598, kept track of her comings and goings. The 1598 casebook records details of nights she had not slept in her bed, a night in which she lay on a bed kissing some of the other inhabitants of Forman's house, days on which she had not gone where Forman had sent her.[52] His concern to document Bess's whereabouts—which started before he began his own sexual relationship with her—was unusual for Forman's casual affairs. Because the woman was his servant, he was in some measure responsible for her behavior. Once she was obviously pregnant, her brothers came to Forman, demanding to know what had happened, and Forman was able to produce his record of her transgressions.[53] He tried to convince himself (and anyone else who asked) that the father of Bess's child was Nicholas Fardell, a man who had stayed at Forman's house during 1598 and whose wife Bess Parker had assisted in childbirth:

> 1598 the 22 of Auguste . . . Besse Parker the mother of this Fenema was sent to Mary Fardell that lai in childbed and Nicolas Fardell did occupie [have sex with] her before she came away. and the 5 of June folowing made 9 monethes & iust 40 wickes. so yt semes to be Nicolas Fardells child.[54]

Although Bess found a husband two months before the child was born, she clearly thought the responsibility for her baby lay more with her repeated sexual partner and former employer than with either Fardell or her new husband. After Fenema was born, a woman came to Forman from Bess (June 28, 1599), and he immediately cast to know whether the child was his.[55] Forman recorded financial details about Bess and Fenema:

Willm Sabells wife nurseth besses child	
Willm fild her brother was here with her	
Itm gaue Besse by Mrs Web for me	30 sh
Itm gaue Besse by Mrs coppleyerd	30 sh
Itm I gau her more the 12 of July at the same time	40 sh
Itm I gaue god wife Sables [Fenema's nurse]	3 sh 4 d[56]

Bess came herself to Forman on July 12 when he gave her the forty shillings. In the margin of his casenotes for that day, Forman wrote "halek Eliz. Parker at 4 pm 12 July."[57] Despite the fairly hefty sums that his earlier sexual encounters with Bess were costing him, Forman once again had sex with her just ten days before his own marriage. Although Forman took some financial responsibility for Fenema and her nursing care, there is no way to determine how long this financial assistance continued because after this encounter both mother and daughter disappear from Forman's records.

Forman mentioned four children by name in his diary whom he regarded as "his" or possibly his. There is some evidence that he took financial responsibility for these children, though only Ann Barker was technically a bastard. Given his widespread sexual activity, he probably fathered others. But Forman usually had sexual relations with married women, or at least with women who were sexually experienced. He became interested in Bess Parker only when he had assured himself that she had been intimate with other men. Therefore, most of the children he may have fathered (like Alexander Allen) could have been palmed off on husbands or the woman's other sexual partners (as he tried to do in the case of Bess). For his legitimate children he expressed tenderness; for those who bore other names he seems to have had some sense of financial responsibility but, with the exception of Joshua his firstborn, little real interest in them as they grew.

☞ Households and Servants

As might be surmised from the discussion of Bess Parker, Forman's house in the late 1590s was full of servants, relatives, and even some recuperating patients. In the 1580s, Forman himself had been the servant, a tutor in other people's homes, staying briefly with clients whom he traveled to treat, following his employers the Penruddocks to London in 1582. In 1588, the diary first records Forman's ability to hire "a man," although he seemed to want John Goodridge more for his ability to "see," to act as scryer in his attempts to call spirits, than as an ordinary servant. Steven Mitchell[58] was bound to him in 1589 but left soon after to go to sea. In 1590, Forman was briefly tempted into Sussex after a profitable trip there during which Mr. Thomas Cumber had promised him a house, land, two beds, and four cows if he would come to Sussex to dwell.[59] Cumber wanted Forman for his occult abilities, and Forman agreed to the arrangement: "after Michelmas I remoued into Sussex wher I went to dwell at Wickham & was at another man's finding, for at alhallowtyd I entred the cirkell for nicromanticall spells."[60] Steven had apparently returned from sea and joined his uncle in Sussex, for it was there in February that he ran away and subsequently told Forman he had been carried off by a spirit (see chapter 5). By that time Forman had a second servant, for Steven's absence was reported by "my man." Forman did not like the location, and on August 4, 1591, he "cam clean from Sussex."[61]

After his permanent move to London in 1592, Forman began to gather the household that continued to grow for nearly two decades. In February, Steven was bound as apprentice to Forman once again, and in March, they moved into Stone House, where he lived in one chamber or another until 1599.[62] Forman summarized his stay at Stone House in a manuscript entitled "Of Taking a house and entring yt to dwelle":

> Anno 1592 the 16 March—I entred first into my first chamber in the stone house. In this chamber I staid a yeare and bettar. and I gote resonable welle & was free from troble. but I had the plague ther and was like to die and the evill stinck of the privy did anoy me moch ther, and because many did resorte ther vnto me I lefte yt because yt was lyttle & to hie vp. & for the stincke and toke that belowe, and I had good neighbours all aboute and frindly.
>
> Anno 1593 the 10 of Aprill—I entred my chamber wher I now liue at ston house belowe. In this chamber I did get moch and the longer I staid ther the more I got. but from the begining of decemb. 1595 & soe forward I got moch after I cam out of prisson whether I was committed by the doctors. . . . I had here good neighbours and frindly all aboute but I was like to haue bin killed in this chamber by a villain and I had mani vexations by the doctors.[63]

In 1594, Forman hired a new servant, William Buck, and used Buck and a second servant, Robert Barnes, as examples in one of his astrological manuscripts. He was explaining how to find out what had happened when servants did not return on time from errands. Forman had sent Buck and

Barnes "among my enimies" and was concerned when they did not return promptly. They turned out to be safe and eventually came home, as the astrological cast had predicted they would.[64]

Forman recorded only one instance of whipping a servant, although others may have gone unrecorded. He did not beat Steven Mitchell when he ran away, but he did "bethong" John Braddege, whose character sketch he offered in his book of nativities:

> Jhon Bradedge born Chepsid—1582.
>
> This boi at 12 yers was put an apprentice he was stubborne and proud & self willd and gaue him selfe to ydelnes, and wold not learn to lyue in any good sorte, but delightyed in play and gamblinge abrod and I kept him 4 yers and then I put him a way for he was giuen to filch and spend & consume & fre harted and 1600 he went from me and went into the low countries, and serued a liftenante, and 1602 about the 29 of Aprill he cam out of flanders very pore & naked and retorninge thither again. 1603 he was a souldiar at ostend.[65] he began to be baudi & lie with wentches at 16 yers old. 1607 he maried a yong woman in flanders a lame wentch and 1608 10 februar he brought her into England gret with child & very pore & cam to lodge at Lambeth. & cam from the Cardinalls camp & he had a bastard by another that he was contracted to before in flanders a boi.[66]

Forman kept in touch with his former servants. Steven (who was a relative as well as a servant) periodically returned to live with Forman; Braddege came back to see him and perhaps to stay with him. Forman even kept in touch with Eustace, a servant he employed for only three months in the fall of 1598. Eustace became lame, and in February 1599, Forman cast to learn "whether it wilbe helped without perrill of his life or legge." Apparently the ailment was serious because Eustace "died in the spittall in Southwark 1599 about October."[67]

Not all master/servant relationships were as free from abuse as the ones Forman recorded in his own household. We remember the maid, pregnant by her master, who had been given something to kill her or abort the fetus (see chapter 3). Forman also made notes about some servants who had been beaten. He described the following case as an example of how to proceed when a mistress asks about the health of a servant "being very sicke, withoute the consente of the Seraunte 1596 the 30 of Septem.":

> This fellowe his Mrs had beten him som 4 or 5 dais before brack his head and som too dais after they sent for a surgeon to dresse him and he said the

skulle was broken. and then the Surgeon dressed yt and after that his face did swelle that he could not see, and withall he had moch pain in his head and stomake. . . . he was very weke and sicke lik to die, but yet he escaped and lyued. But his mistres fearinge he wold die made this question because she had beaten him, fering the daunger that might ensue therof because she had beaten him soe.[68]

Forman's notes on his own household suggest a fairly easygoing, somewhat chaotic atmosphere, not a place where beatings were particularly feared. The tone of that household is perhaps best revealed in a note that Forman made in the process of tracking the behavior of Bess Parker:

1598 the 8 of novem at 10 at night when Steaven lay here Eliz. Parker was on the bed kissing with him & the boyes I being abed. . . . The next morning my boy John [Braddege] told Steaven I watched her every wher & of the bag of stones, and Eustace said yf she wer disposed to pleasure any other good fellowe what had I to doe with yt.[69]

Clearly, a bevy of young servants and relatives filled Forman's bachelor household at this point in his life.

During the final years of the decade, Forman rented two houses most of the time. One was Stone House where he lived and saw his patients. The second housed his books and his occult equipment: whatever he felt might be dangerous if the authorities came to call. The first auxiliary house, "Mrs. Clarkes chamber," he apparently rented in May 1596. "I sent certain thinges thether. . . . I kept yt a quarter of a yere and did put yt of againe / I had al thinges safe ther & was in quiet ther for the tyme."[70]

The following year, 1597, he leased Lambeth House:

This house was ruinouse and the orchard alsoe and the firste yere yt coste me moch money and gret expence for reparations & other charges and the 10 dai of march I was robbed ther & my studi dore broke vp, and divers bockes caried awai.[71]

The former tenant, Mrs. Wodmester, who had died in the house, had left a few scattered possessions: "1 presse, 1 small bed sted, 1 brushing table, 1 yron chest, & a fram for a pair of virginalls, ther is all."[72] Lambeth House was located in Westminster, and Forman allowed his younger sister Joan to live there for a while, though she caused an uproar around Christmas by shutting "Marjery out of dore and Jean into the orchard."[73] His landlady and neighbors did not want Forman, his relatives, or his dangerous books in residence; though he had a seven-year lease, they "made many conspiracies to get me out." Under pressure, he sold his lease and vacated the premises in the summer of 1598.[74]

Forman needed a new place for his books. "At Midsomer I toke the hale wher I dwelt [at] London, but left not the stone house."[75] Thus, he continued to keep two houses. This new house must have been larger than his chamber in Stone House, for at Christmas, 1599, a few months after his marriage, he moved out of Stone House.

In 1600, he increased his household even more, adding Arthur at Michelmas, Frances after Bartholomewtide, and his brother John, who "lai with me this yer oftentymes."[76] Marriage had increased Forman's need for rooms and for servants to help him and his new wife.

The new arrangements cannot have been satisfactory, probably because Forman was still vulnerable to fines and arrest from the College of Physicians. In 1601, he moved his household to Pratt's Piece in Lambeth at the hefty rent of twenty pounds per year, leaving London on May 20. This move was very elaborate, far different from the early move he marked by carrying a book into a new chamber. Forman's manuscripts contain two lists made in conjunction with the Lambeth move. The first recorded "what I lefte in the house at London where I dwelt 1601 the 20 of May, when I went thence." This list gives some sense of the London establishment Forman was leaving:

> Itm. in the gret chamber 12 yerdes of wanscote   16 sh
> Joine dore and a lock & the partition over it   5 sh
> Itm. in the too lowar romes of painted cloth
>   72 yerdes at 4 d   24 sh
> Itm. buttery dores and wanscote & the locke   4 sh[77]

The second list recorded "the charg of my removuell 1601 to Lambeth." Forman had a good deal of work done on the new house between the lease signing in March and the move in May:

> for cariadg of too load stuffe   3 sh 4 d
> for naills   8 d
> for a sawe   8 d
> for bordes   9 sh 6 d
> for going by water to the 2 of Aprill   2 sh
> for dornix[78] at 20d a yerd/ 25 yerdes   44 sh
> & a lyttell peace besydes
> for a joiner [carpenter] for 2 dais and meate
>   and drinke   3 sh

for 7 yeardes mor of dornix	11 sh 8 d
the carpenters for 5 dais a peace at 16 d	13 sh 8 d
to the tiler for 2 daie at 16 d	2 sh 8 d
to the laborer for 2 dais at 12	2 sh
for 2 bordes to find on	18 d
for a doble qrters	8 d
for nailes	9 d
for 4000 lath naille	2 sh 10 d
for doble tens	12 d
for 500 sixpeni naill	2 sh 16 d[79]

Although Forman doesn't say how much space the new house afforded his family, the new quarters seemed to encourage a spate of visitors. In August, Forman's mother-in-law, her husband, and three servants came for an eight-week stay. Forman's older sister Joan and William Brink, her second husband, visited for a week in October. Steven came in late November and stayed through Christmas, and a patient, Mr. Hovelstone, came to be doctored in mid-December. Forman's last diary summary, for 1601, reflected the chaos engendered by ever-greater prosperity and an increasing household:

> This yere I thrived thankes be to god reasonable well. I bought moch houshold stufe & provision for the house & moch apparell, and was at moch charge in keping of my horse, my conies [rabbits]. Divers pigeons which wer gyuen me did not prosper with me but wer kild by cats and stolen & som pigeons flue awaie. My servantes were very disobedient and negligent & carles.[80]

Because both the diary and the casebooks end in 1601, there is no way to follow the growth of Forman's household in the final decade of his life. He remained in Lambeth during the entire period, probably in the same house, though he continued to buy and sell leases of other homes, becoming something of a speculator in real estate. I cannot tell whether he kept a second property for his books as he had done in London, but I think it unlikely since he was now in a less densely populated area with land enough to have outbuildings should he need a separate place for his study.

Chapter 1 contains some examples of Forman's decisions about whether to buy houses. In the 1607 diary, which covers only the period from March through early September, Forman purchased the lease of a property in Swandrop, purchased "more's coppihold" for six pounds per annum, and rented a house (which one he does not say) to a woman for seven pounds per annum.[81] At the moment of his death, according to Lilly, Forman was on his way to look at buildings in Puddledock that "he had in hand."

Forman took Joshua into his house in 1602, only to lose him in 1603. His own children were born in 1605 and 1606, and his nephew John, his brother Richard's oldest son, was living with Forman in 1606 when he, too, died of plague. Forman's financial success had made him an anchor for his relatives, and his moneyed lifestyle and the requirements of his practice necessitated several servants.

Supporting the impression of Forman's increasing material wealth are his references to gardens and gardening. In the mid-1590s during his affair with Mrs. Allen, Forman rented an enclosed garden from Mr. Katerins. The garden immediately began to figure as a meeting place: "the 12 March . . . I went to garden, wher I found A. Al & we becam frindes againe."[82] In this London garden Forman was apparently more interested in assignations than in exercising his skill in horticulture.

Later, however, his interests shifted in the direction of horticulture. One of the reasons for his lease of Lambeth House in Westminster may have been its orchard. During the few months that Forman held that lease, his casebook revealed a new interest in plants and animals. He noted that Jean, his resident virgin, cut hazel rods, useful for his occult practice.[83] He carefully observed the sex life of his rabbits: "my conni was buctred [mated] the 29 of May at 6, five times and she kytted again the 28 of June at night." He made arrangements to sell the fruit of what must have been a sizeable orchard: Robert Fleming would buy all the fruit except that from six trees and the apricots. Fleming signed the agreement, but Forman noted that it was dissolved ten days later.[84]

Once he moved to Pratt's Piece in Lambeth, he again mentioned livestock: conies, pigeons, and his horse. The property must have had sizeable grounds, for several of the manuscripts he wrote during the last decade of his life refer to gardening. In one, Forman provided elaborate instructions for "setting, sowing, planting and grafting, & removing trees." In his directions for setting saffron, Forman sounded almost whimsical:

> yt may be gathered from the natyuity to Simon and Iudes dai, in what tyme of the dai thou wilt. and every fifte year take vp the heades and lay them in a chamber and at the nativity put them in the earth again, and let no wedes growe among yt, and take heed of Robin Redbreste.[85]

He reported a number of his own agricultural successes:

Itm 1610 the moon in [Virgo] the 30 of Januari I set my aple tres in the garden at Lambeth Marsh towardes the lane & the walnut tre & filbert tre and all did prove. The 5 dai of feb . . . betwen 8 and 9 in the morn I set the 6 elmes towardes shepmans garden & they did proue, but slowly.

In the fragment from the 1607 diary, Forman's notes about his agricultural work mix with those of his sexual activity:

halk tronco [Forman's wife] 1607 am at 30 p[ast] 5. the 15 of Juli—that dai at 7 pm I began to cut and bush vp the gret garden of roses at Lambeth marsh & I began in the north west part and made som dossen bushes or better. . . . halk tronco 14 Aug am at 30 p[ast] 5. that dai am at 10 I set the Jilliflowers in the Inner garden. . . . the 20 Aug. 1607. 30 p[ast] 7 I began to dryue my bees and did put them in a newe hiue. Mrs. Bennet did it.[86]

Forman had become a man of property who finally had time to work on his land.

☞ Forman as Consumer

Another reflection of Forman's position in his society can be glimpsed by examining his purchases. In the 1580s Forman spoke frequently of "consuming," but almost always in the negative. He spent more than he earned, but he rarely mentioned purchasing particular items. In 1586, for example, he writes that "I consumed and spent more then I got"; in 1589, "I got lyttle, I spent & consumed all, till Michelmas then yt began to mend with me."[87] Not until 1593 did the tide shift: "The second of Aprill I bought Hugoes ringe for 40 sh[illings]. In May I made my gowne with velvet furr."[88]

The diary entries for 1594–95 are filled with details about the affair with Avis Allen. Forman recorded only the purchase of black stockings for twelve shillings in 1595 and a new fur gown and velvet jerkin in 1596. In 1599, when his determination to wed was in full course, Forman bought much linen, but he also bought a new horse and "harnis and weapons for warr, swordes, daggers, muscotes, corslet, and furnitur, staves howberdes, gantletes, maiells &."[89]

Concurrent with his search for a wife, Forman began to search for a fine horse. Early in 1599, he had cast about whether to buy a particular gelding (the answer was no: "he is all show"). He eventually managed to find a suitable gelding, which he named Bruceldoro, apparently taking the name from Orlando's mighty war horse in *Orlando Furioso*.[90] The list of military equipment that Forman purchased in 1599 might indicate that Forman was investing, buying supplies that he hoped later to sell at a profit. But no records of such transactions appear among his papers. Instead, the military equipment was apparently for himself, part of a self-image he was fashioning. The gelding, or rather the warhorse Bruceldoro, would enable Forman to go to war, not as a foot soldier, but as a knight, properly armed and mounted. He bought this expensive and unnecessary horse (which he had no place to keep in London; he arranged to board him with Richard Napier far off in Buckinghamshire) in order to achieve that image. In 1599, the kingdom was braced for war. Convinced that the Spanish would soon invade, the country prepared: "this yere was the gret muster in August in St. Jeames."[91] An undated entry in the 1599 casebook suggests the lines along which Forman was thinking. Headed "Knightes made in Erland by the E. Essex," the list includes fifty-eight names. Promotion through military service was one way to climb socially. Forman's ambitions in this direction are revealed by a cast in the 1598 casebook, where he asked "whether I shall be a C. [captain] in the fild & lead a band of men or com to greter digniti."[92]

After the death of Avis Allen, Forman seemed to be considering a new direction, searching for a way to get ahead rapidly. In 1598, he had considered going to sea, asking "whether I shall sped well yf I should nowe mak a Voyadg to India & be Captain my self" and "yf I go presently to Sir Willm Monson whether he will let me haue a ship or noe." He had taken the first step: "I went to him forth with but he had noe ship lefte he had sold them, but he vsed me kindly and I found him lame on his bed."[93] He began to compile lists, such as the one on "Howe to vittell a ship":

> In a ship ther go 5 to a mess and every messe is lowed for a dai of flesh, the flesh daies. 3 dais in a wick. Sun. Tues. Thus. the other 4 daies are fish daies.
>
> Yf youe vittell a shipe for on moneth wherin ther ar 40 men then youe must have 84 pounds for every 5 men, for every moneth. that is 14 shillings for 5 men in flesh for a moneth. at 16 d a stone [a stone equals 14 pounds]. Itm for 50 men ther must be for one moneth of flesh 84 pounds.
>
> Thinges necessary to victell a shipe with all for a long viage: peas mustard seed flesh [such] as bakon otmell candells bef fish as butter Bisket pork poor Ihon chease Beare mealle stockfish oylle water beanes viniger.[94]

Forman was searching for a way to "come to credit." In 1598, he thought seriously of captaining a ship. By 1599, he was interested in military service, seriously enough to lay out considerable cash on the horse and weapons of war.

By 1600, Forman's focus had shifted once again. With the threat of a Spanish invasion abated and after his marriage, he dropped his interest in military matters. He sold Bruceldoro in 1601, but he never says what he did with all the armor and weapons. In 1600, he recorded a different kind of purchase in his diary:

> This yere I bought many pictures about our Lady dai. This sommer I had my own pictur drawn,[95] and mad my purple gowne, my velvet cap my velvet cote my velvet breches my taffety cloke, my hat & many other thinges & did let my hear & berd growe. . . . I bought my swachele[?] sword this yer & did the hangers with siluer.[96]

In 1600, Forman's personal appearance seemed uppermost in his mind; his new clothes were as close as possible to the purple gown and velvet cap that the College of Physicians prescribed for its members. Although he bought a sword, it was clearly for show with its silver hangers. That year Forman envisioned himself not as a sea captain or as a knight on horseback but as a reputable physician, dressed as befitted his calling. By 1601, with the new house in Lambeth uppermost in his mind, Forman's attention, as we have seen, turned to domestic purchases and livestock.

☞ Leisure

The Formans' attempts to behave as gentlepeople were reflected by the activities in which they engaged. They stood as godparents; they traveled to visit friends and relatives in Greenwich; occasionally they were entertained at dinner both in Lambeth and in London.

The portrait that Forman mentioned having had drawn in his 1600 diary entry was probably the same one that was engraved and published in 1776 "from the Original Drawing in the Collection of the Right Honble Lord Mountstuart" (figure 10).[97] It shows Forman, looking very serious, dressed plainly in a dark gown (perhaps his purple velvet) with a large flat white collar. His dark hair is brushed back from his lined face and falls just below his ears. A neat mustache and well-trimmed beard complete the picture of a sober, thoughtful gentleman.

Forman not only commissioned his own portrait; he also purchased "many pictures." The diary note implies that Forman bought a collection of pictures all at once "about our Lady dai." These may have been a group of miniatures, for an astrological cast for a theft provides a vignette of the Formans displaying their new acquisitions in their home. The cast was made

FIGURE 10: Forman's portrait, engraved in the eighteenth century, perhaps from the portrait that Forman mentions having "drawn" in 1600.

by a certain gentleman for certain picturs gon out of his closset. Ther came diuers gentlewomen of her old acquaintance to see her, and she had them vp into her chamber and into her closset wher ther hanged certain fiue smalle pictures. And they toke the pictures out of the clossete to loke on them, and wold haue begged them, but she wold not giue them awai for any thinge but bad them lay them into the closset again, and a kinsman of hers standing by, toke the picturs and put them into his hose & forgettinge them went awai with them.

A kinsmans of the gentell womans of the house coming in whill the gentlewomen wer ther & coming vp into the chamber among them whill they wer loking on the pictures, toke them to loke on & put them in his hose in gest & forgetting them with talke carried them a waie, but after brought them again.[98]

Forman was careful about his details. He wrote about a gentleman and a gentlewoman entertaining old friends at home by displaying pictures, desirable possessions that the friends "wold haue begged." During the visit, the pictures were stolen by a kinsman of the gentlewoman, but Forman claimed, it was done "in gest"; after all, no kinsman of a gentlewoman could be a real thief. In the passage quoted above, Forman recounts the story of the forgotten pictures twice, changing it in the second version to emphasize the "gest" and to mention that they were returned. It is difficult to imagine a gentleman forgetting that he was carrying five small pictures in his hose, but the story was Forman's to tell.

Forman cannot have had a great deal of leisure time. The steady stream of patients, his reading and writing, the preparation of his oils, waters, and other medicines, along with his magical and alchemical experiments, must have consumed most of Forman's time. But one avocation that can be glimpsed through his manuscripts is theatergoing. In 1597, Forman had a dream in which he was attacked by a group of men with daggers drawn. Searching for what this dream signified, as he did for each of his dreams, he could only say, "that daie I hard of a plaie."[99] He had seen enough drama to connect his violent dream with stage action.

In April 1599, Forman met a prospective bride twice at the Curtain theater. Shakespeare's company would have been sharing it at that time with the Lord Admiral's Men while awaiting completion of the Globe later in 1599. He did not mention the play he saw, only that he walked in the fields with Sarah Archdell after the performance on April 19 and negotiated with her uncle at the same theater on April 22. The next year he attended two plays at the Rose theater, *Sir John Oldcastle* and *Cox of Cullinton* (recorded in Henslowe's diary as *Cox of Collumpton*), for which he gave a plot summary.[100] The casual way in which these references crop up in his notes amid patient records makes it fairly likely that, before he decided in 1610 to keep a record of the plays he attended, he rarely bothered to mention his theatergoing.

Rowse argued that Forman lived among theater people and treated many of them. A few are mentioned in the casebooks. He treated the first wife of William Kendall, a member of the Admiral's Men, casting her nativity and recording what he knew about her life.

> Margaret the daughter of Thomas Redman & of Margaret Wordalle—b. 1579—wif of Wilm Kendall. She list her maidenhead about 13 yers, and had many sutors at 15 yers or 16 of age and was in diuers humors and might haue had many good matches, & yet maried non, but in thend was with child by on, and soe maried to another, to a player & ther began her confusion. She was wild & gyuen to dansinge & Iolity.[101]

Kendall had bound himself in 1597 to Philip Henslowe to play for two years at the Rose theater. Little else is known of him.

Henslowe himself consulted Forman. On the 5th of February, 1597,

> Mr Philip Henslowe . . . diz [a medical consultation] himself [he came to Forman rather than sending a messenger]. . . . Yt is in the reins sid & hed . . . a tincling & ytching in his hed face moch melancoly . . . water with his stomak prepare 2 daies & purge & kill venomous humers.[102]

Philip Henslowe does not reappear in the casebooks, but Forman treated several women whose last name was Henslowe.

The other identifiable theater people came to Forman about a theft. In 1601, on February 10 and again on February 12, Frances and George Somerset inquired about the theft of a doublet. Forman told them it had been stolen by a woman, but later added a note that admitted his own mistake: "Town on of their compani had yt & confessed yt." Forman used this case again as an example of how to set an astrological question about theft, and included a bit more information: "the plaiers wife" made the request for information, with the result: "Yt was on of their own company that stolle yt his nam was Towne a player & at laste confeste yt of himselfe, but the good was not had again, but recompence made for it."[103]

There were two men by the name of Towne acting in London at the time of the theft. George Somerset belonged to the Lord Admiral's Men, where he played in 1600–1601 in *The Battle of Alcazar* with fellow actors Thomas Towne and William Kendall.[104] Since the thief was "on of their own company," Thomas Towne is probably the actor to whom Forman's notes referred. Rather than having a general acquaintance among theater people, Forman seems to have been consulted primarily by members of Henslowe's company, on matters ranging from illness to theft. Surely it would have been natural for Forman to go to watch these clients perform on the stage.

Not until a decade later, however, did Forman begin his theater diary, "The Bocke of Plaies and Notes therof per Forman for common Pollicie." Much has been written about Forman's truncated, four-play record, especially about the mistakes it contains.[105] Macbeth did not have trouble washing Duncan's blood from his hands. He and Banquo were not on horseback in Shakespeare's play, although they were on horses in the woodcut in Holinshed, which illustrates the meeting with the three witches (I have found no references to Holinshed among Forman's notes). Cloten was not banished from court by Cymbeline for loving Imogen. And *The Winter's Tale* ended with the revival or return of Hermione, a major plot detail which Forman failed to mention. This casualness about the details of someone else's work seems entirely characteristic of Forman. Just as he related the play he heard of in 1597 to his own dream, so he saw on the stage either reflections of himself or cautionary events from which he could learn. In *Macbeth*, he clearly derived satisfaction from the observant, note-taking doctor: "and the doctor noted her words," he concluded, hardly the detail most audience members would have singled out. In *Cymbeline*, he found nothing much of interest, so he concluded his jumbled plot summary with a bored "&c.," completely omitting Posthumus's oracular dream and, indeed, most of act 5.

In the non-Shakespearean *Richard II*, he found both cautionary lessons and a figure with whom to identify. "Never admit any party without a bar betwen," he wrote, "for a man cannot be to wise, nor kepe him self to safe." Forman empathized with the wise man whom the Duke of Lancaster hung for predicting that his son should be king:

> I sai yt was a villains parte and a Judas kisse to hange the man for telling him the truth. Beware by this example of noble men, and of their fair words & sai lyttell to them, lest they doe the like by thee for thy good will.[106]

Forman, too, was a wise man whose profession forced him to tell dangerous truths. I suspect that Forman also saw himself among Autolycus's victims. He had been cozened, and his warning, "be ware of trusting feigned beggars or fawning fellows," was heartfelt. He had said much the same thing in his plague treatise, warning of beggars who falsely claimed to be wounded soldiers:

> how manie roges and vagrante persons, that liue by the highe waies vnder the name of souldiars which never served at all nor came wher any service was done, which take away that allmes and lyuing manie tymes that pore souldiars should haue which in deed oughte to be mainteyned and reliued.[107]

Forman's account of the plays he attended illustrates Sidney's claim that literature was a "medicine of cherries," a tasty way to ingest a moral lesson.[108] Forman was intent on the didactic messages he could squeeze from what he saw onstage, particularly if those messages could be directly related to his own experience. What he reported tells us more about Forman than about the performances themselves.

Forman's ability to ignore all but what was in his own interest has been apparent throughout this chapter. Women should be chaste, but he never reflected on his own sexual profligacy. He bought a warhorse—never mind that he had nowhere to keep him and that he soon sold him. He leased an extra house for his dangerous books and quarrelsome relatives—how unfair that the neighbors conspired to get rid of him. All too often, in fact, people disappointed, betrayed, or angered Forman. He seems to have preferred the company of his books.

Forman and Public Events

THUS FAR, THE FORMAN of this study has been the character Simon Forman himself constructed. His choices of books, a wife, consumable goods, medical theories, the patients he would treat, and ultimately, what he would write down and preserve, have determined the parameters of my exploration. In this final chapter, I consider some public events and subjects in which Forman himself is not center stage, but about which he concerned himself or in which he was implicated. I focus on three examples: Forman's awareness of the New World, specifically the colonization of Virginia; his response to political figures and events; and finally, Forman's posthumous role in the Overbury trials.

☛ The New World

One public subject that attracted Forman's interest was the New World, specifically, the colony of Virginia. As we might have anticipated, Forman focused on a few subjects in the news from Virginia that seemed of particular relevance to his own work: flora and fauna, issues of health and, to a lesser degree, the habits of the indigenous New World people. Forman's Virginia notes are in no apparent order, perhaps jottings from memory of what Forman had read or been told. He wrote of the Indians planting wheat [corn] and beans in the same hill "and when yt groweth vp the bean doth clasp about the whete and every wheat will haue 3.4 or 5 ears & every ear will haue 300 or 400 grains and they clear the ground in March, and set their corn in Aprill, and rep yt in auguste."[1] He mentioned the maricoke[2] with its lemon flavor, comparing it in appearance to pumpkins and cucumbers, and noting that when it is ripe its sharp flavor changes to something "sweet and lussius." He also wrote of bean-bearing trees; the bean husks were sweet and good to eat, but the grains within them "doe purge moch."

In addition to notes on fruits and vegetables, Forman wrote of birds, insects, and animals. He describes an insect immediately recognizable as a finefly:

> Ther is also a kind of flie of som half inch longe that flyeth vp and down in the wodes in the night with f[ire] in their taills, like candells, or ar thes glowe[worms] and they ar seen ther in the sommer tyme bu[t not] in the winter.

The opossum, staple of several published New World accounts,[3] had slightly different features in Forman's description:

> Ther is also a Beaste called a opossum and yt is as bige as an old cat, but a taill lik a Rat and his head also lik a rate 4 leges and is foted lik a rat and of grayesh collor both the malle and the femalle & ar both of on bignes in a manner and this beaste doth carry her yonge ons in her belly, and she hath vnder her belly a bag in which she carrieth her yong ons. vp and down after they be varowed and they will go out of that bag and feed and then goe into yt again and they liue by grasse & herbes, and by ded fish on the Sea side. & they never suck & they slynk like a rat.[4]

Forman's additional details are probably due in part to his habit of repetition and expansion, but both in the opossum description and in that of the maracock he offers details not found in the published narratives. These additions raise the question of where Forman got his information about Virginia. Neither Smith nor Strachey's accounts were published until after Forman's death, so he must either have got his details from a manuscript source or from some firsthand account.

When he spoke of Jamestown, and its unfortunate physical location, Forman came close to the details of Strachey's 1609 account, "A True Reportory of the Wreck and Redemption of Sir Thomas Gates, Knight,"[5] but Forman again gave more details than Strachey, specifically those about the health of Jamestown's citizens: in May through August they were troubled with "a kind of burning feuer . . . swelling in theyr bodies & face," but in winter they were free of disease.

In a similar vein, Forman was interested in the prophylactic measures taken by the Indians to preserve their health:

> The Indians doe alwais in March boill the harte or pith of a pine tre in water

thorowly and then straine yt and drink the water therof and yt makes them
purge vpwardes and donwardes. and this doe they alwais doe in march and
at no tyme ells. and then in that moneth they purge all the whole contrie
over. and they bind their yonge children and make them drink yt then also.[6]

Forman recorded details of the New World culture that interested him;
he does not mention his sources, nor do his descriptions match, except
in their general topics, the printed accounts of the Virginia discoveries.
Rowse theorized that Forman got his material from his acquaintance among
the sailors who had made trips to Virginia, and this may be the explanation. He recorded dreaming that Steven, his stepnephew, brought him
"more" tobacco,[7] suggesting that Steven might have been to Virginia on
one of his sea voyages and brought back tobacco. Forman was certainly
able to obtain certain drugs, like tacamahac, which were available only from
the Americas.

Further speculation is fruitless, but Forman's knowledge about Virginia,
selective though it may have been, adds additional weight to what has been
increasingly evident throughout this study. Forman was privy to an enormous
amount of information—personal, public, and political—through his web of
patients and clients. His profession demanded that he find out things, from
the stars or from any other source that presented itself. Forman got a good
deal of his information from books, of course, but his practice also gave him
an information network in which news relayed by one patient might be used
to advise another or be recorded in Forman's ever-expanding books of notes
for some future use.

Political Interest and Awareness

Given his lively interest in so many topics, Forman's lack of comment on
politics and the court is somewhat surprising. He used political connections
to help himself in his quarrel with the College of Physicians, by urging
some of his noble patients to write letters interceding in his behalf. His
interest in the general political climate, on the other hand, seems quite
limited. Perhaps Forman rarely wrote about politics or the court because they
were too remote from the subject that principally concerned him: himself.
He occasionally mentioned the monarch, but when he did it was almost
always in passing. Elizabeth had become queen when Forman was five; he
remembered no other monarch. The queen intersected his life a few times
but always at a distance. He perhaps gave an oration before her just at the
time he left Oxford University; she apparently wrote a letter in 1579 that got

Forman released from his first long imprisonment. Occasionally Forman dreamed about her. In a now canonical article, Louis Montrose analyzed the most detailed of Forman's three recorded dreams about Elizabeth, in which Forman exchanged bawdy remarks with her and offered to make her pregnant.[8] Forman's two other recorded dreams about her are both less detailed and less salacious:

> Itm the 21 of feb [1597] I drempt of the quene that she came to me all in black & a french hode. that dai I had anger by dority and mrs pennington that cam to me about wordes my man spake.
>
> Itm 1598 the 9 of Januari am at 3 I drempt that the Quene did commend me moch for my skille & Judgment in phisick & chid with the docters and railed on them moch, for trobling me.[9]

In this last dream, the queen offered a possible escape from Forman's troubles with the doctors. In 1601, he speculated about getting an appointment as the queen's physician, as replacement for Dr. James.[10] In other words, the queen was an accepted part of the background canvas of Forman's life, as was the case when he was consulted in 1600 by Elizabeth Sparrow, twenty-eight, a servant who had the "quenes evil," otherwise known as scrofula. "The quene hath blessed it & is neuer the better,"[11] Forman wrote. In another manuscript Forman noted that the queen had proclaimed a reward for anyone providing "ashen kayes."[12] These seeds were apparently extremely scarce in 1591 and were in great demand, probably as part of some medical recipe.[13]

Although Forman occasionally mentioned major political crises or political executions, he never referred to Elizabeth or gave her agency in the executions. For example, he briefly recorded the death of Mary Queen of Scots and the atmosphere of the year of her execution, but Elizabeth was not mentioned:

> This quarter in the begininge of Feb. 1587 & in all that moneth ther was many lies and sleinge talles & strange Newes & rumors verie many like to mak an vproar which made many folkes almoste at their wites end to hear therof, & yet it was all or for the moste parte all falls rumors & talles & in this moneth the Quen of Scots was behedded & ther was moch nois of wars & our shipes staid in Fraunce.[14]

Similarly, in Forman's several notes on Essex's troubles, Elizabeth receives no mention.

The one exception to Forman's matter-of-fact acceptance of Elizabeth's presence is a poem that Forman wrote in 1578 about Henry VIII and Elizabeth. The narrator of the poem canvasses Earth and Hell looking for a subject worthy of poetic praise. Finally he spies the royal tree:

Too kindes of frute out of this tree
Ther did sumtime forthe springe
The on yealdes frute yet to this daie
Thoughe thother none doe bringe
The firste frute that this tre did yeld
Wase worthines of fame
The other frute whiche from him spronge
weer pearlese princes thre
Which afterward bye course did rulle
when withered was the tree.

In marginal notes to these lines, Forman wrote "2 kindes of frut on is wisdome in ruling the Realm & defending it, 2 encreas of childrene. wisdom raignes in our queene though encres of children do not." He goes on in the poem to celebrate Henry VIII as David, a warlike king ready to lead his nation in military exploits. Elizabeth follows as Solomon, noted for wisdom rather than for war.

Though David kinge in thee be dead
yet Sallomon dothe live:
To whom straunge peaple com from fare
and Princlye giftes doe giue
Of whom her people doe reioice
As of a father dear:
And wishinge her with willing harte
To raign a thousand year.

The comparison of Elizabeth to males—to Solomon and a "father dear"— is not consistent throughout the poem. In fact, the narrator makes a point about how much more perfect Elizabeth is than famous women of antiquity and mythology—Dido, Cleopatra, Helen, Pandora, Phyllis, etcetera. Forman does not say that all these women were in some way identified with or made famous by the men in their lives, though perhaps that is one reason why Elizabeth, the only virgin in the group, is superior to the others. Claiming to be running out of inspiration, wishing for Chaucer's pen and then for Tully's, unable to do the subject justice, Forman brought his poem to a limping close:

whos worthines a brod to blase
my witte I feell to faint
Sir Chaucers pene hit woold amase
hir praise in verse to paint.[15]

Forman's uncertainty about the queen's appropriate metaphorical gender suggests that her subjects (or at least this subject) had, to some degree, adopted Elizabeth's own adroit switching between masculine and feminine images when she spoke of herself. Like his praise of her wisdom and chastity and his regret that there would be no second fruit, no children, his double gendering of Elizabeth is strictly conventional. Even his dreams about Elizabeth seem less remarkable when we note that he also dreamed about King James in one of the few dreams after 1603 of which he left records:

> Anno 1607 the 22 aprill wensdai night I drempt the king came to my house with a halk on his fiste & said he had bin at the bishops. that dai cam to my house many of my old friendes that I had not seen longe before. yt showeth the comminge of strangers & old acquaintance.[16]

Because there are no daily notebooks for 1603, we do not know Forman's thoughts on the death of the queen and the ascension of the new king, events of such magnitude that it is difficult to imagine that they did not evoke some response from Forman.

One political story that captured Forman's interest was that of Robert Devereux, earl of Essex, whose rise and fall Forman followed with close attention. Essex's name had surfaced in Forman's notes once or twice before 1599, when clients questioned whether it would be safe to join an Essex expedition or whether Essex might grant a knighthood to a client's husband. When Essex prepared to set out for Ireland, however, Forman began to display a personal interest in the earl's success. On March 14, 1599, Forman set a horoscope, no client present, "to know how my L Robt Deverex E of Essex shall speed in his voyadge into Ireland & wher he shall prevaill or no 1599." He recorded his answer in unusual detail:

> Ther seames to be in thend of his voyadg negligence treason hunger sicknes & death, and he shall not doe moch good to bring yt to effecte, but at his retorne moch treachery shall be wroughte againste him & thend wilbe evill to him selfe for he shalbe Imprisoned or haue great troble for he shall find many enimies in his retorne & haue gret losse of goodes & honor & moch villainy and treason shalbe wroughte against him to the hazard of his life . . . yeat he shall escape yt with moch adoe after long tyme & moch infami & troble.[17]

So accurate was Forman's prediction about the hot-headed Essex that one might reasonably suspect that he wrote it after the earl's troubled return from Ireland later in 1599. But the note is in its proper place, fitting in naturally among casenotes written on the same day, so I believe that on this occasion at least the stars were nearly accurate in their forecast.

Forman was in the street at 1:00 P.M. on March 27, 1599, to see Essex and his company depart London for Ireland. He then hurried home to cast yet another horoscope. Though he gave great detail in his description of the ominous weather that blew up for Essex's leave-taking, he did not record what the stars foretold on this occasion:

> howe he shall speed er he retorne from Ireland in his wars. he went with som hundred horses in his compani. . . . He toke horse at the toware about on of the clocke and vp the crutched fryars and vp chepsyd with som hundred horse and about 2 of the clok yt begane to raigne. and at 3 till 4 ther fell such a haille shower that was very great. And then yt thunderd withall and the wind turned to the north and after the showar was paste yt turned to the south est again. And ther wer many mighty cloudes vp. but all the day before on of the clock was a very fair day & cler and 4 or 5 dayes before bright and clere & very hote lyk somer.[18]

Forman felt that the abrupt change in the weather was ominous for the earl, as did other observers.

A few months later, Forman included, on a separate page in his casebook among materials dated in August 1599, a meticulously copied and numbered list of fifty-eight knights made in Ireland by Essex. This was the year when Forman purchased his warhorse and his armor and, I suspect, fantasized about serving with Essex, from whom he might receive the recognition he hungered for. Ironically, the massive bestowal of knighthoods was one of the acts that would get Essex in trouble with the queen and her advisors.

By the time of Forman's next astrological cast about Essex, the earl's situation had altered radically. Rushing back to England unsummoned and leaving a debacle behind in Ireland, Essex was imprisoned from October 1599, until the following August. Forman, however, did not forget him. On November 27, 1599, Forman cast "Essex quid sibi accidit et quid de eo evenit &c."[19] He recorded no answer.

Essex does not reappear in Forman's casenotes until February 1601, immediately after his failed rebellion. But Forman had remained interested in Ireland. On September 19, 1600, Forman cast to know "Jeames Fitsgerall,

Erel of Dessmond howe he shall spead in Irland when he comes ther & what will come of him."[20] The young man about whom Forman cast had been a prisoner in the Tower most of his life, shut up because he was heir to the traitorous [i.e., sympathetic to the Irish] earl of Desmond, now deceased. Elizabeth's council had decided to give young James the title and send him to Ireland under very close supervision in the hope that the Irish people would receive him and be influenced by him to be more tractable. The scheme failed, but Forman knew about and was interested in the earl's departure. Though he recorded no astrological judgment, Forman did note "he went awai to erland som 8 dais after." I assume Forman was recording the young earl's exit from London, since the party embarked from Bristol for Ireland on October 13, about twenty-four days after Forman's question.

The 1601 casebook reveals Forman's strong interest in the fate of Essex and his co-conspirators. On Monday, February 9, the day after Essex's plot to seize the queen had been foiled, Forman cast: "Quid L Essex. vita aut mors." On February 12, he again cast: "Utrum nobiles [illegible] mort." On February 20, the day after the trial, he asked whether "hampton" [Henry Wriothesley, earl of Southampton who was tried with Essex] would die. On February 21, he asked the same question about Essex. On February 25, sprawled across a casenote, appears the notation: "Essex was beheaded this dai about 30 p 7 am."[21]

Even after Essex's death, Forman's interest in the fate of the Essex conspirators persisted. On February 26, Forman asked "pro hampton utrum decol." In fact, Southampton's death sentence was commuted to life in prison, a sentence that James promptly revoked when he came to the throne. Southampton long outlived Forman. Two other conspirators were less fortunate, however, and Forman noted in his casebook "that Sir christopher blunt and sir charells danvers were behedded at Towar hill 1601 the 18 of march betwen 8 and 9 of the cloke am."[22]

Not quite ready to forget the trial, Forman also made a careful list of the peers who were appointed to try Essex and Southampton. Beside this list of twenty-five "Errells and Lordes," Forman wrote:

> and ther were alleadged againste them 25 articles. and of 24 [of] them they did very well acquite them selfs and for the 25th [he] was caste & condemned. w[hich] was for that he yelded not him [self] after the proclimation was made.[23]

Forman's sympathies were still with Essex; he never mentioned his attempt to seize the queen. Indeed, Forman's notes about Essex and his conspiracy make no mention of the monarch. Related probably to his concern for Essex and his reputation was a list, on the page following that listing Essex's jury, of prominent English families that "haue bin attainted of treason." Nine family names appeared, including "the shellies, the hawards the hungerfords."[24] The Essex story is unique in Forman's records because it is the only story in which Forman seemed to take more than a passing interest in something that does not directly involve himself.

☞ The Overbury Trials and Forman's Reputation

Forman had nothing to do with the murder of Sir Thomas Overbury, arguably the most scandalous crime of King James's reign and certainly the one that touched the court most intimately.[25] Yet Forman's name is popularly associated with that murder. At the time of Forman's death in September 1611, Overbury was in excellent health and performing his duties as courtier and as advisor to King James's royal favorite, Robert Carr. In April 1613, nearly two years after Forman's death, Overbury was committed to the Tower of London for refusing an ambassadorship to Russia offered him by King James. On September 14, 1613, Overbury died while still a prisoner in the Tower and was quickly and quietly interred.

How Overbury came first to the Tower and then to his death is a convoluted story of which I will give only the briefest summary. Frances Howard had been married while very young to the earl of Essex (son of the executed earl in whose fate Forman had been so interested). The young couple at first did not live together, and Frances spent several years in the court while Essex traveled abroad. At court she met men—most specifically, Robert Carr—who seemed more attractive than her young husband. When the young earl and his wife at last came to live together, severe problems surfaced. Frances claimed that the marriage was never consummated and demanded an annulment. While her annulment case was being decided, Frances and Robert Carr began a relationship and then to talk of marriage, much to the dismay of Carr's friend and close political advisor, Sir Thomas Overbury. Feeling that Overbury's opposition to their marriage was trouble-some, Carr and Howard apparently persuaded King James to offer Overbury an ambassadorship to Russia. Should he accept, he would be away from the court for some time; should he refuse, he would incur James's displeasure and perhaps be punished. In fact, Overbury did refuse, and James sent him to the Tower of London.

Perhaps still worried about his interference even from the Tower, or perhaps angry that she should be so obviously scorned by Carr's friend and advisor, Howard seems to have plotted Overbury's death by poison and to have hired people to help her carry out her scheme. Whether Carr himself was a party to the poison scheme has never been conclusively determined.[26]

How did Forman come to be connected in popular opinion and in most written commentary with this death? By the summer of 1615, escalating rumors that Overbury had been poisoned prompted King James to appoint Lord Chief Justice Edmund Coke to investigate the circumstances surrounding his death. As Coke assiduously pursued his inquiries, the circle of those implicated widened, and by October 1615, the first of the indicted, Richard Weston, was brought to trial. He was found guilty and executed.

Next to be tried was Anne Turner, widow of a physician and a friend of Frances Howard. Turner was accused of having helped Howard procure poisons that were administered to Overbury during his imprisonment. Here Forman's name enters the record. As part of the background to Turner's case (a part that was quickly foregrounded by the attorney presenting the State's case), two letters from Frances Howard were read in court; one was written to Anne Turner and the other allegedly to Simon Forman. The letters no longer exist, and we have only the record of the state trial as evidence of what they said.

The letters as printed in the trial transcripts are very ambiguous. Howard rarely used a proper name and never mentioned Forman's. In the letter to Turner, whom she does name, she wrote: "You may send the party word of all; he sent me word all should be well, but I shall not be so happy as the lorde to love me." The court was told that "the party" referred to Forman and that "the lorde" was Robert Carr whose affections Howard was trying to secure to herself. At the letter's end, she remarks that she cannot be happy "so long as this man [presumably her unwanted husband the earl of Essex] liveth." "Let him [Forman?] know this ill news," she concludes.[27] The letter was read in court and was followed by a second letter beginning "Sweet Father," which, the record assures us, was addressed to Forman. This letter is a masterpiece of obfuscation. Clearly Frances Howard was following her own advice about the need for caution. "Remember the galls," she writes,

> for I fear though I have yet no cause but to be confident, in you, yet I desire to have it as it is yet remaining well; so continue it still, if it be possible, and if you can you must send me some good fortune, alas! I have need of it.

Keep the lord [Carr?] still to me, for that I desire; and be careful you name me not to any body, for we have so many spies, that you must use all your wits, and little enough, for the world is against me, and the heavens favour me not, only happy in your love; I hope you wil do me good, and if I be ingrateful, let all mischief come to me.[28]

Howard goes on to complain about the earl of Essex ("my lord") and closes, "Your affectionate, loving daughter, FRANCES ESSEX." In a postscript, she urges the person to whom she writes to warn Turner of all things but not to contact "the lord" [Robert Carr?].

The Turner letter suggests that Howard had been consulting Forman about her future and had gotten a mixed prediction "all should be well, but I shall not be so happy as the lord to love me." In the "Sweet Father" letter, Howard's requests are difficult to decipher. As we have seen earlier, Forman made sigils that, in addition to relieving medical problems, could promote love and good fortune. Something of this sort might "keep the lord [Carr?] still to [her]."

In themselves the letters are fairly innocuous, suggesting that Forman had been consulted on the astrological side of his practice, this time by a very highly placed member of James's court who wanted both a prediction about the future and some help with her love life. But Sir Laurence Hide, the attorney who was presenting the case, contextualized the letters to make them much more sinister than a first reading of them indicates. As he opened Turner's trial, even before introducing the letters,

he shewed further, that there was one Dr. Forman, dwelling in Lambeth, who died very suddenly, and a little before his death desired that he might be buried very deep in the ground, or else (saith he) I shall fear you all—To him, in his life-time, often resorted the Countess of Essex [Frances Howard] and Mrs Turner, calling him father: their cause of coming to him was, that by force of magick, he should procure the now earl of Somerset, the viscount Rochester, [Robert Carr] to love her, and sir Arthur Manwaring to love Mrs. Turner, by whom, as it was there related, she had three children.[29]

The gratuitous remark about Forman desiring to be buried deep sets up an atmosphere of guilt into which the letters themselves are read. That Turner and Howard were Forman's clients would not be surprising, though no record remains among Forman's papers of either woman.

After printing the two letters, the trial record lists items that had been taken from Mrs. Turner; a black scarf full of white crosses and "pictures of a man and woman in copulation, made in lead" were shown in court. The record implies, but does not state, that Turner obtained these objects from Forman. As these exotic items were displayed,

> there was heard a crack from the scaffolds, which caused great fear, tumult and confusion among the spectators, and throughout the hall every one fearing hurt, as if the devil had been present, and grown angry to have his workmanship shewed, by such as were not his own scholars; and this terror continuing about a quarter of an hour, after silence proclaimed, the rest of the cunning tricks were likewise shewed.[30]

The courtroom atmosphere was highly charged. As the editorial remarks make clear, Turner was associated, by the prosecution or by the narrator of the record, with the Devil. This amounted almost to an accusation of witchcraft.

Though they had no direct bearing on the Overbury murder, Turner's dealings with Forman continued to be the focus of the court's attention. Mrs. Forman was called to testify. As Forman's "administratrix," she had found "letters in packets, by which much was discovered." Mrs. Forman testified that, after her husband's death, Mrs. Turner had come to demand "certain pictures which were in her husband's study." Later, after the trial indictments, Turner had sent her maid Margaret, according to Mrs. Forman, to gather letters and papers concerning Frances Howard and Robert Carr. These papers were burnt, yet "[Mrs. Forman] kept some without their privity."[31] Mrs. Forman also reported that her husband and Turner would sometimes be locked up in his study for three or four hours at a time.

In addition to testimony that involved Turner, Mrs. Forman added some apparently irrelevant details about her husband. For example, he "had a ring would open like a watch." Also a "Note was shewed in the Court, made by Dr. Forman, and written in parchment, signifying what ladies loved what lordes in the court; but the Lord Chief Justice would not suffer it to be read openly in the court."[32]

Perhaps this testimony helps to explain the gaps in Forman's records after about 1603. If some papers had been burnt and others taken to court by Mrs. Forman, never to be returned, the absence of the later casebooks and letters may be accounted for. Unfortunately, their absence makes corroboration of the allegations made in court impossible. One wishes for Forman's lists of clients or even his sexual records, which might lend insight into those hours spent shut up with Mrs. Turner. Lacking these, however, we have simply the gratuitous details, which reflect negatively on Forman, dead but on trial just the same.

In the trial, detail is heaped on detail. The record speaks of parchments: on one the names of the Trinity were written, on another, devils' names, and on yet another, the mysterious inscription "+B+C+D+E." Another parchment had a drawn figure labeled "corpus" with a piece of "the skin of a man" attached. None of these items seems particularly surprising to someone who has examined Forman's papers, but they were used during the trial to present Forman as a devilish, corrupt creature who preyed upon women. No mention is made of his medical practice, for example, though that might help explain the figure labeled "corpus." Nor is there any acknowledgement that he was consulted by men as well as by women.

In a patriarchal society, the idea that a young noblewoman—Frances Howard—might have herself planned the poisoning of a prominent courtier was unthinkable.[33] It was more credible to portray her as corrupted by the older, less noble, "witchy" Anne Turner, who herself was controlled by a male sorcerer. Before the jury deliberated Turner's guilt or innocence, Justice Coke himself made the point:

> Then the Lord Chief Justice told Mrs. Turner, that she had the seven deadly sins: viz. a whore, a bawd, a sorcerer, a witch, a papist, a felon, and a murderer, *the daughter of the devil Forman.*[34]

The jury returned a verdict of guilty, surely to no one's surprise. Part of the displacement of blame from Frances Howard to her subordinates may be seen in the fact that Weston, Turner, and two others were executed, while Howard—though found guilty after a guilty plea—was merely imprisoned and later pardoned by King James.

The destruction of Forman's reputation (already questionable because of his feuds with the College of Physicians and his occult activities) was thorough and continued to reverberate throughout the century. Retellings of the incidents surrounding Overbury's death gave Forman two quite distinct characters. In one version of the story, he appeared as a devilish creature, empowered by the necromantic arts.[35] In the alternative version, he was a charlatan, fooling silly women into thinking he had occult powers. In both versions, he is despicable.

In *Sir Thomas Overbury's Vision*, a long poem apparently composed by Richard Niccols on the heels of the trial itself in 1616, the demonic Forman is featured. Overbury appears to the narrator of the poem in a dream vision, followed by the ghosts of three of those executed for his murder: Anne Turner, Weston, and one of Turner's servants, Franklin. Turner's ghost explains her fall into evil:

> I left my God t'ask counsel of the devil,
> I knew there was no help from God in evil:
> As they that go on whoring unto hell,
> From thence to fetch some charm or magick spell;
> So over Thames, as o'er th'infernal lake,
> A wherry with its oars I oft did take,
> Who Charon-like did waft me to that strand,
> Where Lambeth's town to all well known doth stand;
> There Forman was, that fiend in human shape,
> That by his art did act the devil's ape:
> Oft there the black inchanter, with sad looks,
> Sat turning over his blasphemous books,
> Making strange characters in blood-red lines:
> And, to effect his horrible designs,
> Oft would he invocate the fiends below,
> In the sad house of endless pain and woe,
> And threaten them, as if he could compel
> Those damned spirits to confirm his spell.[36]

Even Franklin's ghost has something to say about Forman, though Forman's name was not mentioned in Franklin's trial. His ghost, however, claims to have learned evil by Forman's side:

> Forman, that cunning exorcist, and I
> Would many times our wicked wits apply
> Kind nature, in her working, to disarm
> Of proper strength; and, by our spells, would charm
> Both men and women, making it our sport
> And play to point at them in our report.[37]

Forman has become an exorcist, playing with men and women, distorting nature. Gone is any reference to his medical practice. He is portrayed as the enticer of women like Anne Turner, not as a practitioner whose advice, medical as well as occult, was sought by thousands of Londoners.

In a pamphlet first printed in 1643, "The Five Years of King James," attributed erroneously on its title page to Fulke Greville,[38] Forman's participation in the schemes of Turner and Frances Howard is amplified once more. Here he is first responsible for making Essex—the unwanted husband—

impotent, and then credited with enchanting Carr—the desired lover—to fall in love with Frances Howard.

> For this purpose [making Essex impotent] Dr. Forman is consulted, for the procuring of means; pictures in wax are made, crosses, and many strange and uncouth things for what will the devil leave unattempted to accomplish their ends? Many attempts failed, and still the earl stood it out. At last, they framed a picture of wax, and got a thorn from a tree that bore leaves, and stuck upon the privity of the said picture, by which means they accomplished their desires.[39]

After printing a slightly altered version of the "Sweet Father" letter, this account continues:

> This letter, coming to the hands of the old master, procures a new attempt, and now he goes and inchants a nutmeg and a letter; one to be given to the viscount [Robert Carr] in his drink, the other to be sent unto him as a present; these things being accomplished, he [Forman], not long after, died, leaving behind him some of those letters, whereby the countess had intercourse with him, in his pocket, which gave some light into the business.[40]

For the first and only time, we are told that Forman died with incriminating letters in his pocket. The pamphlet never mentions the nutmeg again, but the enchanted letter had its desired effect.

> [Frances Howard] sends congratulations to the viscount, and with those, the letter sent her by Dr. Forman; he reads it, and, the more he reads it, the more is intangled: For no man knows the miseries that are contained in evil arts, and who can withstand the words of evil tongues?[41]

While this author does not show Forman as controlling spirits, he does identify him as an enchanter who is ready to use whatever means necessary to produce impotence in Essex and passion in Robert Carr.

In Anthony Weldon's midcentry account, on the other hand, Forman is merely a "silly fellow," dangerous because of his influence over women:

> . . . among those tricks, Formans book was shewed. This Forman was a fellow dwelt in Lambeth, a very silly fellow, yet had wit enough to cheate ladies and other women, by pretending skill in telling their fortunes, as whether they should bury their husbands, and what second husbands they should have, and whether they should enjoy their loves, or whether maids should get husbands, or enjoy their servants to themselves without corrivals; but before he would tell any thing, they must write their names to his alphabetical book with their owne hand writing. By this trick, he kept them in awe, if they should complain of his abusing them, as in truth he did nothing else.

Weldon cannot resist a bit more gossip about Forman and about the response in court to his books of records.

> Besides, it was believed, some meetings were at his house, wherein the art of a bawd was more beneficial to him then that of a conjurer, and that he was a better artist in the one then other; and that you may know his skil, he was himselfe a cuckold, having a very pretty wench to his wife, which would say, she did it to try his skill, but it fared with him as with astrologers that cannot foresee their owne destiny. I well remember there was much mirth made in the court upon the shewing this book; for it was reported, the first leafe my Lord Cook lighted on he found his owne wives name.[42]

Yet another early historian of the reign of James, William Sanderson, offers an alternative version of the events of the trial, claiming the perspective of an eyewitness:

> I was present at their arraignments, and the pictures, puppets, for magick spells, were no other but severall French babies, some naked, others clothed; which were usuall then, and so are now a dayes, to teach us the fashions for dresse of ladies tyring and apparrell. And indeed Foremans book was brought forth, wherein the mountebanck had formerly, for his own advantage and credit, sawcily inserted the countesses name, so of many others that came to seek fortunes, which she cleared by her own protestation and Foremans confession that she was never with him.[43]

In this account, by an apologist for James's court, Frances Howard was never a client of Forman's. Rather the "mountebanck" had fabricated the connection with the countess in order to elevate his social status. Forman's "confession" must have been a bit difficult to retrieve from the grave, but Sanderson has no difficulty in asserting that it existed.

It is perhaps not surprising that this scandalous set of murder trials which reached so high into the ranks of the Court should be retold and refashioned by political factions in the seventeenth century. What is surprising is that, in the nineteenth century, a writer such as Hawthorne could still call up Forman's name and diabolic reputation as a way of characterizing his own villain.[44] Forman's refashioning reached its nineteenth-century apogee, however, in England. In 1819, an anonymous three-volume novel entitled *Forman: A Tale* was published in London and dedicated to Sir Walter Scott. The author, now identified as Abel Moysey, admits to having found his "original hint" for the novel in the trial of Anne Turner.

In his preface, he reminds readers that in the period of James I, people believed in the reality of necromantic arts, and therefore he has not hesitated to use "real, downright sorcery, fiends, and spectres."[45] All of these occult trappings are connected with Forman, a figure to whom Moysey gives no Christian name in the novel. Dressed in black, Forman pops up intermittently in the novel, always causing dread and foreboding in the hearts of those around to witness his activities. For example, as the young, romantic noble-man who is the novel's hero approaches a "low obscure house" in Lambeth to ask directions, "he saw, or believed he saw, in a vivid blaze of lightning, several strange shapes glide towards the hut, and could not help fancying that they never touched the ground."[46] The house, of course, is Forman's Lambeth residence, much transformed from the spacious house and garden of Forman's own accounts.

In the course of the narrative, Forman attempts two conjurations of spirits for the purpose of killing living characters (one is Overbury; the other is the novel's hero). Both operations are interrupted and thus fail, but earthquakes and storms result from Forman's forbidden necromantic activity. His power to call fiends and to strike terror into the hearts of all those who behold him is explained by a Faustian pact that he has made with the Devil. Moysey's descriptions of his demonic conjurations are designed to produce a romantic shudder of horror:

> The wizard prostrated himself before the fiend, and again, with the ve-hemence of the most earnest supplication, pronounced some words from the volume in his hand, accompanying them with gestures of worship and adoration.[47]

Forman meets his bad end in volume three, dying, of course, miserably. It is soon revealed that he is a neglected second son of minor nobility, twisted by thwarted ambition and jealousy into a creature of total evil. Near the novel's end is a phrase that makes an appropriate epigraph for the post-Overbury Forman: "Forman the wizard; a name by this time universally known, and already a byword and term of reproach."[48]

Ironically, the Forman whose writings this study has examined was outflanked by writers who took advantage of print publication to offer their accounts of "Forman" to a broad general audience. The widely disseminated accounts of the Overbury murder and its subsequent trials, printed both in official accounts and as gossipy history, completely eclipsed Forman's own writings preserved in one or two copies in manuscript collections.[49]

He wished to "come to account," to have a place in history, to reestablish the Forman name. But the "Forman" who lives on in print is largely the posthumous creation of a patriarchal culture, a demonic character who can shoulder the blame for the crimes of the nobility, and only occasionally the "silly fellow" first suggested by Jonsonian lampoons. "The astrological physician of Lambeth," Forman's favorite description of himself, has been totally eclipsed by "Forman the wizard" and "Forman the charlatan."

🙊 A P P E N D I X 🙊

This appendix lists the contents of the Ashmole manuscripts, housed in the Bodleian Library, Oxford University, Oxford, referenced or consulted for this study. Because there are so many fragments, unfinished texts, and short notes, listing the manuscript contents accurately is difficult, and I make no claim that the following list is exhaustive. I hope that it will prove helpful to scholars looking for Forman material on a particular topic. For more precise and detailed description of the contents of Ashmole manuscripts, see William H. Black, comp., *A Descriptive, Analytical and Critical Catalogue of the Manuscripts Bequeathed . . . by Elias Ashmole* (Oxford, 1845). Unless otherwise noted, all references are to leaves not pages.

MS. Ashmole 174: Primarily a manuscript of Richard Napier whose material I omit. The manuscript contains the following Forman materials (paginated).

    pp. 375–379 Who will live longest, a man or a woman

    380 How to know if someone sick can be cured

    381 Of compounding medicines, for surgery and physic

    382 How to determine the length of an imprisonment by the position of the moon

    479 Clement Forman's letter to Richard Napier, August 20, 1628, "from Saint Christophers in America"

MS. Ashmole 195: Casebook from February 1598 to February 1599. The following nonpatient notes are included.

    ff. 9r Personal astrological casts

    69r–73v Personal notes, Forman nativities

    90v Notes on Doctor Poor's fatal doses

    101v Personal notes

    141r Forman's own illnesses

    150r–151v Notes

    195r–196v Forman's conflicts with the "doctors"

    245v–246r Value of coins; payments "for soldiers"

MS. Ashmole 205: A book of instruction about casting for astrological questions.

ff. 1r–120v About people and goods lost or missing

122r–208v Various questions: whether a wife is honest, whether a servant is trusty, how one shall speed on a journey,; etcetera

209v–230r "De Planetis"

231r–245r Questions: whether a woman is pregnant, about the philosopher's stone, etcetera

245r–276r "Of the absente"

282r–285v Lists of medicines and cures

286r–289v Forman's own nativities and predictions

290v–309v Questions on theft, with astrological tables

313v–314v Two personal casts (1610–11)

315v–326v "De Luna"

327r–330v Leaves that are probably part of the volume's first essay

MS. Ashmole 206: A book of nativities (both leaves and pages are numbered; I use the pagination).

n.p. An unpaginated, inaccurate index to the volume

pp. 1–4 "The Comment of Jhon of Saxon upon the Text of Alcabitius translated by S.F, 1601"

5–7 Notes on the location of planets

8–436 Text on nativities (on 218 there is a change from listing rules determining nativities to giving examples of particular nativities beginning with Forman's (218–25) and that of his illegitimate son, Joshua Walworth (226)

MS. Ashmole 208: A miscellaneous collection of papers.

ff. 1r–74r Forman's diary to 1602

78r–93v "Of Cako [antimony, a mineral necessary for alchemy]"

94r–97r "Of the Mineral Stone"

98r–101r "Opus minerale"

102r–103r "Of the Vegetable Stone"

104r–107v Fragment of a treatise on the elixir

108r–111v List of animals, plants, and people influenced by the moon

110r–134r "A Discourse of the plague writen by Simon Forman gent. 1593. and verie necessary for all men to reade and truely to remember"

136r–142r Forman's autobiography (to 1574)

143r–144r Letter to Forman from Frances Haiward

145r–199v Miscellaneous instructions: how to find stolen goods, where an absent person is, etcetera

200r–207v "The Bocke of Plaies and Notes therof per Forman for common Pollicie"

214r–227r "Of the Name of Forman" (genealogical material)

228r–231r "The Letters and Vowells" (an attempt at ciphers, cf. MS. Ash. 244: 1–22)

235r–248v "The Argument betwen fforman and death in his Sicknes"

250r–260r Poem about Henry VIII and his children

260v–261v Poem of praise to a "Noble Lord"

262r–v "Thomas Ellis in praise of [Martin] Frobisher"

263r–264v "John Kirkham of Martin Frobisher"

265–266 Heavy parchment sections of circles inscribed with the names of Hebrew letters and numbers

MS. Ashmole 219: Casebook from February 1599 to January 1, 1600. The following nonpatient notes are included.

ff. 47r "She is a pug of perles price" (poem signed by Forman)

47v "Of sneezing"

53r–54r Personal notes on slander case and book theft

133r "Knights made in Ireland 1599 by the E. Essex"

133v A payment agreement for treating Margaret Snow

134r A list of nineteen cases in which Forman correctly predicted death

135r–136v Personal notes about his wife, mistress, and illegitimate daughter; a dream

227r "Kings of England since Lud" (with the length of their reigns)

228r–229v "When Arter first in court began" (poem about Lancelot)

MS. Ashmole 226: Casebook from January 20, 1597, to February 20, 1598. The following nonpatient notes are included.

ff. 43v "Charges of the matter I have in suit against Peter Sefton" (1596)

44r–45r Dreams from 1597, including two about Queen Elizabeth

89v Personal notes including a dream

120r Note signed by Ann Waller that she will not marry without Forman's permission or forfeit 500 pounds

180r–v Notes on how to get to Linford, Buckinghamshire (home of Richard Napier), recipe for "Oil of Swallowes"

310r–v Dreams, including one about Queen Elizabeth. Personal notes

MS. Ashmole 227: Richard Napier's casebook, which includes the following material relevant to Forman.

ff. 85v Note about Clement Forman's visit to inform Napier of the plan to sell Forman's books

275r Note by Napier about receiving an "acquittance" for all the Forman materials in his possession from Clement and Mrs. Forman (now Mrs. Neale)

MS. Ashmole 234: Casebook from March 18, 1596, to January 20, 1597. The following nonpatient notes are included.

ff. 47r "A Note of things I put in my strong water. 1596"

48v What a pregnant woman's desires indicate about the child she carries

123r–124v Dreams from 1596, most involving Avis Allen

126v A prophetic poem

127r–v Personal notes, mostly about money
156v–157v Dreams; note on wind direction; notes on charges for arresting "Atkins"

MS. Ashmole 236: Casebook from January 20, 1600, to December 17, 1600. The following nonpatient notes are included.

ff. 27v Notes
76v [Legal agreement]: Forman will drop charges against Sefton if Sefton promises never again to molest him
77r–v Notes on the giant Gogmagog, on the play *Cox of Crillinton*, on Ledsom going to Forman's privy "privily"
124v Notes, mostly about particular women's sexual activity
151r Poetic proverbs
151v Notes
201r Notes on women bewitched and a witch
201v "Halek" notes; notes on an eclipse (June 30, 1600)
246v Notes recording medical gossip
263r–v Dreams (about A.Y, Steven Mitchell, etc.); his wife's first menstrual period; gossip; patient payment notes

MS. Ashmole 240: Miscellaneous materials.

ff. 1r–7v Astrological questions for one who is absent
8r–9v "De Luna"
11r–v Personal cast about future fortune
12r Rules to observe when judging by an astrological figure
13r Brief injunctions against hopyards, glass houses, iron mills, and printing
13v Casts about animals strayed or stolen
14r Cast about a man deciding whether to marry; cast about a lost greyhound
17r Questions about servants
18r–21r Miscellaneous astrological judgments
23r–v Forman genealogy
24r–v Miscellaneous astrological leaf
25r–27r "Forman his Repetition of the troble he had with the Docters of Phisick in London and of his delivery in the plague. 1592" (unfinished poem)
28r–v "Orations" (prayers in Latin and English)
31r–v Nativity for Joshua Walworth
32r–35v Meditation on darkness and the creation
37r Notes on planting trees and bushes
38r–v Remedies to remove hair
39r Question about a possible marriage
40r–v Miscellaneous leaf from a prophetic treatise
41r–v How to find minerals buried in the Earth
103r–106r Letters from Forman to Napier (1599–1611)

107r Letter from "Jane Forman" to Napier dated February 26, 1611 (1612 new calendar)

MS. Ashmole 244: Miscellaneous collection of Forman's writings.

ff. 1r–22r Cabala

25r–33v Calculations about the age of the world

34r–60r Of the motion of the three superior heavens (primum mobile, eighth, and ninth heavens)

72r–75v "De 4 Elements per Forman"

77r–90v "Of the Fixed Stars"

91r–92v "De horis planetariis"

94r–105v Of the eighth and ninth heavens

106r–117v "Demon Invenire geniture" (partly from Ficino's "de vita coelitus"; tables of cabalistic letters and motions of the stars)

143r–145r "Of finding Hyleg and Alcoden in a Nativity"

160r–165v "Of the Splen or Milte"

166r–171r How to predict illness and disease from heavenly configurations

172r–175v Herbs and minerals and their medicinal application ("aloes" through "gipsum")

176 Miscellaneous leaf, perhaps belonging with ff. 166–171

179r "To drawe out the proportion of any man"

184v Fragment from "Of Giants" (ff. 192r–199r)

187r–187v "Of Adam and Eve"

192r–199r "Of Giants"

MS. Ashmole 338: Richard Napier's manuscript. Napier notes the following information concerning Forman and his relatives.

ff. 23r "Mr. Forman, sodenly taken [ill]," October 6, 1608

95v Napier visits Forman, February 23, 1609

116r Nativity for "Josua, filius Ag. Young, March 27, 1585" (Forman's illegitimate son)

116v Nativities for Ann Baker, February 1581 (Forman's wife), Fenema Parker, June 9,1599 (Forman's illegitimate daughter)

117r Nativity for "An Barker, D. Forman's kinswoman," March 11, 1594 (Forman's illegitimate daughter)

MS. Ashmole 354: A volume of instruction in how to cast for nonmedical questions.

ff. 1r–198v "S. Forman de arte Geomantia 1589 " (explains how to ask about things stolen, the safety of ships, marriage, etcetera; includes many examples taken from his casebooks)

198r–198v An index to the volume

MS. Ashmole 355: A beautifully prepared medical text with lots of blank pages interspersed.

ff. 1r–428v "Liber Juditiorum Morborum secundum cursus Caelorum & Astrorum factus per Simonem Forman secundum Experientiam suam 1600 pro seculo futuro" (signed at the bottom of the title page "Simon Forman D in Astronomy & Phisick"). The volume is organized by first treating the four humors, then the seven planets, and the twelve astrological houses; it concludes with recipes for waters, purges, and plasters.

428r–428v An index to the volume

MS. Ashmole 363: A copy in Sir Richard Napier's hand of Forman's astrological/medical text (MS. Ashmole 389; cf. also MS. Ashmole 403). This version is the fullest and most complete of the three in the Ashmole collection.

MS. Ashmole 384: Miscellaneous astrological papers, erratically numbered.

ff. 1r–2r Lists of countries and cities under the influence of particular astrological signs

2v List of Forman's New Year's gifts, 1604

10r–25r "De Revolutione Mundi"

27r–36r "To knowe by . . . the years revolution what shall befall here in England"

38r–91v "Eclipses of the Sun and Moon [written] 1592"

92r–101r "A Table of the principal stars according to their Longitude and Latitude," 1602

102r–113v "Of setting thy figure . . . to know what sickness shalbe"

116r–186r Notes about weather, crops, diseases from mid–1580s to 1594. Particular notes in 1592 and 1593 about plague deaths

187r–v Index to volume

187r (Second leaf so numbered) miscellaneous notes

187v–192v Monthly calendar (December is missing) with a quatrain of poetry at the bottom of each page

193r–194v "Of the places where the effects of the eclipses shall appear"

MS. Ashmole 389: Medical text (mostly paginated).

pp. 1–879 "The Astrologicalle Judgmentes of Phisick & other Questions . . ." 1606. A version of this work containing additional exemplary cases occurs in the hand of Sir Richard Napier (MS. Ash. 363), and a third version, which has the theoretical explanations but no examples, occurs in the hand of Richard Napier (MS. Ash. 403).

MS. Ashmole 390: Nonmedical astrological text, resembling MS. Ash. 354.

ff. 1r Partial index on ships at sea

2r–49r Questions involving love

52r–54r When a man should flee for an offense

55r–64v "Of Taking a house and entring yt to dwelle"

65r–70v Questions about arrest

66r–72r More questions about love

74r–v "In Electione Ludorum"

75r–104v "De Fugitivo"

105r–120v Of law and controversy

125r–130v "Of trouble and Imprisonment"

131r Concerning a case of a woman with an abscess

132v A dream about the philosopher's stone
133r–136r "Best to take one in cure that is diseased?"
143r–v Whether a man shall overcome his enemies
151r–160v "De Itinere" (on whether to travel)
161r–173r Questions about conception and childbirth
175r–185r "Matrix and the pain thereof"
190r–199v Whether a woman is pregnant
202r–203v Short Latin pieces
204r–205r Recipes for medicines
207r–208v Miscellaneous horoscopes

MS. Ashmole 392: A late manuscript containing mostly nonmedical astrology.

ff. 1r–3r Questions about seeking hidden treasure
5r–39r "Of Treasure hid or any such thing"
41r–v "Best for a woman to take such a man"
46r–254r "Of Astronomy": treats topics such as "conjunction," "translation," "of Occupation," "Of Company," "Of buying land or houses," "Best to stai in a place or to remove," "Of law and controversy," "Matrimony," "Theft," "De Amore illigittimo," "Of Revenge," and "De Lapide philosophia." Includes much blank paper.

MS. Ashmole 403: A copy in Richard Napier's hand of Forman's astrological and medical text (MS. Ashmole 398; cf. MS. Ashmole 363).

MS. Ashmole 411: Casebook from December 26, 1600, to November 29, 1601 and from May 11, 1603, to September 5, 1603. The following nonpatient material is included.

ff. 49v "The names of the honorable Iurie Impannyled 1601 . . . for the tryall of the . . . Earl of Essex and Southampton"
50r Families attainted of treason (nine are listed). Notes on expenses for wax and thread charged by a tailor for a doublet
50v Miscellaneous notes
100r "A note what I lefte in the house at London wher I dwelte 1601 the 20th of May"
100v Accusations against John Pet. Notes about his wife's absence and his sexual activity
101r–102v List of patients who took diet
103r–v Notes, including the cost of his move to Lambeth
141r Note of "lycenses" granted on items such as playing cards
142v Notes, including some patient fees
163r–v "The Names of the Giants . . . when Brutus came"; notes of addresses

MS. Ashmole 802: Miscellaneous texts, mostly nonmedical and nonastrological in content.

ff. 1r–12r Creation
19r–49r Adam and Eve to Noah and his children

51r–55v Giants after Noah

56v–58r Descriptions of Arthurian knights

59r–v Notes on giants

66r–82r Consultation of devils after Christ harrows hell; their decision to beget Merlin, 445 A.D.

86r–89v Years of the world

90r Eagles, crows, and other prodigies

91r–v Index to a different manuscript

103r–v "How the Jewes shalbe called before the last daie to the faith of Christ" (poem)

111r–118v "Of Antichrist" (poem with notes)

121r–122r "Forman his thankesgyuinge and acknowledgmente of the poware of god after his firste & second troble. 1579" (poem)

123r–125r "Forman A Rehersale of his firste troble and his thanksgyvinge to God for his deliverie. 1576" (poem)

126r–128r "Psalme per formann of the wickednes of the Tyme"

131r–133r Poem about plague (its opening lines are missing)

134r Single stanza of a poem

135r–140v "Forman 1604 January 19. To be songe at his burialle" (poem)

141r–148v Prayers

151v–152v Fragment from Forman's 1607 diary

155r–156v Notes about building a brick wall

157r–158r Notes about various longitudes and latitudes

159r Notes about a patient

161r Notes about the Sun

163v Notes about planets

165r–170v "The Ninth Sphere" (place of the art of love)

171r–175v Notes on Virginia

181r–191v Notes and drawings about heraldry

206v–216r Notes about the arms and genealogy of the Formans

224r–225v "The Thirde parte of this bocke showeth howe and when the dyuell doth plague men"

226r–227v "De fugitivo & re Amissa"

234r–275v "To know what State a Ship is in at Sea"

MS. Ashmole 1403: A partial version of MS. Ashmole 1436, Forman's treatise on the plague.

ff. 1r–101v (Begins with a detailed table of contents in which "Epistle to the Reader" and "Testament of the author" were inserted as the two first entries after the page had been completed. Neither section is included in this manuscript. The text ends in midsentence.)

102r–103v A complaint about the length of medical treatment

104v "Sleepe" (recipe for a sleep-inducing potion)

MS. Ashmole 1429: "September 1611. Doctor Formans booke reserved for the use of Clement his sonne." This is a general compendium of basic medical information probably written by a professional hand. The inscription quoted above is on a prefatory leaf and in Napier's hand.

ff. 1r–2v Table of contents

1r–34r "Here followeth good documents for the preservation of the helthe of man"

35v–75v "The mansions of the moon"

76r–77r Origins of medicine (beginning with the children of Lamech)

78r–89r Herbs and their uses

90r–99v Recipes for purges, plasters, oils, etcetera

100r–101v How to read urine

102r–106r Herbs

107r–113v Recipes

MS. Ashmole 1430: An alphabet book, primarily alchemical. This seems to be a shorter verion of MSS. Ashmole 1494 and 1491.

ff. 1r–243v Includes a number of alchemical poems and diagrams of alchemical equipment

MS. Ashmole 1436: Treatise on plague.

ff. 1r–147v "Of the plague generally and of his sortes" (both introductory prefaces "Epistel to the Reader" and the "The Testament of the Author" have had text restored, in Ashmole's hand, where leaves 1–3 have been half torn away).

147r–150r A detailed index

MS. Ashmole 1453: Richard Napier's recipes for treating various conditions.

ff. 461r–463r Recipes in Forman's hand, the final leaves of the volume

MS. Ashmole 1457: Many pieces of paper pasted onto larger sheets comprise this volume. Most material is not Forman's.

ff. 53r–54v Fragment on what makes a good physician, includes a denunciation of uroscopy and diagnosis by pulse or sedge [feces]

55r–56v Recipes for potions made with roses

MS. Ashmole 1472: Alphabet book; an alchemical manuscript with a lot of Latin but the examples and practical procedures in English.

n.p. Preliminary notes on unnumbered leaves include "The Names of the Auctors mentioned in this book per Forman"

ff. 1r–914v "Simon Forman compositor huius libri ad lectorum 1597. All thinges seame harde when wee doe begine"

Sample headings: "antimony," "borax," "chaos," "distillation," "ignis," "painting of women's faces," "sal peter"

Alchemical poems: "mercury" (350r); "Imbibition" (396r–v); "Tempus operandi" (400r)

"Of certain dremes and visions that I haue sene totching the philosophers stone" (807r–813v)

918r–945v "Tabula" (a huge index containing some topics not in the text, leaves numbered 1–14 in lower right)

16r–24v "The Kalender of the principle of earthly planets" (the new numbering continues)

MS. Ashmole 1488: Richard Napier's cures and medicines, including the following items in Forman's hand.

ff. 37r "A most costly precious balme to cure all fresh wounds in 3 daies"

47v "Sweet water that I made 1596 the 18 Jun"

89r–90v Letter from Forman to Richard Napier

MS. Ashmole 1490: Collection of works or fragments of works (mostly alchemical) copied by Forman.

ff. 28r "A dialogue of Egidius de Vadius betwene nature and the disciple of philosofie of the serching of the philosophers stone"

38r–41r Notes about the philosopher's stone

42r–45v Robert Frimitor (1496) (sayings of philosophers)

46r–v "Tractatus de Mercurio" (poem narrated by Mercury; in English)

47r–v Alchemical poems by "Geuer of Spain" and "Arnold of the newtoune"

49r–52v Notes on alchemical processes

53r–54v "Opus de Argentio" (concludes "explicit liber Ehenius")

49r "De ponderibus" (second leaf so numbered)

56r–v "De rotatione rerum elementat scriptum per Simon Forman. 1593"

57r–61v "Incipit liber de Anaxagore Convertionis naturalis"

62r–v "Pro operere maior"

66r–74v "Tractatus Institulatis medulla alkimiae" (George Ripley, 1476)

78r–80r "To calcine"

81r–84r "Scoller and Master" (alchemical dialogue)

84v–87v Notes on alchemical processes

88r "The whole effect in brief of this book"

89r–101v Medical and alchemical recipes

102r–106r "Incipit Prophia Sibille"

106v Forman's prophecies

108r–113v Alchemical notes extracted from authorities

114r–136v "The Book of Alcamie . . . by the Channon of Briglington [Ripley]," heavily annotated

137r "Norton of Magnesia"

138r–139v "De Quartuor Elements"

140r–141v Dialogue between "Master and Child"

142r–153v Alchemical notes, including charts and diagrams

154r–163v Practice of Raymond Lully (dated 1590)

164r "Sayings of the Philosophers . . . out of Norton's book"

165r–168v "Sir Robarte Greene touching the philosopher's stone"

169r–170v "Practica Blomfield"

171r–v "Verses of Sir Edward Kelli"

173r–180r "Prologus Johannis de Meduno" and other fragments

181r–198v Material from a 1422 text by Herbert Branckenberger, copied 1590

199r–216r "7 bockes of Aurelius Theophrastus parracelsis," dated 1592

217r–220r "2 Bookes of the Nature of Man" by Paracelsus

221r–236r The Philosopher's Stone by "Reverente doctor Almante and Lord Barnard Erell of March and Trevison"

236v–241r Appendices to the previous item (lists of writers)

242r–276v "Testament of J. J. D[octor] of Physicke" (incomplete work on the philosopher's stone)

277r–289r "Liber Thomas Norton [Ordinal of alchemy]. 1447." (copied 1592)

291r–306r Alchemical treatise dedicated to William Cecil, Lord Burghley (poetic dedication 292r–293r), signed by Forman, 1590

307r–331v Appendices to the previous item

332r–335r Extracts on the philosopher's stone

336r–342v "Pater sapientiae" (120 stanza alchemical poem) signed by Forman, 1590

343r–345r "The opening of Secrets done by the arte of philosophy," signed by Forman, 1599

350v Note of the bill and names of items "mr parke was to buy for mulleneux 1595"

352v "Forman preface speaking in the bockes behaulf"
The volume's remaining pages are not in Forman's hand.

MS. Ashmole 1491: Continuation of MS. Ashmole 1494, alphabetical alchemical manuscript.

ff. 671r–1426r foliation is continuous from MS. 1494.
This volume begins with "Mundus"; last few entries are out of alphabetical order: "Termes" and "Gun powder."

1390r–1422v An index to both volumes

MS. Ashmole 1494: Part one of an alphabetical alchemical manuscript (see MS. Ashmole 1491 for part two].

ff. 52r–644r "Of Appoticarie Druges writen by Simon Forman"; contains much alchemical and some practical information (recipes for glue and curing leather); alphabetical entries go from "antimony" to "leaves, flowars, Barkes, Sods"

MS. Ashmole 1495: A medical text.

ff. 1v–2v Cures and who may be cured

3r–9r Poem on urine and then a preface about climacteric years, dated 1594

11r–v "The Groundes of Arte"

12r–15v On the twelve houses, twelve signs, seven planets

16r–17v "De gradibus siccitatis calliditatus aet humiditatus & frigiditatis est sciendum"

29r–519r "Judgmente of diseas and of Life and Death after our experience. Forman"

After a general introduction to signs and planets, this text follows each planet through the twelve houses, listing diseases and treatments for each configuration.

522r–523v "Of the planets" (fragment)

MS. Ashmole 1763: A large-format scrapbook with a number of documents pasted in; only one item is associated with Forman.

f. 44r Forman's license to practice medicine, issued by Cambridge University, 1603

MS. Ashmole 1790: Elias Ashmole's manuscript with the following material relevant to Forman.

ff. 78r Digest of MS. Ashmole 244, labeled "Forman abbreviated"

102r–103v Repaired leaves of a Forman plague manuscript

❧ N O T E S ❧

INTRODUCTION

1. Paul Delany, *British Autobiography in the Seventeenth Century* (London: Routledge & Kegan Paul, 1969), 133.

2. Ashmole Manuscript Collection, Bodleian Library, Oxford University, manuscript no. 208: 110r, 134r. Citations to manuscripts from this collection will henceforth be referred to as "MS. Ash." plus the manuscript number and folio or page number. Unless otherwise noted, all references are to folios (leaves), not pages.

3. MS. Ash. 389 (in Forman's own hand and dated 1606), MS. Ash. 363 (in the hand of Sir Richard Napier, the nephew of Forman's friend Richard Napier), and MS. Ash. 403 (in the hand of Richard Napier). There is at least one more version in the British Library, MS. Sloane 99.

4. Some early modern writers with a similar penchant for adding to their texts, however, chose to have their works printed, with successive editions becoming larger and larger. Two well-known examples are Robert Burton's *Anatomy of Melancholy*, which grew steadily larger in the five editions printed in his lifetime, and Francis Bacon's *Essays*, which numbered ten in the first edition but had grown to fifty-eight by the 1625 edition.

5. MS. Ash. 200: 167r.

6. MS. Ash. 200: 170r, 172r.

7. MS. Ash. 227: 85v, 275r.

8. C. H. Josten, *Elias Ashmole (1617–1692)* 5 vols. (Oxford: Clarendon Press, 1966), 1: 209–10.

9. Josten, 4: 1454–55. This binding of Forman's papers for Ashmole explains the rather uniform external appearance of the manuscripts, bound in tooled brown leather with metal clasps. The bound volumes differ considerably, however, in size.

10. Josten, 4: 1663–64 (fraxinella), MS. Ash. 1790: 102r–103v (plague), 78r (digest).

11. Forman's lack of introspection and lack of any expression of inner conflict or guilt about his many sexual encounters, his illegitimate children, or his adultery contrast markedly with the introspective autobiography composed by Forman's somewhat older contemporary, Thomas Whythorne (1528–1596). For example, Whythorne reports having many opportunities for adulterous sex which, after much internal debate, he prudently

refuses. *The Autobiography of Thomas Whythorne*, ed. James M. Osborn (London: Oxford University Press, 1962), esp. 63, 80–90.

12. Stephen J. Greenblatt, *Renaissance Self-Fashioning: From More to Shakespeare* (Chicago: University of Chicago Press, 1980).

13. Meric Casaubon, *A True and Faithful Relation of What Passed between Dr. John Dee and Some Spirits* (London, 1659).

14. David Lindley, *The Trials of Frances Howard: Fact and Fiction at the Court of King James* (London: Routledge, 1993).

CHAPTER ONE

1. "Epicoene," in *Ben Jonson*, ed. C. H. Herford and Percy and Evelyn Simpson, 11 vols. (Oxford: Clarendon Press, 1925–52), IV.i.145–50.

2. *The Devil Is an Ass*, in *Ben Jonson*, II.viii.30–33.

3. A. L. Rowse simply assumes so: "It is obvious that *The Alchemist* was inspired by Forman." *Simon Forman: Sex and Society in Shakespeare's Age* (London: Weidenfeld and Nicolson, 1974), 17. S. P. Cerasano offers evidence for her belief that Forman is figured in Jonson's play, see "Philip Henslowe, Simon Forman, and the Theatrical Community of the 1590s," *Shakespeare Quarterly* 44 (1993), 146–47.

4. Charles Goodall, *The Royal College of Physicians of London . . . and an Historical Account of the College's Proceedings Against Empiricks and Unlicensed Practisers* (London, 1684), 337–39.

5. Thomas Bayly Howell, comp., *Cobbett's Complete Collection of State Trials*, 34 vols. (London, 1809–26), 11: col. 935.

6. Nathaniel Hawthorne, *The Scarlet Letter*, in *Novels* (New York: Library of the Americas, 1983), 227.

7. [Abel Moysey], *Forman: A Tale*, 3 vols. (London: Ogle, Duncan, and Co., 1819).

8. Simon Forman, *The Autobiography and Personal Diary of Dr. Simon Forman*, ed. James Orchard Halliwell (London, 1849), [i].

9. Lynn Thorndike, *A History of Magic and Experimental Science*, 8 vols. (New York: Columbia University Press, 1923–58), VI, 219. The word "empiric" had several connotations by the late sixteenth century. Empirics were those people who relied on personal observation and experience, rather than book learning, in the practice of medicine (or other sciences). But the term also could suggest "quack," as it does in Thorndike's context, and was beginning to be used to indicate outright fraud and charlatanism. With regards to Forman and his peers it could be used as a neutral descriptor of them as a particular kind of practitioner or it could suggest that they were inept, irresponsible, or even fraudulent in their practice of medicine.

10. Michael MacDonald, *Mystical Bedlam: Madness, Anxiety, and Healing in Seventeenth-Century England*, Cambridge Monographs on the History of Medicine (Cambridge: Cambridge University Press, 1981), 25.

11. MS. Ash. 208: 221r–221v.

12. Paul Delany characterized this text as "the amusing and flamboyant self-presentation of Simon Forman." *British Autobiography in the Seventeenth Century* (London: Routledge & Kegan Paul, 1969), 16.

13. MS. Ash. 208: 111v.

14. The question of what constitutes an autobiography has been much discussed. Karl J.

Weintraub distinguishes among "memoirs," "diaries," "literary self-portraits" and genuine "autobiographies." According to these categories, this second text would be classified as a diary, and the autobiography discussed above would be a memoir—"in memoir external fact is . . . translated into conscious experience, but the eye of the writer is focused less on the inner experience than on the external realm of fact." See "Autobiography and Historical Consciousness," *Critical Inquiry* 1 (1975), 823. Forman's autobiographical materials might more properly be classified as "ego-documents (a broader category [than autobiography] including diaries, journals, memoirs and letters)," Peter Burke, "Representations of the Self from Petrarch to Descartes," in *Rewriting the Self: Histories from the Renaissance to the Present*, ed. Roy Porter (London: Routledge, 1997), 21. For further discussion of the definition of autobiography in the early modern period, see James M. Osborn, *The Beginnings of Autobiography in England* (Los Angeles: William Andrews Clark Library, University of California, 1959).

15. MS. Ash. 208: 45v.

16. MS. Ash. 208: 45v.

17. MS. Ash. 802: 151v–152v.

18. Rowse reprinted a brief segment under the heading, "Forman's notes on his family." Rowse, *Simon Forman*, 300–302. According to Delany, a transition from genealogy to autobiography was often a feature of early British autobiography. Delany, *British Autobiography*, 9.

19. MS. Ash. 208: 22r.

20. The term "commonwealthes men" probably refers to a specific political/social allegiance. Though the existence of "commonwealth men" has been much debated among historians, most seem to agree that it refers to men who advocated a program of social and economic help for the "commonwealth." Whitney R. D. Jones quotes a letter written during the reign of Edward VI that asks that "men seek not their own wealth, nor their private commodity, but as good members, the universal wealth of the whole body." Jones suggests that one of the items on the agenda of the commonwealth men may have been the use of former church property for the common good (i.e., hospitals for the sick and poor or free schools for poor children). *The Tudor Commonwealth, 1529–1559* (London: The Athlone Press, 1970), 35, 39. This would seem to fit the context in which Forman speaks of his grandfather's rejection of former church land. For other views on commonwealth men, see Joan Thirsk, *Economic Policy and Projects: The Development of a Consumer Society in Early Modern England* (Oxford: Clarendon Press, 1978), 16–17, and G. R. Elton, "Reform and the 'Commonwealth-Men' of Edward VI's Reign," in *The English Commonwealth, 1547–1640: Essays in Politics and Society* (New York: Barnes & Noble, 1979), 23–38.

21. MS. Ash. 208: 218r.

22. MS. Ash. 208: 220r–227r.

23. MS. Ash. 208: 225v.

24. William Lilly, *Mr. William Lilly's History of His Life and Times from the Year 1602 to 1681* (London, 1715), 12. In the manuscript of Lilly's *History*, Elias Ashmole added a note: "only in Holland for a month 1580. a mistake" (MS. Ash. 421: 184v).

25. MS. Ash. 208: 65v.

26. MS. Ash. 208: 225v.

27. MS. Ash. 208: 226r.

28. MS. Ash. 802: 123r–125r, 121r–122r, 126r–128r; MS. Ash. 208: 235r–248v; MS. Ash. 802: 135r–140v.

29. MS. Ash. 240: 103r–106r; MS. Ash. 1488: 30r or 359r (double numbers on this leaf).

30. Though I have found no other references in the manuscripts to Forman's working with men who came to learn astrology or medicine, a casual remark by Elias Ashmole reminds me that there may have been such relationships that are simply not visible in Forman's records. Ashmole wrote in a letter to Anthony Wood, who had asked for information about Sir John Davis, that "I was intimately acquainted with Sir John Davis his Son . . . from him I have heard, that he [Sir John Davis, Sr.] spent much time in the Mathematicks & astrology, he being instructed in the later by Doctor Forman (a very able Astrologer & Phisitian, as appears by the manuscript bookes he left behinde him which are now in my possession)." Quoted in C. H. Josten, *Elias Ashmole (1617–1692)*, 5 vols. (Oxford: Clarendon Press, 1996), 4: 1809.

31. MS. Ash. 208: 214r–214v.

32. MS. Ash. 802: 211r. Forman's forays into family genealogy also appear in MS. Ash. 240: 23r–23v and MS. Ash. 802: 181r–216r.

33. A section recording many dreams, including the one about King James, appears in MS. Ash. 1472: 807v–813v. More dreams, including two about Queen Elizabeth, are recorded in MS. Ash. 226: 44r–45r. MS. Ash. 234: 123r–124v has additional dreams, and a note about a third Elizabeth dream occurs in MS. Ash. 226: 310r.

34. MS. Ash. 1436: 72r–72v. Leaves here have two sets of numbers. I follow the pencilled foliation on the lower corner of the recto.

35. MS. Ash. 354: 230r.

36. MS. Ash. 411: 8v.

37. MS. Ash. 354: 236r.

38. MS. Ash. 219: 122v.

39. MS. Ash. 206: 99r.

40. MS. Ash. 208: 139r, 140r.

41. MS. Ash. 208: 140r.

42. MS. Ash. 208: 142r.

43. Although Forman never mentioned Oxford in his later papers, a vestigial interest may be indicated by his inclusion of the arms of Magdalen College among his colored drawings of coats of arms. MS. Ash. 802: 187r.

44. MS. Ash. 208: 112r. Robert Burton had similar views of the activities of wealthy university students. In *Philosophaster*, his Latin drama satirizing universities and their pedants, a naive young scholar is advised not to study but rather to "worry about a hunting dog, about song, dance, hunting and fowling, about fencing, and about a mistress. These studies are more suited to you." Robert Burton, *Philosophaster*, ed. and trans. Connie McQuillen (Binghamton, N.Y.: Medieval & Renaissance Texts & Studies, 1992), II.iv.625–27.

45. MS. Ash. 208: 28v.

46. MS. Ash. 208: 27v.

47. Perhaps since the weather was bad during the queen's visit (John Nichols, *The Progresses and Public Processions of Queen Elizabeth*, 3 vols. [London, 1823], I: 409–10), Forman never got to deliver the speech. Forman's date and those recorded by Nichols for the Salisbury visit differ by a matter of some days.

48. David Cressy, "A Drudgery of Schoolmasters: The Teaching Profession in Elizabethan and Stuart England," in *The Professions in Early Modern England*, ed. Wilfred Prest (London: Croom Helm, 1987), 137.

49. MS. Ash. 208: 30v.

50. MS. Ash. 208: 32v.

51. MS. Ash. 208: 42v.

52. MS. Ash. 208: 48r.

53. MS. Ash. 208: 34v.

54. MS. Ash. 802: 124r.

55. The Fleet was a well-known London prison.

56. MS. Ash. 802: 124v.

57. All these events are noted in the diary entries for 1580 to 1585 (MS. Ash. 208: 34v–40v).

58. MS. Ash. 390: 125r.

59. MS. Ash. 219: 135r.

60. Rowse, *Simon Forman*, 242–43.

61. MS. Ash. 208: 127v.

62. These details are noted in diary entries (MS. Ash. 208: 36v, 40v, 42v, 45v).

63. MS. Ash. 208: 41v.

64. The only *OED* citation for "swachele" is to Forman's usage here. Perhaps it is a variant of "swash," meaning "swagger."

65. MS. Ash. 208: 62v. "Hangers" are the straps on the sword belt from which the sword hangs.

66. MS. Ash. 802: 133r.

67. MS. Ash. 1472: 662r.

68. MS. Ash. 392: 137v.

69. MS. Ash. 392: 136r, 139r.

70. Each version of the anecdote differs. Cobbett said simply, "there was also a Note shewed in the Court, made by Dr. Forman, and written in parchment, signifying what ladies loved what lords in the court; but the Lord Chief Justice would not suffer it to be read openly in the court." *State Trials*, 11: col. 935. Weldon wrote: "I well remember, there was much mirth made in the Court, upon shewing this book [according to Weldon, an "Alphabet Book" in which Forman made all his clients sign their names], for it was reported, the first leafe My Lord *Cook* lighted on, he found his own wives name." Anthony Weldon, "The Court and Character of King James," in *Secret History of the Court of James the First*, 2 vols. (Edinburgh: James Ballantyne, 1811), iii. By the time Rowse retold the story it had become: "A telltale note by Forman was exhibited, 'signifying what ladies loved what lords in the Court.' Chief Justice Coke opened it, and then refused to have it read: he had seen that the first name was his own wife's, Lady Hatton, whom he had married for her money" (261).

71. Cobbett, *State Trials*, 11: col. 932.

72. An exception to this claim might be the sigils he created. Used primarily as amulets to protect against various medical problems, such engraved sigils could also assist in amatory matters (see chapter 5).

73. Rowse, 23.

74. MS. Ash. 802: 152v.

75. MS. Ash. 338: 23r, 114r, 95v, 98r.

76. MS. Ash. 392: 175r.

77. Lilly, *History of His Life and Times*, 16.

78. MS. Ash. 1429. The hand that wrote this note was surely Napier's. He uses the same phrase "for the use of Clement his sonne" in a casebook note about Forman's books (MS. Ash. 200: 172r).

79. Napier seems to have been much involved with Forman's family in the year after his death. As noted in the introduction, he took Clement to Linford with him three weeks after Forman's death; he took custody of Forman's books; and he was the recipient of a letter from Mrs. Forman, written February 26, 1611 [old style calendar; this is about five months after Forman's death]. She asks Napier for his opinion of Mr. Tommes, a lawyer, who is her suitor and who claims to know Napier. Mrs. Forman describes herself as defenseless in her widowhood "with greefes and trobles which I fynd by the want of a defender which I neuer knowd before till now" (MS. Ash. 240: 107r). Mrs. Forman clearly regards Napier as a friend and advisor.

80. The two notes about the sale of Forman's books in 1627 have been mentioned (MS. Ash. 227: 85v, 275r). A year later Clement wrote from "Sant Christophers in America" a note dated August 20, 1628. The money realized from the sale of the books had apparently not financed legal study. Clement's letter suggests that he continued to regard Napier as a close friend: "I cannot write at large yet the desire I haue to know of your welfare that made me to write a few lines to you my special frend" (MS. Ash. 174: 479r). The letter may have been a thinly disguised request for financial support as well as a greeting to his "special frend."

81. MS. Ash. 802: 118v.

82. Delany, *British Autobiography*, 21. For more discussion of the autobiographical impulse in the period see Burke, "Representations of the Self," 17–23.

83. Stephen J. Greenblatt, *Renaissance Self-Fashioning: From More to Shakespeare* (Chicago: University of Chicago Press, 1980), 7.

84. The manuscripts may fail, of course, to reveal significant relationships, just as they failed to mention Forman's instruction of Sir John Davis (see n. 30).

85. Forman was by no means alone in his avoidance of the "standard" route to medical practice; for a discussion of the varied backgrounds of unlicensed practitioners see Margaret Pelling, "Knowledge Common and Acquired: The Education of Unlicensed Medical Practitioners in Early Modern London," in *The History of Medical Education in Britain*, ed. Vivian Nutton and Roy Porter (Amsterdam: Rodopi Press, 1995), 250–279.

86. Rowse cites Lilly's claim that Forman was worth about 1,200 pounds at his death without the numerous real-estate holdings that he had acquired (*Simon Forman*, 259). The same information is included in a note in MS. Ash. 208: 60r: recorded in a hand not Forman's, it reads, "After Dr. Forman dyed (who left his wife worth 1200 pounds) she married on Mr. Neale a Northamptonshire gentleman & had a son by her."

87. MS. Ash. 1763: 44r.

88. MS. Ash. 208: 201r.

89. MS. Ash. 208: 202r.

90. Writing of the autobiographical papers left by Lady Grace Mildmay, Linda Pollock remarks on the problem of using autobiography as historical evidence. "A comparison of

her life with other available sources reveals that her memoirs are not entirely accurate; not in the sense of deliberate falsification but in that of concealing details which detracted from the image she wished to present." *With Faith and Physick: The Life of a Tudor Gentlewoman, Lady Grace Mildmay* (New York: St. Martin's, 1995), 4. Forman's manipulation of detail may have been even more deliberate than Lady Mildmay's.

CHAPTER TWO

1. Forman was not the only practitioner of astrological medicine in England during the sixteenth and seventeenth centuries. Michael MacDonald discusses the principles and practice of astrological medicine, using Forman and Richard Napier as his primary examples. "The Career of Astrological Medicine in England," in *Religio Medici: Medicine and Religion in Seventeenth-Century England*, ed. Ole Peter Grell and Andrew Cunningham (Aldershot: Scolar Press, 1996), 62–90.

2. Quoted in Eric Sangwine, "The Private Libraries of Tudor Doctors," *Journal of the History of Medicine and Allied Sciences* 33 (1978): 170, n2.

3. Harold J. Cook, *The Decline of the Old Medical Regime in Stuart London* (Ithaca: Cornell University Press, 1986), 56, 59.

4. For general discussions of this framework, see Nancy G. Siraisi, *Medieval and Early Renaissance Medicine: An Introduction to Knowledge and Practice* (Chicago: University of Chicago Press, 1990), 97–114, and F. David Hoeniger, *Medicine and Shakespeare in the English Renaissance* (Newark, Del.: University of Delaware Press, 1992), 71–116.

5. Peter Murray Jones, "Reading Medicine in Tudor Cambridge," in *The History of Medical Education in Britain*, ed. Vivian Nutton and Roy Porter (Amsterdam: Rodopi Press, 1995), 154. I am grateful to Mr. Jones, not only for allowing me to see his manuscript in typescript but also for providing me access to King's College MS. 16 during a time when the library was closed.

6. Mary Edmond, "Simon Forman's Vade-Mecum," *The Book Collector* 26 (1977): 46. For purposes of easy identification, I will refer to the original manuscript as "Cokkis's text" in my discussion since we are uncertain of the author of the second Latin text.

7. MS. King's College 16: 25v ("Emoroyde"), 107v ("sputum"), 46ar–46av ("formica").

8. MS. King's College 16: 146ar.

9. MS. Ash. 1491: 938. Such self-experimentation was quite common among the experimental philosophers of the mid-seventeenth century; Simon Schaffer graphically summarizes these experiments: "they blinded themselves with sunlight, gassed themselves into states of ecstasy and insensibility, and electrified their limbs into paralysis or spasm." "Self Evidence," *Critical Inquiry* 18 (1992): 329. Forman's self-experimentation was not so dangerous, perhaps, but he seems to be one of the first Englishmen to have used himself to test his remedies.

10. MS. King's College 16: 146hr.

11. MS. King's College 16: 146kv.

12. Scrofula was tuberculosis of the lymphatic glands, usually in the neck, and characterized by massive swelling and eventual disintegration of those glands. Its alternative name, "the King's evil," came from the belief that it would be cured if the sufferer were touched by the English monarch. Both Elizabeth I and James I "touched" for the disease.

13. MS. Ash. 208: 34v.

14. MS. King's College 16: 130br.

15. MS. King's College 16: 130bv.

16. Sections on wounds appear on folios 22A–22C and 143r. Directions for the oil are on folio 22Av.

17. MS. Ash. 208: 36v.

18. MS. Ash. 208: 49r.

19. MS. Ash. 205: 146r.

20. MS. Ash. 1495: 501r.

21. MS. Ash. 1491: 1366r.

22. For Napier's balance between surgery and medicine, which seemed to include more minor surgery than Forman's, see Ronald C. Sawyer, "Patients, Healers, and Diseases in the Southeast Midlands, 1597–1634," (Ph.D. diss., University of Wisconsin, 1986), 103. Siraisi notes that the omission of surgical procedures, other than cautery and phlebotomy, from physicians' *consilia* does not mean they shunned surgical interventions: "It may, however, owe a good deal to a desire to present their practice in the most scientifically interesting and intellectually respectable light." *Taddeo Alderotti and His Pupils: Two Generations of Italian Medical Learning* (Princeton: Princeton University Press, 1981), 299.

23. The anonymous author of a slightly later manuscript (ca. 1640) implies as much when he writes in "Advyse to a young physitian" that a physician should also know some surgery "so that, being in the country, thou do not be ashamed for want of a surgeon." Quoted in Cook, *Decline*, 65.

24. Edmond, "Vade-Mecum," 55.

25. MS. Ash. 1495: 3r.

26. MS. Ash. 1495: 486r. Lauren Kassell, whose perceptive article reached me too late to be fully integrated into my text, also remarks on this case. "How to Read Simon Forman's Casebooks: Medicine, Astrology, and Gender in Elizabethan London," *Social History of Medicine* 12 (1999): 9.

27. For Forman's negative opinion of contemporary diagnostic techniques, including uroscopy, see MS. Ash. 1457: 53r–54v, MS. Ash. 355: 48r, and MS. Ash. 1436: 143v–145v. The College of Physicians eventually came to a view of urine inspection that coincided with Forman's and cautioned its members about its use as a diagnostic technique. George Clark, *A History of the Royal College of Physicians of London*, vol. 1 (Oxford: Clarendon Press, 1964), 178.

28. MS. King's College 16: 146Av.

29. MS. Ash. 1491: 1248.

30. MS. King's College 16: 79v–80v.

31. MS. King's College 16: 80r.

32. Goodall, *Proceedings against Empiricks*, 337.

33. MS. Ash. 1490: 199r–216r. The note about Falowfild's copy appears on 216r. Forman went on to copy another extract from Paracelsus's "The Nature of Man" (217r–220r), noting that he finished this section on February 10, 1591.

34. MS. Sloane 2550: 3r.

35. MS. Ash. 1495: 503v.

36. See Audrey Eccles, *Obstetrics and Gynaecology in Tudor and Stuart England* (Kent, Ohio: Kent State University Press, 1982), plate 7, for a reproduction.

37. MS. Ash. 390: 175r.

38. MS. Ash. 390: 181r.

39. MS. Ash. 390: 181v.

40. Eccles, *Obstetrics and Gynaecology*, 74–75. See also Beryl Rowland, ed. and trans., *Medieval Woman's Guide to Health: The First English Gynecological Handbook* (Kent, Ohio: Kent State University Press, 1981), 61–69, where the first recommendation for amenorrhea is bleeding "a considerable quantity of blood at their big toe one day, and another day at their other big toe" (67).

41. MS. Ash. 1488: 89r.

42. MS. Ash. 390: 178r.

43. MS. Ash. 390: 179r–179v.

44. MS. Ash. 390: 183r.

45. MS. Ash. 355: 133v.

46. MS. Ash. 1488: 90v.

47. MS. Ash. 208: 138v.

48. MS. Ash. 195: 167r.

49. MS. Ash. 195: 39r.

50. Goodall, *Proceedings against Empiricks*, 374.

51. MS. Ash. 208: 48r.

52. MS. Ash. 208: 112v.

53. MS. Ash. 208: 121r.

54. MS. Ash. 208: 127r.

55. The notion that plague was the result of human sin was widespread in early modern England. Forman's treatise simply expounded upon a commonplace reiterated, for example, in another essay written during the plague of 1593: "Every man say, my sinnes, as our sinnes are the causes of this malady. Our rebellions, presumptions, scorning, Athe-istical, our Romane sinnes, our carnall apetites, present, past, remembred, and forgotten sinnes. . . . There is no plague but for sinne, and the Lyon roareth not, without his prey." Anthony Anderson, *An Approved Medicine Against the Deserved Plague* (London, 1593), A3r, A4r. Similar sentiments appear in a pamphlet by Frances Herring, first published in 1603 and reprinted in 1625: "Let not Gentlemen & rich Citizens by flying (vnlesse they likewise flie from their sinnes) thinke to escape Scotfree. So long as they carie their sinne with them, the Lord will find them out, & his hand will reach them wheresoeuer they are." Herring, *Rules for Pestilentiall Contagion*, reprinted as *The English Experience*, no. 527 (Amsterdam: Theatrum Orbis Terrarum, 1973). I owe these references to Kathleen Ann Mosher, whose just-completed Ph.D. dissertation studies early modern plague literature.

56. MS. Ash. 1436: 65v–66r.

57. MS. Ash. 1436: 66r.

58. MS. Ash. 1436: 66v–67r.

59. MS. Ash. 1436: 72r.

60. Cook talks about five primary ways a practitioner might establish himself: earning a degree from a university; having one "good" case that brought him patronage; publishing; developing a secret remedy; or getting a position such as royal physician or fellow of the Royal College of Physicians (*Decline*, 52–55). Forman may fit this pattern in one way: he developed his "strong water," which he claimed had therapeutic value in treating plague.

61. MS. Ash. 355; the section on melancholy is 115r–146v.

62. MS. Ash. 226: 125r. See Barbara Traister, "New Evidence about Burton's Melancholy?" *Renaissance Quarterly* 29 (1976): 66–70, for a detailed discussion of Burton's case.

63. See J. B. Bamborough, "Robert Burton's Astrological Notebook," *Review of English Studies* n.s. 32 (1981): 280.

64. MS. Ash. 355: 130v. Forman did not cross out the names very carefully, and many are still legible. This woman was the mother of John Braddege, Forman's young apprentice whom he eventually dismissed and who served at Ostend in 1601–1603 with other English troops.

65. MS. Ash. 355: 132v.

66. MS. Ash. 355: 132v.

67. MS. Ash. 355: 133r.

68. MS. Ash. 1491: 1088r, 1090r, 1095r.

69. Harriet Joseph, *Shakespeare's Son-in-Law: John Hall, Man and Physician* (Hamden, Conn.: Archon, 1964), 25–26, comments on Hall's use of antiscorbutics to treat scurvy sufferers. Clearly a remedy for scurvy long preceded an understanding of what caused the condition. In Hall's use of scurvy grass, watercress, and brooklime to combat scurvy, however, the effect must have been minimal because he did not prescribe the fresh herbs but infused them in medicinal drinks, destroying the vitamin C in the heating process. Joan Lane, *John Hall and His Patients: The Medical Practice of Shakespeare's Son-in-Law* (Stratford-upon-Avon: The Shakespeare Birthplace Trust, 1996), xxxviii–xxxix.

70. MS. Ash. 1453: 461r.

71. MS. Ash. 1453: 462v–463r.

72. MS. Ash. 390: 178r.

73. Eccles, *Obstetrics and Gynaecology*, 80.

74. Hoeniger, *Medicine and Shakespeare*, 245.

75. MS. Ash. 389: 446r.

76. Siraisi, *Medieval and Early Renaissance Medicine*, 133.

77. MS. Ash. 389: 656r.

78. MS. Ash. 226: 51r (on Slaughter), 105r (on Heiborn).

79. MS. Ash. 226: 96r (on Webster), 84v (on Griffeth).

80. MS. Ash. 1495: 500v.

81. MS. Ash. 363: 187r–188r.

82. Two such Biblical examples are found in the Book of Mark. In Mark 2:1–5, a paralyzed man is carried by his friends and lowered through a hole in the roof for Jesus's healing, and in Mark 5:25, a woman, who has suffered from hemorrhages for many years and who has seen many physicians, is brought before Jesus for healing.

83. See Kassell, "Simon Forman's Casebooks," 16–17, for analysis of another extended case narrative. These two cases are representative of a kind of medical narrative quite different from casebook records. Kassell emphasizes the female gender and the relatively high social status of the patients whose cases receive such narrative treatment.

84. MS. Ash. 1457: 53r.

CHAPTER THREE

1. The extant casebooks include MS. Ash. 234 (March 18, 1596, to January 20, 1597); MS. Ash. 226 (January 20, 1597, to February 20, 1598); MS. Ash. 195 (February 1598

to February 1599); MS. Ash. 219 (February 1599 to January 1, 1600); MS. Ash. 236 (January 20, 1600, to December 17, 1600); and MS. Ash. 411 (December 26, 1600, to November 29, 1601). Cases from May 11 to September 5, 1603, written in a hand not Forman's, appear at the end of MS. Ash. 411. Since familar patient names appear, the cases are quite clearly Forman's, perhaps recorded by one of his assistants.

2. Clark, *A History of the Royal College*, 197.

3. Goodall, *Proceedings against Empiricks*, 339. The trial records of Anne Turner mention a book with patient names—presumably a casebook—which is made to seem scandalous. Anthony Weldon recorded that Forman made his clients write their own names in a book before he would treat them ("The Court and Character of King James," 417). Not only is there no evidence of such a procedure in Forman's papers, but also many of Forman's patients would have been unable to write their own names, and many consulted him by messenger.

4. MS. Ash. 363: 2r–3v.

5. *On the Precautions that Physicians Must Observe*, trans. Henry E. Sigerist, in *A Source Book of Medieval Science*, ed. Edward Grant (Cambridge, Mass.: Harvard University Press, 1974), cited by Siraisi, *Medieval and Early Renaissance Medicine*, 125.

6. MS. Ash. 389: 388v. Kassell, "How to Read Simon Forman's Casebooks," provides a more detailed reading of Forman's introduction to his methods and a valuable account of what happened during a patient's astrological consultation.

7. W. R. LeFanu, "A North-Riding Doctor in 1609," *Medical History* 5 (1961), 178–88. A few patient records are also preserved in the manuscript notebook of John Crophill, a fifteenth-century physician. Descriptions of that manuscript indicate, however, that only a few patients are named, no symptoms or diagnoses are recorded, and what were once thought to be patient fee records are actually rent records. See Ernest William Talbert, "The Notebook of a Fifteenth-Century Practicing Physician," *Tennessee Studies in English Literature* 21 (1942): 5–30, and James K. Mustain, "A Rural Medical Practitioner in Fifteenth-Century England," *Bulletin of the History of Medicine* 46 (1972): 469–76. The casebook of John Hall, Shakespeare's son-in-law, who practiced in Stratford from about 1607 to 1635, begins with a 1622 case but offers no dates for most of the cases it records. Hall's book, his own selection of some of his most interesting and successful cases, emphasized his therapeutic response rather than the patients' complaints or symptoms. It was clearly intended to be instructional. In *John Hall and His Patients*, Joan Lane reprints a facsimile of the casebook along with historical and medical annotations about the various patients and therapies it describes. See also Joseph, *Shakespeare's Son-in-Law*, 19–30.

8. MacDonald, *Mystical Bedlam*, 26.

9. These figures and those throughout this chapter are based on my calendar of Forman's patients in two casebooks. Kassell has different figures (though often our percentages are very close); her figures are based on a count of all six of Forman's casebooks. In some instances, the figures differ because the questions they respond to were framed in slightly different ways.

10. The Broughton visits begin on MS. Ash. 226: 21v and are scattered thereafter. Rowse provides a mildly laudatory biographical sketch of this persistent client, who never did receive his deanship (145–50).

11. Digby's first visit is recorded on January 31 (MS. Ash. 411: 17r).

12. MS. Ash. 411: 30v.

13. MS. Ash. 411: 32r.

14. MS. Ash. 411: 49r, 51r.

15. MS. Ash. 411: 62r.

16. MS. Ash. 411: 76v.

17. MS. Ash. 411: 83v.

18. Robert Burton in *The Anatomy of Melancholy* lists dryness, paleness, leanness, lack of sleep, and burning [fever] among the symptoms of love melancholy. See *The Anatomy of Melancholy*, ed. Holbrook Jackson, 3 vols. (New York: Dutton, 1932), 3: 133–141.

19. MS. Ash. 226: 37r, 40r, 80v, 103r, 107r.

20. MS. Ash. 411: 12r, 13v.

21. MS. Ash. 411: 108v, 112v, 118v.

22. MS. Ash. 226: 26r.

23. MS. Ash. 226: 80r, 82v, 83v, 86v, 93v, 102v.

24. MS. Ash. 411: 24v, 25v.

25. MS. Ash. 411: 157v.

26. MS. Ash. 411: 67v.

27. MS. Ash. 411: 108r.

28. Even William Lilly, who was interested primarily in Forman's nonmedical astrology, wrote that "He was a person that in Horary [astrological] Questions (especially thefts) was very judicious and fortunate: so also in Sicknesses, which indeed was his Master-piece." Lilly, *History of His Life and Times*, 12.

29. MacDonald also speculates about why so few children were brought for medical treatment (*Mystical Bedlam*, 42–43).

30. See Philippe Ariès, *Centuries of Childhood: A Social History of Family Life*, trans. Robert Baldick (London: Jonathan Cape, 1962), 38–39. Lawrence Stone, *The Crisis of the Aristocracy, 1558–1641* (Oxford: Clarendon Press, 1965), 590–593, puts the case for parental indifference in even stronger terms than Ariès, though his work has frequently been challenged.

31. MacDonald suggests that early modern mothers and fathers may have responded somewhat differently to the death of their child (*Mystical Bedlam*, 80–85).

32. I owe this suggestion to Gail Paster of George Washington University, offered in the midst of extended conversation about the physical treatment of children in the period. Her suggestion finds support in Thomas Phayer's *The Regiment of life wherunto is added a treatyse of the pestilence with the booke of children* (London, 1543) in which Phayer promised to address the illnesses of children who were "desolate of remedye for so moche as manye do suppose that ther is no cure to be ministered vnto them, by reason of theyr weaknesse" (Biv).

33. "Fairy-pinched" and the stronger "fairy-blasted" (see p. 65) refer to children who have been blighted by supernatural agency. These adjectives usually describe children who show excessive bruising (Forman often describes their skin as "black").

34. MS. Ash. 226: 2r (Carter), 56v (Waldorn).

35. MS. Ash. 226: 120v (Spensar), 122r (Smith), 230r (Commin).

36. MS. Ash. 411: 47v (Bigs), 73v (Palmer), 140v (Campion), 158r (Kelly).

37. Though using the neuter pronoun to refer to young children is common in Forman's casebooks, I have not seen it mentioned by scholars who have worked with other casebook notes from this period, so it may have been one of Forman's idiosyncrasies. I have not read

enough of Napier's cases where children were the patients to know, for example, whether he follows this practice.

38. MS. Ash. 411: 83v.

39. MS. Ash. 226: 153r.

40. MS. Ash. 236: 202v (Hil), MS. Ash. 234: 3v (Starker), MS. Ash. 226: 162v (Heiborne).

41. MS. Ash. 195: 9v.

42. Sawyer is similarly unsure how to understand the many menstrual disorders and high rate of amenorrhea among the patients seen by Napier ("Patients, Healers, and Diseases," 485–9). Forman's particular interest in this subject is evidenced by his treatise on the matrix, discussed above in chapter 2.

43. MS. Ash. 389: 232r.

44. MS. Ash. 389: 232r.

45. Looking at much the same evidence, Kassell leans in the opposite direction, believing that the astrological information was most important and that patient reporting of symptoms was secondary ("Simon Forman's Casebooks," 9–10). MacDonald addresses the same question for astrological physicians in general: "analysis of the stars did not pre-empt clinical evidence. . . . It was a flexible tool. . . . The horoscope did not produce an unambiguous diagnosis nor foreordain an appropriate therapy. . . . [I]t did not and could not *impose* a significance on the patient's illness" ("The Career of Astrological Medicine," 66).

46. Siraisi writes of the uncertain fit between written disease descriptions and the symptoms physicians actually encountered: "conditions described in earlier texts might recur in a practitioner's own experience; but even when personal observations were made, textual tradition was likely to govern the understanding and interpretation of what was seen." *Medieval and Early Renaissance Medicine*, 128. Though Forman was not formally trained in medicine, his knowledge of medical texts made it likely that he, too, translated symptoms of his patients into familiar paradigms described in medical texts as well as into astrological paradigms.

47. MacDonald, *Mystical Bedlam*, 117.

48. MS. Ash. 206: 331r.

49. John Dee reports a similar case of spirit possession, which led to repeated attempts at suicide. Ann Frank "my nurse had long been tempted by a wycked spirit: but this day [August 22, 1590] it was evident how she was possessed of him." Dee anointed her several times with holy oil to help her resist the spirit, but she attempted to drown herself in a well on September 8. On September 29th, Frank finally satisfied the "wycked spirit" by eluding her keeper and cutting her throat (*The Private Diary*, 35–36).

50. MS. Ash. 411: 129v.

51. Siraisi addresses this issue as a general problem for the twentieth-century student of early medicine (*Medieval and Early Renaissance Medicine*, 130).

52. In the alphabetical medical manuscript of John Cokkis, which Forman annotated, he commented: "None may be let blud except he or she be 17 yeares of age. or 14 at ye leste. Yet I Simon Forman the coter of this bocke haue let children blod of 5 yers old & lesse" (MS. King's College 16: 146gr). In the casebooks I have calendared, the youngest patient for whom Forman prescribed bloodletting was Godolphin Casswell, age 6. At his consultation in May 1601, Forman predicted that the illness would get worse and that the child would eventually die. But he prescribed four days of dietary drink and then a

bloodletting. A note added later recorded the child's death at the end of July (MS. Ash. 411: 88r).

53. MS. Ash. 226: 9r (Weston), 55r (Carde).

54. I can find no definition for "bonoshawes." In Forman's context, they seem to indicate lumps or swellings on the shin bone.

55. MS. Ash. 226: 149v (Cole), 145r (Bull).

56. MS. Ash. 226: 136r.

57. MS. Ash. 411: 57r.

58. Siraisi, *Medieval and Early Renaissance Medicine,* 133.

59. MS. Ash. 226: 119v, 134v, 135r (Hoon), 146v (Bolter).

60. Sawyer, "Patients, Healers, and Diseases," 198.

61. MS. Ash. 411: 77r.

62. MS. Ash. 411: 91v, 129r.

63. MS. Ash. 226: 109r.

64. Sawyer finds evidence in Napier's papers that Napier and Forman referred patients to one another. These patients consulted Napier when in Buckinghamshire and Forman when in London ("Patients, Healers, and Diseases," 90). Forman's papers show that the two consulted by letter about particular cases, and since they visited each other's homes, they were able to talk about individuals in both locations whom they both knew. On at least two occasions, Forman recorded patient consultations in Napier's casebooks. He was either seeing Napier's Buckinghamshire patients himself while visiting Napier or recording Napier's patient sessions for him (MS. Ash. 228: 11v–12r, 172r–177r).

65. MacDonald sees a large, lower-status patient base as a feature of an astrological medical practice: "In crass economic terms . . . MDs tried to limit their practices to relatively few rich people, whereas astrological physicians grew rich treating the masses for small sums" ("The Career of Astrological Medicine," 68).

66. Among Napier's patients, as well, servants are those most frequently identified by profession (MacDonald, *Mystical Bedlam,* 50).

67. MS. Ash. 240: 25r.

68. MS. Ash. 1495: 486v. Note that this case record is not part of a casebook, but rather a case chosen as an illustrative example in a book of medical instruction.

69. Quoted in Steve Rappaport, *Worlds within Worlds: Structures of Life in Sixteenth-Century London,* Cambridge Studies in Population, Economy and Society in Past Time, 7 (Cambridge: Cambridge University Press, 1989), 221, n.6. Other figures offered here are based on charts Rappaport supplies in appendix 3, 401–407.

70. Rappaport, *Worlds within Worlds,* 221.

71. Lauren Kassell has suggested that Forman may have kept the financial records of his practice separate from the casebooks.

72. MS. Ash. 226: 53r (Smallwood), 39v (Mitchell), and 47r (Boes).

73. MS. Ash. 411: 101r–102v.

74. Sawyer, "Patients, Healers, and Diseases," 545.

75. MS. 411: 102v. This is Forman's total of the bill and includes the item now illegible.

76. MS. Ash. 411: 82v (Thomas), 76r (Edward and Mary).

77. MS. Ash. 236: 225v.

78. MS. Ash. 236: 73v, 113r. Note that Forman doesn't mention "the doctors," who had diagnosed correctly here. He was happy to include them when he thought their opinion

was wrong, but omitted them when he turned out to be in error.

79. MS. Ash. 219: 119v (first consultation), 133v (agreement).

80. Clark, *A History of the Royal College*, 96. Margaret Pelling offers an explanation for this stand by the College: "London physicians demanded payment for advice, regardless of outcome. This was part of the campaign to give primacy to their intellectual attainments, but it was also an attempt to copy the liberal professions by evading the slur of having to earn a livelihood. Fees were to look like unearned income. Thus, like the clergy, physicians wanted to be paid simply for talking and being." Margaret Pelling, "Compromised by Gender: The Role of the Male Medical Practitioner in Early Modern England," in *The Task of Healing: Medicine, Religion and Gender in England and the Netherlands, 1450–1800*, ed. Hilary Marland and Margaret Pelling (Rotterdam: Erasmus Publishing, 1996), 109–10.

81. MS. Ash. 208: 49r. In Rowse's version of this diary entry he inserts "[not]" in the final sentence—"and did [not] bargain with him first" (288). Thus he obscures Forman's point that he could not prosper no matter what he tried.

82. Clark, *A History of the Royal College*, 180.

CHAPTER FOUR

1. "Medical Practitioners," in *Health, Medicine and Mortality in the Sixteenth Century*, ed. Charles Webster (Cambridge: Cambridge University Press, 1979), 168.

2. John Henry writes that "[Licensing] had the effect of enhancing the practitioners' status and their market value," but he goes on to remark that "No amount of rhetoric was able to overcome the everyday experience that irregular practitioners were, generally speaking, just as successful as the regulars"; see "Doctors and Healers: Popular Culture and the Medical Profession," in *Science, Culture and Popular Belief in Renaissance Europe*, ed. Stephen Pumfrey, Paolo L. Rossi, and Maurice Slawinski (Manchester: Manchester University Press, 1991), 190, 210. Lucinda McCray Beier comments that the learned physicians were more upset by the successes of their unlicensed competitors than they were by the failures: "Unable to prove they were the only healers able to cure diseases and heal wounds, licensed practitioners were forced to rely upon social and political clout and the powers of the pen in their competition with unlicensed practitioners." *Sufferers and Healers: The Experience of Illness in Seventeenth-Century England* (London: Routledge & Kegan Paul, 1987), 47, 49. Allen Debus, on the other hand, believes the College of Physicians was fair in its admission of members and prosecution of empirics. Without explaining the basis for his judgment of Forman, Debus remarks, in a discussion of why so few alchemical treatises were published in England, that "the frauds of alchemical tricksters and the escapades of men such as Simon Forman were enough to disturb any honest searcher for the truth." *The English Paracelsians* (New York: Franklin Watts, 1965), 14, 91.

3. Clark, *A History of the Royal College*, 137.

4. MS. Ash. 208: 62v.

5. Leah S. Marcus, *Puzzling Shakespeare: Local Reading and its Discontents* (Berkeley: University of California Press, 1988), offers some idea of the legal and statutory morass in which the disputes over jurisdictional power took place:

> London and its environs were a crazy quilt of different legal jurisdictions, some inextricable from topography, others more global, independent of topical

boundaries. The former would include city ordinances and customary laws. London's liberties and franchises were jealously guarded by her citizens and, in general, protected by English common law. But there was another system of law interlayered with the "local" law of the city and increasingly in competition with it during the early Jacobean period: that was the amorphous, pervasive, "unlocalized" jurisdiction associated with ecclesiastical law and the canons of the church, with royal prerogative . . . and with the royal "dispensing power" to exempt individuals from the provisions of statute law. (171)

6. Goodall, *Proceedings against Empiricks*, 331.

7. Clark, *A History of the Royal College*, 180.

8. Goodall, *Proceedings against Empiricks*, 335.

9. Goodall, *Proceedings against Empiricks*, 333.

10. Goodall, *Proceedings against Empiricks*, 337.

11. MS. Ash. 208: 50r.

12. MS. Ash. 195: 195r (Barnsdell), MS. Ash. 208: 56v, 67v (Stamp), MS. Ash. 234: 31r (the proctor).

13. MS. Ash. 234: 102v, 104v (the Counter), MS. Ash. 195: 195r (reimprisoned).

14. MS. Ash. 234: 111r.

15. MS. Ash. 195: 195r.

16. Goodall, *Proceedings against Empiricks*, 337.

17. Pelling and Webster mistakenly identify "Cokkis" as a reference to Francis Cox's *Treatise of the making and use of divers oils, unguents, emplasters and distilled waters* (1575) in "Medical Practitioners," 326. Rowse follows them in this identification, *Simon Forman*, 32.

18. MacDonald addresses this issue in a footnote: "Assuming—and it is a big assumption —that the examination was fair, the judgment of Forman's astrological competence may have been due to the fact that there was no single, authoritative text that all astrologers followed." "The Career of Astrological Medicine," 82, n7).

19. MS. Ash. 208: 157v.

20. MS. Ash. 234: 127r (money supply), MS. Ash. 208: 57v (to Sandwich), MS. Ash. 234: 132v (return to his home).

21. Goodall, *Proceedings against Empiricks*, 337–38.

22. MS. Ash. 208: 61r.

23. MS. Ash. 219: 170r.

24. MS. Ash. 236: 238r.

25. MS. Ash. 208: 62v. Forman's own notes do not mention this arrest, which probably occurred in 1600.

26. Goodall, *Proceedings against Empiricks*, 338.

27. Rowse, *Simon Forman*, 118–139.

28. Clark, *A History of the Royal College*, 78.

29. Goodall, *Proceedings against Empiricks*, 338–39.

30. John Strype, *The Life and Acts of John Whitgift*, 2 vols. (Oxford: Clarendon Press, 1822), 2: 458. Strype had earlier referred to Forman as "a great imposter."

31. Goodall, *Proceedings against Empiricks*, 339; Strype, *John Whitgift*, 2: 458.

32. MS. Ash. 422: 110v.

33. Rowse, *Simon Forman*, 134.

34. Strype, *John Whitgift*, 2: 485, 505.

35. MS. Ash. 1472: 807v.

36. Bulls of Bashan (Ps. 22:12–13).

37. MS. Ash. 240: 105r–105v.

38. MS. Ash. 802: 132v–133r.

39. Forman's challenge to debate is more within the academic and the occult than the medical tradition. Giordano Bruno's performance at Oxford in 1583 is an English example of this tradition, and it is memorialized in a number of dramatic magical competitions such as those in Greene's *Friar Bacon and Friar Bungay* and Munday's *John a Kent and John a Cumber.*

40. Pelling and Webster remark on the conduct of such university examinations: "Although the College was apt to accuse the universities of abusing their licensing privileges by granting degrees and licenses to illiterate empirics, there is very little evidence to support this accusation. On the whole . . . licenses were granted with care and discrimination" ("Medical Practitioners," 192).

41. Harold J. Cook, "Institutional Structures and Personal Belief in the London College of Physicians," in *Religio Medici: Medicine and Religion in Seventeenth-Century England,* ed. Ole Peter Grell and Andrew Cunningham (Aldershot: Scolar Press, 1996), 97.

42. Clark, *A History of the Royal College,* 210; Cook, "Institutional Structures," 98.

43. MS. Ash. 802: 151v.

44. MS. Ash. 392: 130v.

45. Clark, *A History of the Royal College,* 216.

46. MS. Ash. 392: 175r.

47. Beier comments that the licensed practitioners launched a campaign to sell their own two-pronged point of view: a favorable image for licensed healers and destruction of the reputations of the unlicensed. "As its main agencies it used the powers of its occupational organizations and the vernacular medical literature"; see *Sufferers and Healers,* 33.

Chapter Five

1. Nancy Siraisi, "Girolamo Cardano and the Art of Medical Narrative," *Journal of the History of Ideas* 52 (1991), 581.

2. David Carlson, "The Writings and Manuscript Collections of the Elizabethan Alchemist, Antiquary, and Herald, Francis Thynne," *Huntington Library Quarterly* 52 (1989), 204–205.

3. MacDonald, "The Career of Astrological Medicine," 64.

4. Rowse, *Simon Forman,* 188–189.

5. Peter W. G. Wright, "A Study in the Legitimisation of Knowledge: The 'Success' of Medicine and the 'Failure' of Astrology," in *On the Margins of Science: The Social Construction of Rejected Knowledge,* Sociological Review Monograph 27 (Keele: University of Keele, 1979), 85–101. For a similar argument about the success of medicine put somewhat more moderately, see Cook, *Decline,* 42–45.

6. Cook, *Decline,* 42–45.

7. H. R. Woudhuysen, *Sir Philip Sidney and the Circulation of Manuscripts, 1558–1640* (Oxford: Clarendon Press, 1996), 120. On the occultists' reluctance to publish in print, see also Harold J. Love, *Scribal Publication in Seventeenth-Century England* (Oxford: Clarendon Press, 1993), 177, 179.

8. MS. Ash. 355: 48v. In Forman's manuscript, the last two words, "nor magick," are

crossed out.

9. The terminology is confusing because Forman uses the word "sigil" in two senses. The first is as a seal or signet, referring to the amulet itself and interchangeable with "lamin" meaning "a thin plate of metal used as . . . an astrological charm" *(OED)*. The second use is as "an occult sign"*(OED)*, so that he also writes of engraving the "sigill of Jupiter" onto a coral stone. Either metals or stones could be used in making these protective amulets.

10. Lilly, B6r–B6v.

11. MS. Sloane 3822: 13r, 15r.

12. Because the creation of images to attract celestial power was considered one of the most damnable of magical activities, Ficino uses great caution in talking about this topic. In his address to the reader, he writes, "If you do not approve of astronomical images, albeit invented for the health of mortals—which even I do not so approve of as report—dismiss them with my complete permission and even, if you will, by my advice!" Only after another disclaimer—"you must not think I approve the use of images, only recount it"—does Ficino actually discuss the power of these images: "the material for making an image, if it is in other respects entirely consonant with the heavens, once it has received by art a figure similar to the heavens, both conceives in itself the celestial gift and gives it again to someone who is in the vicinity or wearing it." Marsilio Ficino, *Three Books on Life*, ed. and trans. Carol V. Kaske and John Clark (Binghamton, N.Y.: Medieval & Renaissance Texts & Studies, 1989), book 3: 239, 321, 333.

13. Ficino writes of an image made in the hour of Jupiter: "for a long and happy life, [the ancients] made an image of Jupiter in clear or white stone. It was a man crowned, sitting on an eagle or dragon, wearing a yellow robe, made in the hour of Jupiter when he was fortunately ascending in his exaltation," *Three Books on Life*, 337.

14. I was unable to find a definition of "bailif."

15. MS. Sloane 3822: 11r. Forman's casebook for 1599 has a heading "Of my sigill of Jupiter with the red corall stone" and notes his payment for the stone and its engraving: 8 shillings "for making of yt" and 6 pence for the stone. His sigil may have been less expensive than Jean Shelly's because some barter was involved. He recorded giving the workman "two lamins" (MS. Ash. 219: 48r).

16. MS. Ash. 392: 46r–46v.

17. MS. Ash. 226: 291v.

18. MS. Ash. 226: 206v.

19. MS. Ash. 226: 56v (invasion), MS. Ash. 195: 177r (peace treaty), MS. Ash. 219: 23r (Essex). Forman's fascination with Essex is discussed in chapter 8.

20. Clark, *A History of the Royal College*, 168.

21. Goodall, *Proceedings against Empiricks and Unlicensed Practisers*, 337.

22. MS. Ash. 389.

23. "Forespeaking" means prophesying but within a context that suggests that the prophecy must come to pass because it was spoken. To forespeak someone's illness, in effect, causes that person to become ill. "Overseeing" means looking at someone with an evil eye.

24. MS. Ash. 389: 716r; also MS. Ash. 363: 299r.

25. MS. Ash. 206: 8r–208v (mispagination makes this appear as 436v).

26. MS. Ash. 205.

27. MS Ash. 802: 234r–275v.

28. MS. Ash. 240: 104v. Forman indicates the astrological signs, here as elsewhere, by their symbols, which I have replaced with their names in brackets.

29. MS. Ash. 240: 104v.

30. MS. Ash. 1491: 1074v.

31. MS. Ash. 384: 116r–186r.

32. MS. Ash. 390: 29r. Compare Prospero's similar concern with the appropriate astrological moment in *The Tempest:* "I find my zenith doth depend upon / A most auspicious star, whose influence / If now I court not, but omit, my fortunes / Will ever after droop" (I.2.182–5).

33. MS. Ash. 208: 32v.

34. MS. Ash. 208: 38v.

35. MS. Ash. 208: 42v. Forman's descriptions of employing a scryer, or crystal gazer, are very similar to those that appear in the diary of Dr. John Dee. For example, on May 25, 1581, Dee recorded: "I had a sight in crystal [transliterated in Greek letters] offred me, and I saw." John Dee, *The Private Diary of Dr. John Dee,* ed. James Orchard Halliwell (London, 1842),11. Dee's extensive conversations with angelic spirits, carried on with the help of the scryer Edward Kelly, are recorded in *A True and Faithful Relation of what Passed for Many Yeers Between Dr. John Dee and Some Spirits,* ed. Meric Casaubon (London, 1659). Forman's attempts to contact spirits were neither as extensive nor as successful as those of Dee.

36. MS. Ash. 208: 43v.

37. MS. Ash. 354: 236v.

38. MS. Ash. 354: 237r.

39. MS. Ash. 354: 236r.

40. MS. Ash. 244: 74r–75r.

41. MS. Ash. 244: 1r–v. Forman here follows distinctions made by Pico della Mirandola as he attempted to pick his way among the acceptable and unacceptable aspects of magical and cabalistic power. See the discussion of Pico's belief system by Frances Yates in *Giordano Bruno and the Hermetic Tradition* (London: Routledge & Kegan Paul, 1964), esp. 86–106.

42. MS. Ash. 1472: 812v.

43. MS. Ash. 226: 172v.

44. This John was probably John Goodridge. But it could also have been "John Ward our clark" who appeared in one of Forman's dreams in the 1599 casebook as a summoner of spirits, or John Braddege his servant (of whom Forman remarked in 1599 "in my distillations [John] was negligent," MS. Ash. 219: 135r). Forman's magical activities involved several people and do not seem to have been particularly secret.

45. Forman here mentions a series of basic alchemical operations. "Sublime" means to subject a substance to heat in a vessel so that it is converted into a vapor, which is carried off and, on cooling, is deposited in solid form; "congelle" (congeal) means to solidify; "conioyne" (conjoin) means to combine; "sept" apparently means to separate.

46. MS. Ash. 1472: 1v. Despite the direct address employed in the poem, there is no evidence about its intended audience.

47. MS. Ash. 1472: 810r–812v. Once again, Dee's autobiographical notes parallel Forman's; Dee writes in his diary on August 6, 1600, that "I had a dream after midnight of my working of the philosopher's stone," *The Private Diary,* 62.

48. MS. Ash. 1490: 28r–36v.

49. MS. Ash. 1491: 1268r–1278v.

50. In The Edgar Fahs Smith Collection, Annenberg Rare Book and Manuscript Library, University of Pennsylvania.

51. MS. Ash. 219: 30v.

52. MS. Ash. 219: 122v.

53. MS. Ash. 205: 236v.

54. MS. Ash. 1472: 438r.

55. Theoretically, men could also be witches. But in Forman's papers, no male name is ever suggested as a witch, even in the cases where clients report their suspicions that a particular person is bewitching them. The suspected person is inevitably a female. Scholars agree that women vastly outnumbered men as the subjects of witchcraft accusations and trials, though they disagree about why this was so and about whether gender was a determining factor in accusing a witch or merely a demographical coincidence. See Stuart Clark, "The 'Gendering' of Witchcraft in French Demonology: Misogyny or Polarity," *French History* 5 (1991), 426–437; Clive Holmes, "Women: Witnesses and Witches," *Past and Present* 140 (1993), 45–78; Christina Larner, *Witchcraft and Religion: The Politics of Popular Belief* (Oxford: Basil Blackwell, 1985), esp. 84–88; Deborah Willis, *Malevolent Nurture: Witch-Hunting and Maternal Power in Early Modern England* (Ithaca: Cornell University Press, 1995), esp. 6–25.

56. MS. Ash. 219: 136r.

57. In this, as in other matters, Forman's practice tallied with that of his friend Napier. Ronald Sawyer remarks, "Napier, like many cunning people and diviners, seldom issued a diagnosis of bewitchment unless the patient or the patient's family had already focused on that cause." Sawyer, " 'Strangely Handled in all her lyms': Witchcraft and Healing in Jacobean England," *Journal of Social History* 22 (1989), 467.

58. MS. Ash. 411: 90v.

59. MS. Ash. 236: 201r.

60. Sawyer (" 'Strangely Handled,' " 461–485) provides statistical data about the gender, age, and symptoms of all Napier's bewitchment cases. Since Forman's cases resemble Napier's closely in their statistical profile, I have chosen, instead of statistics, to examine individual cases involving witchcraft, how Forman speaks of them, and how much attention he gives them.

61. MS. Ash. 226: 149r.

62. MS. Ash. 411: 77r.

63. MS. Ash. 411: 87r.

64. The version of this advice in MS. Ash. 389 reads "triuet" instead of "trenate" (765r). "Trenate" does not appear in *OED*.

65. MS. Ash. 363: 309r–v; also MS. Ash. 389: 765r–765v.

66. MS. Ash. 411: 105r.

67. MS. Ash. 208: 131r.

68. The "glass delusion" was apparently quite common both in real life and in the literature of early modern Europe. A subset of those who believed their bodies made of glass were convinced that they were glass urinals. On this topic see Gill Speak, "An Odd Kind of Melancholy: Reflections on the Glass Delusion in Europe (1440–1680)," *History of Psychiatry* 1 (1990), esp. 192–197.

69. MS. Ash. 363: 141r.

70. MS. Ash. 390: 102v. Dee's servant's more tragic encounter with a spirit caused her suicide (see chapter 3, note 49).

71. MS. Ash. 206: 371r.

72. James Sharpe, *Instruments of Darkness: Witchcraft in Early Modern England* (Philadelphia: University of Pennsylvania Press, 1997), 56–57.

CHAPTER SIX

1. MS. Ash. 208: 139r.

2. MS. Ash. 208: 141r.

3. MS. Ash. 208: 141v.

4. MS. Ash. 205: 146v.

5. MS. Ash. 195: 186v.

6. Forman recorded astrological casts and notes about the stolen books in MS. Ash. 195: 9r, 72r, 95r, 96v, and 151v. In MS. Ash. 219: 54r, he gave the names of the thieves along with the names of the books that they tried to sell.

7. MS. Ash. 206: 1r–2v. According to Lynn Thorndike in *A History of Magic and Experimental Science During the First Thirteen Centuries of Our Era* (New York: Columbia University Press, 1925), John of Saxony contributed the commentary (1331) to a Latin translation by John of Spain (2: 97).

8. MS. Ash. 208: 28v, 48r.

9. MS. Ash. 390: 125r. Because Forman says nothing about his religious beliefs, except for asserting faith in God, it is difficult to understand what sort of "prayer book" could have been responsible for his imprisonment. Perhaps he is speaking about a Roman Catholic manual of some sort or an occult book full of invocatory prayers to spirits. He does record one dream about attempting to call spirits in a church. Either sort of text might have got him in trouble.

10. MS. Ash. 208: 56v, 57r. *Picatrix* is a medieval compilation of occult texts, described by Thorndike in the chapter he devotes to it as "openly and professedly a book of magic" (*History of Magic*, 2: 815). John Dee worried similarly about letting people know he possessed certain books. In one diary entry, he wrote, "I gave Mr. Richard Cavendish the copy of Paracelsus, twelve lettres, written in French with my own hand; and he promised me, before my wife, never to disclose to any that he hath it; and that yf he dye before me he will restore it agayn to me; but if I dy befor him, that he shall deliver it to one of my sonnes, most fit among them to have it." *The Private Diary*, 35.

11. MS. Ash. 226: 89v (books at the wake), MS. Ash 219: 146r (hiding the books).

12. MS. Ash. 208: 62v. Forman may be referring to a text dealing with the *Ars Notoria*, a "magical art of memory sometimes attributed to Appollonius." Frances Yates, *The Art of Memory* (London: Routledge & Kegan Paul, 1966), 43. John Trithemius (1462–1516) is credited with writing *Steganographia*, a book about language and secret writing (Thorndike, *History of Magic*, 4: 524–25).

13. MS. Ash. 411: 163v.

14. MS. Ash. 227: 275r.

15. MS. Sloane 3822: 114v.

16. A copy of this publication is bound into MS. Ash. 802 at the very end. STC 11185.

17. J. B. Bamborough remarks in passing that "the orderliness of the similar notebook [similar to Robert Burton's astrological notebook] by Simon Forman in the Bodleian (MS. Ash. 205) . . . , as it is now found at least, might almost form the copy for a printed book on the different aspects of judicial astrology." In "Robert Burton's Astrological Notebook," *Review of English Studies*, n.s. 32 (1981), 271.

18. MS. Ash. 240: 103r.

19. Napier's "A Treatise Touching the defens of astrologie" is probably the work Forman was alluding to here. Drafts of at least part of this defense appear among Napier's manuscripts, but it was never printed (MS. Ash. 205: 50r–63v).

20. MS. Ash. 195: 151r. Though I first read this little note as one of Forman's enigmatic remarks, the more I work with his manuscripts and remark the scarcity of references to printed books, the more I feel that this note reveals Forman's fairly strong opinion about print publication.

21. Forman, *The Groundes of Longitude*, B2r.

22. Forman, *The Groundes of Longitude*, B3v.

23. Forman, *The Groundes of Longitude*, A4r.

24. Forman, *The Groundes of Longitude*, A2v.

25. Forman, *The Groundes of Longitude*, B1r.

26. Forman, *The Groundes of Longitude*, B1v.

27. Forman, *The Groundes of Longitude*, A3v.

28. For a more detailed discussion of this matter, see Stephen Johnston's informative article, "Mathematical Practitioners and Instruments in Elizabethan England," *Annals of Science* 48 (1991), 319–344.

29. MS. Ash. 208: 47v. In E. G. R. Taylor's account of this episode, *The Mathematical Practitioners of Tudor and Stuart England* (Cambridge: Cambridge University Press, 1954), she also places Emery Molyneux, the mapmaker, in opposition to Forman: "[Forman] refused to reveal the method when publicly challenged to do so by Emery Molyneux" (182). She offers no source for her comment, but apparently based her claim on Forman's own text. In *The Groundes*, he writes: "there hath beene heretofore diuers proffers made in the absence and behalf of the Author, by Maister *Emery Mulleneux* & others, for the trueth and triall hereof and hath not beene accepted hetherto: because some haue thought it eyther to be doone vpon presumption or on a Brauado, &c. But whatsoeuer they before haue offered in the premises, I the Author here of am ready at all times to performe the same, God willing" (B3r). Surely Forman meant that Molyneux had been spreading the word, acting as his agent, and urging people to come learn Forman's method. In the diary, Forman noted that he had gone to London and stayed with Molyneux to teach him the longitude several months before he put the book to press (MS. Ash. 208: 47v). That Forman probably continued contact with both Parker and Molyneux is suggested by a later manuscript entry: "A note of the bill and names of the thinges that Mr. Parke was to buy for Mulleneux 1595 the 11 of March" (MS. Ash. 1490: 350v). Forman's reputation (Taylor refers to him as "notorious") influences readers to interpret comments by and about him negatively.

30. Johnston, "Mathematical Practitioners," 335, n. 65.

31. William Sherman, *John Dee: The Politics of Reading and Writing in the English Renaissance*, Massachusetts Studies in Early Modern Culture (Amherst: University of Massachusetts Press, 1995), esp. 29–52.

32. Sherman, *John Dee*, 45.

33. Deborah Harkness discusses Jane Dee's central role in managing the Dee household and in enabling her husband's work in "Managing an Experimental Household: The Dees of Mortlake and the Practice of Natural Philosophy," *Isis* 88 (1997), 247–62. Partly because Forman's marriage came long after his work and study patterns were well established, partly because his wife was extremely young relative to himself, and partly because he needed to be firmly in charge of his milieu, Forman's relationship with his wife was more distant than Dee's with his. Mrs. Forman functioned more as an acquisition than as a domestic partner.

34. MS. Ash. 360: 116–128.

35. MS. Ash. 390.

36. MS. Ash. 208: 94–97, (Avicenna), MS. Ash. 1423: 1–78 (Bacon), MS. Ash. 1490: 66r–74v and 114r–136v (Ripley), 154r–164r (Lull), 277r–289r (Norton).

37. MS. Ash. 208: 106r (Maplet), MS. Ash. 802: 59v (Elyot).

38. MS. Ash. 208: 131r.

39. MS. Ash. 208: 262r–263r (Frobisher), 112r (Lyly).

40. MS. Ash. 802: 111v.

41. MS. Ash. 802: "Forman his Thankesgyuinge and acknowledgmente of the poware of god after his firste & second troble," 121r–121v.

42. MS. Ash. 802: 126v.

43. *King Lear* IV.vi.165–66.

44. MS. Ash. 802: 127v.

45. As with many of his nonmedical writings, Forman here follows a well-established tradition of eschatological writing, including a number of specific treatises on the coming of the Antichrist. See Stuart Clark, *Thinking with Demons: The Idea of Witchcraft in Early Modern Europe* (Oxford: Clarendon Press, 1997), 335–62, and especially chapters 22 and 23.

46. Clark remarks: "Witchcraft and demonism were spoken of as aspects of that final period of time in which men and women were currently living. Though initially puzzling, they became perfectly intelligible as features of a decaying world." *Thinking with Demons*, 320.

47. MS. Ash. 802: 116r.

48. MS. Ash. 802: 120r.

49. Forman's choice of 1666 was not original. Clark notes, for example, that Sieur Paul de Perrieres-Varin had predicted the arrival of the Antichrist in 1626 and the end of the world in 1666. *Thinking with Demons*, 342.

50. MS. Ash. 802: 118v.

51. MS. Ash. 802: 33v.

52. MS. Ash. 802: 33v.

53. MS. Ash. 802: 1v.

54 H. F. D. Sparks, ed., *The Apocryphal Old Testament* (Oxford: Clarendon Press, 1984), 141–67. I owe the identification of Forman's source to Lauren Kassell.

55. MS. Ash. 802: 20v–21r.

56. MS. Ash. 802: 6r (final copy), 10r (draft copy).

57. MS. Ash. 802: 39v–40v.

58. MS. Ash. 802: 23r.

59. Forman's manuscripts contain two copies of his lists of giants. I quote from MS. Ash. 802 where the account of giants is suggestively juxtaposed with the creation account

and with a list of Arthurian characters. But a more careful copy of the giant text is MS. Ash. 244: 192r–199r. Forman titled and dated this copy: "The Bocke of Giantes and huge and Monstrose Formes gathered by Simon Forman. ann. 1610."

60. MS. Ash. 802: 53v.

61. Walter Stephens, *Giants in Those Days* (Lincoln: University of Nebraska Press, 1989), 64–84.

62. Stephens, *Giants*, 6.

63. Stephens, *Giants*, 107.

64. Another brief list of giants in Forman's 1601 casebook is headed "The Names of the giants that were in England when Brutus came in." Kent was home to Evarne and a woman named Jillabery. In Wiltshire were Memmyne and Chesse. Dorsetshire had Hod, Hambeldene, and Melborowe (MS. Ash. 411: 163r). Forman's interest in giants stretched over at least a decade.

65. MS. Ash. 802: 51r (also MS. Ash. 244: 194r).

66. MS. Ash. 802: 51v (also MS. Ash. 244: 195r).

67. The relevant section in Geoffrey is book 8, chapters 10–12.

68. MS. Ash. 244: 196r. The corresponding section in Geoffrey's account is book 1, chapter 16.

69. MS. Ash. 802: 58r.

70. Henry B. Wheatley, ed., *Merlin or The Early History of King Arthur* (1899; reprint, 2 vols., New York: Greenwood Press, 1969), 1: 14.

71. MS. Ash. 802: 74v.

72. MS. Ash. 802: 80v.

73. Clark, *Thinking with Demons*, 375.

74. MS. Ash. 802: 59r.

75. MS. Ash. 802: 59r.

76. See Arthur Marotti's introductory chapter in *John Donne, Coterie Poet* (Madison: University of Wisconsin Press, 1986), 3–24, for a brief discussion of manuscript transmission. Given Forman's social aspirations, I could suggest that his lack of interest in taking his books to press grew at least partially from the "stigma of print" felt by gentlemen authors. But there is no real evidence among Forman's writings to support such a theory. Harold Love, in *Scribal Publication in Seventeenth-Century England* (Oxford: Clarendon Press, 1993), discusses the tradition of scribal publication. Especially relevant to Forman's situation is Love's notion that scribal publication served to define "communities of the like-minded" (33).

77. MS. Ash. 1491: 1309.

CHAPTER SEVEN

1. Beier notes, "The extent to which diaries reflect general experience is frequently and deservedly questioned. . . . Diarists and autobiographers were unusual in any age, feeling a need most people never feel to commit thoughts and experience to paper. Their attitudes and behavior can be taken as representative neither of general experience nor of the experience of others at their social level." "In Sickness and in Health: A Seventeenth-Century Family's Experience," in *Patients and Practitioners: Lay Perceptions of Medicine in Pre-Industrial Society*, ed. Roy Porter (Cambridge: Cambridge University Press, 1985), 101.

2. I use "Simon" when referring to the character Forman calls by that name in his

autobiography because that figure represents, but is not the same as, Forman the author.

3. "Yard" here means a stick, perhaps a stick used for measuring such as would be available in a merchant's shop.

4. MS. Ash. 208: 139r.

5. MS. Ash. 208: 139v.

6. MS. Ash. 208: 141r.

7. Steven R. Smith comments on the confusing roles that occurred when young apprentices were subjugated to the wives and maids of their masters, and he suggests that "the frequency of complaints about the domination by women indicates the sexual confusion which is a part of adolescence." "Communication: The London Apprentices as Seventeenth-Century Adolescents," *Past and Present* 61 (1973), 149–161. Forman's own sexual confusion may be indicated by his choice of the word "yeard" in his account of retributive attacks on the two women of Commins's household. Though its primary meaning is "stick" in his narrative, "yeard" was also frequently used, as we have seen in some of his medical cases, to mean penis.

8. MS. Ash. 208: 141r.

9. MS. Ash. 208: 141r.

10. MS. Ash. 208: 140v.

11. MS. Ash. 208: 140v.

12. The phrase "halikekeros harescum tauro" is Forman's coded phrase for sexual intercourse. He frequently shortened it to the single word "halek" in his notes. I have been unable to discover where the phrase comes from or to figure out what code Forman used, but he repeats the expression so frequently in explicit contexts that its meaning is clear, even though its derivation is not.

13. Ann Young eventually married Ralph Walworth, and Joshua assumed his stepfather's name. He always appears in Forman's notes as "Joshua Walworth."

14. The diary references to Ann Young occur in MS. Ash. 208: 37v, 39r–v, 42v, 43v, and 53v.

15. MS. Ash. 208: 54v, 62r. Rowse offers a detailed discussion of Forman's affairs with Ann Young and Avis Allen (53–69, 70–73).

16. MS. Ash. 234: 123r, MS. Ash. 226: 132r.

17. MS. Ash. 226: 132r.

18. MS. Ash. 354: 186v.

19. MS. Ash. 208: 37v.

20. MS. Ash. 208: 31v.

21. MS. Ash. 208: 46v.

22. MS. Ash. 208: 48r.

23. Rowse, *Simon Forman*, 51–69.

24. MS. Ash. 208: 54r, 168v.

25. MS. Ash. 208: 57r.

26. MS. Ash. 390: 69r.

27. MS. Ash. 226: 112r, 119r.

28. MS. Ash. 208: 58r.

29. MS. Ash. 226: 224r.

30. MS. Ash. 206: 269r.

31. MS. Ash. 354: 74r.

32. MS. Ash. 389: 81.

33. MS. Ash. 219: 47r.

34. Rowse says that she was a new servant in Forman's house (*Simon Forman*, 92), but provides no evidence. The only shred of support I can find for Rowse's claim is a cast on July 6, 1599, where he phrases the question: "best to kepe Jeane et conducr illum nec non" (MS. Ash. 219: 100v). I think it unlikely that Forman would have married his servant.

35. MS. Ash. 219: 100r.

36. MS. Ash. 802: 151v–152v.

37. MS. Ash. 208: 226r.

38. MS. Ash. 219: 141v, MS. Ash. 236: 77v. Forman "reads" the signs of his wife's infidelity in her open mouth (the conversation with Ledsom) and in the invasion of his (and her) house (the trip to the privy). In so doing, he illustrates quite dramatically Peter Stallybrass's argument that the "normative" woman of the renaissance is "rigidly 'finished': her signs are the enclosed body, the closed mouth, the locked house." "Patriarchal Territories: The Body Enclosed," in *Rewriting the Renaissance: The Discourses of Sexual Difference in Early Modern Europe*, eds. Margaret Ferguson, Maureen Quilligan, and Nancy Vickers (Chicago: University of Chicago Press, 1986), 127. Forman's wife, by opening her mouth and her house, led her husband to assume that she had also opened her body to Ledsom.

39. MS. Ash. 236: 76r. This enigmatic astrological answer seems to mean that, though it is in his wife's nature to be a whore, she has not yet been unfaithful to Forman.

40. MS. Ash. 236: 263r.

41. One post-Overbury discussion of Forman refers to adulterous behavior by Mrs. Forman: "that you may know [Forman's] skil, he was himselfe a cuckold, having a very pretty wench to his wife, which would say, she did it to try his skill." Anthony Weldon, "The Court and Character of King James" (1650); reprinted as *Secret History of the Court of James the First*, 2 vols. (Edinburgh: James Ballantyne, 1811), 1: 418. Weldon is inaccurate about many details in his account of the Overbury trial, and I find no support elsewhere for his account of Mrs. Forman.

42. MS. Ash. 390: 161r.

43. MS. Ash. 208: 63, MS. Ash. 802: 152v.

44. MS. Ash. 208: 121v–122r.

45. MS. Ash. 206: 102r–103r.

46. The dangerous "bag" associated with an impostume, or abscess, occurs elsewhere in Forman's papers. Writing of a woman troubled with an impostume in the pit of her stomach, he told how a physician

> gaue her a vomite, of asarabacca or som such thinge that shee did vomite mightily & soe moch that at laste the velme or bag that thimpostum was in cam vp & out at her mothe and he had prepared at a smithes an yron instrument of a quarter of a yerd long croked at on end barbed thus, like a fish croke or fishe hocke and euer as the velm or bag cam forth he caughte it still with that Instrument and held it fast that it retorned not in again, but it came forth alle. (MS. Ash. 390: 131r)

A reference to a similar bag occurs in the poetry of Forman's contemporary, John Donne:

> When no Physician of Redresse can speake,
> A ioyfull casuall violence may breake

A dangerous Apostem in thy brest;
And whilst thou ioyest in this, the dangerous rest,
The bag may rise vp, and so strangle thee.
("The Second Anniversary," ll. 477–81)

Despite these other references, I still cannot determine exactly what this "bag" was. Several physicians have suggested to me that it may have been a throat membrane associated with diphtheria.

47. MS. Ash. 240: 31v.

48. All these details about Ann are from MS. Ash. 208: 50r.

49. MS. Ash. 208: 54r.

50. Forman was apparently not secretive, at least to his friend Napier, about his illegitimate children. In a manuscript of nativities, Richard Napier records several pages of names and dates of Forman's family and friends. Among them are the names and birth dates of Mrs. Forman and Forman's three illegitimate children: "Ann Baker, Mrs. Forman," February 1581; "Josua filius Ag. Young," March 27, 1585; "An Barker, D. Forman's kinswoman," March 11, 1594; and "fenema Parker," June 11, 1599 (MS. Ash. 338: 115v–117r).

51. MS. Ash. 206: 276r. Forman seems to be accusing the nurse of giving the child a head injury by manipulating too vigorously the soft bones of the skull. Such injuries often occurred in childbirth.

52. MS. Ash. 195: 101v, 147r, 196r, 203r, 237r.

53. MS. Ash. 219: 49v.

54. MS. Ash. 206: 236r.

55. MS. Ash. 219: 94r.

56. MS. Ash. 219: 136r.

57. MS. Ash. 219: 105v.

58. Forman called Steven "his sister's son" (MS. Ash. 390: 102v). According to the genealogical account of his family (MS. Ash. 208: 222r), Steven was actually the son of Forman's stepsister from his mother's first marriage. Phyllis married Henry Mitchell, and Steven was one of their four children. Forman noted that he was killed at age 27, slain by the Spanish in 1601 in Sir William Monson's ship. Forman had two full sisters, both named Joan. The eldest had two husbands but no children. The younger Joan did not marry until 1610 when she was 53.

59. MS. Ash. 390: 158r.

60. MS. Ash. 208: 46v.

61. MS. Ash. 208: 47v.

62. Rowse identified Stone House as "the re-vestry of the parish church of St. Botolph, Billingsgate. . . . now secularized and let out as chambers and apartments" (91, 83). Forman spoke of living in Philpot Lane, quite close to St. Botolph on Thames Street, but not at the location Rowse suggests. Rowse's identification is made appealing, however, by John Stow's description of the revestry given by John Rainwell in the early fifteenth century as "a stone house to be a revestrie to that church for ever," *A Survey of London written in the year 1598* (1598; reprint, London: Chatto and Windus, 1876), 78. Whether he lived in this revestry or in another stone house in Philpot Lane, Forman remained for years in this section of London described disparagingly by Stowe: "This parish of St. Buttolph is no great thing notwithstanding divers strangers are there harboured." Stow quoted someone

who declared, "In Billingsgate ward were one and fifty households of strangers, whereof thirty of these households inhabited in the parish of St. Buttolph, in the chief and principal houses, where they give twenty pounds the year for a house lately letten for four marks" (78). Such a note makes the twenty pounds a year Forman would later pay for his Lambeth house seem plausible.

63. MS. Ash. 390: 60v.

64. MS. Ash. 240: 17r.

65. Braddege was one of more than three thousand Englishmen dispatched to Belgium in an attempt to lift the Spanish siege against Protestant Ostend in the period 1601–03. See Wallace T. MacCaffrey, *Elizabeth I: War and Politics, 1588–1603* (Princeton: Princeton University Press, 1992), 293–97.

66. MS. Ash. 206: 249v.

67. MS. Ash. 195: 244r, 180v.

68. MS. Ash. 389: 65v.

69. MS. Ash. 195: 196r. I have no idea what "the bag of stones" refers to.

70. MS. Ash. 390: 64v.

71. MS. Ash. 390: 61r.

72. MS. Ash. 226: 268r.

73. MS. Ash. 208: 59v.

74. MS. Ash. 390: 61r.

75. MS. Ash. 208: 59v.

76. MS. Ash. 411: 62v.

77. MS. Ash. 411: 100r.

78. Dornix [dornick] was a silk, worsted or woollen fabric used for hangings, carpets, etc. Forman was moving up from the cheaper "painted cloth" of his London house.

79. MS. Ash. 411: 103v.

80. MS. Ash. 208: 64r.

81. MS. Ash. 802: 152r–152v.

82. MS. Ash. 208: 57r.

83. Hazel rods were used for occult purposes and Forman believed, as did others in the period, that to have their full effect they had to be cut by a virgin. Jean was an unmarried servant in Forman's household (perhaps she is the servant named Jean whom Rowse assumed became Forman's wife). "1598 the 8 of Feb . . . juste betwen [sun] rising which was just at 7 of the clok & a qrter after I did let to be cut 8 hazell wan[d]s of on yers growth. in the dai & howar of [Mercury?]. Jean did cut them instanti being a virgin & in that howar they wer whited & writen on" (MS. Ash. 226: 303r). Reginald Scot in *The Discoverie of Witchcraft* recounted how hazel wands marked with three crosses—"certaine words both blasphemous and impious must be said over it"—were used to find buried treasure: "if the time of digging be neglected the diuell will carie all the treasure awaie" (x.vii, 183). Scot then added a marginal gloss: "Note this superstitious dotage." Forman, however, took the treasure hunting seriously: "Cut a hassell rod that is forked of on years growth, that groweth Easte and weste the forkes and let them be of on length, and hould the 2 spriges in the handes and so goe wher mettall is and the end will bowe down to the place wher it is" (MS. Sloane 3822: 84r).

84. MS. Ash. 195: 47v (hazel rods), 101v (rabbits), and 151v (orchard).

85. MS. Ash. 1491: 1071v.

86. MS. Ash. 802: 151v.

87. MS. Ash. 208: 41v, 45v.

88. MS. Ash. 208: 49r.

89. MS. Ash. 208: 61v.

90. Rowse, *Simon Forman,* 152.

91. MS. Ash. 208: 61v. Some historians believe that this groundless panic, which "triggered the largest English mobilization since 1588," was stimulated by the fear that Essex, in Ireland with troops, might bring them back against England. In fact, the scare seems to have been caused by faulty intelligence reports (MacCaffrey, *Elizabeth I,* 133).

92. MS. Ash. 219: 133r (list of knights), MS. Ash. 195: 124r (on whether he will be captain).

93. MS. Ash. 195: 173v, 177r.

94. MS. Ash. 195: 195v.

95. Forman's matter-of-fact statement about having his picture drawn contrasts markedly with Thomas Wythorne's reflective meditation on having his portrait painted for the third time, asking himself why men, no longer young and attractive, would have "their pictures or counterfeits to be painted from time to time" (*Autobiography,* 115–17). Wythorne's introspective tone is characteristic of his entire autobiography, just as Forman's plain statement of fact characterizes his autobiographical records.

96. MS. Ash. 208: 62v.

97. A cutout copy is preserved in the Folger copy of Halliwell's edition of Forman's *Autobiography.* This extra-illustrated book contains handwritten notes supplying the diary portions that Halliwell silently omitted as well as other associated Forman material. Rowse also reproduced the engraving in his book on Forman.

98. MS. Ash. 389: 544v. Another, almost identical version of this story is in MS. Ash. 205 on a misnumbered leaf between folios 77 and 79. But in an astrological manuscript, Forman uses this example in questions about theft and is more direct. The theft occurred on a Monday, and on Wednesday Forman questioned the female guests about the loss "but they denyed ym absolutely." Not until five days had passed did the "gentleman" remember to return the pictures (MS. Ash. 354: 276r).

99. MS. Ash. 226: 45r.

100. MS. Ash. 236: 77v.

101. MS. Ash. 206: 349r.

102. MS. Ash. 226: 13v.

103. MS. Ash. 411: 24v, 25v (consultations), MS. Ash. 354: 273r (Forman's example).

104. Edwin Nungezer, *Dictionary of Actors,* Cornell Studies in English, vol. 13 (New Haven: Yale University Press, 1929), 377–78.

105. The diary is located in MS. Ash. 208: 200r–207v. A recent study by Don LePan, *The Birth of Expectation* (London: Macmillan Press, 1989), devotes its entire final chapter to analysis of Forman's brief diary (280–302).

106. MS. Ash. 208: 201r–201v.

107. MS. Ash. 208: 122r.

108. Philip Sidney, "A Defense of Poetry," in *Miscellaneous Prose of Sir Philip Sidney,* ed. Katherine Duncan-Jones and Jan van Dorsten (Oxford: Clarendon Press, 1973), 93.

CHAPTER EIGHT

1. MS. Ash. 802: 174v.

2. According to the *OED*, "maracock" refers to certain American passionflowers or to the fruit which they produce.

3. The published accounts of William Strachey, *The Historie of Travell into Virginia Britania 1612*, ed. Louis B. Wright and Virginia Freund, The Hakluyt Society, n.s. 103 (London, 1953), and John Smith, *A Map of Virginia with a Description of the Country* (Oxford, 1612); facs. Theatrum Orbis Terrarum (Amsterdam, 1973), both include descriptions of the maracock and the opossum, but they seem closer to one another in detail than either does to Forman's. Note the difference between the description of Strachey:

> An Oppusum is a beast as big as a pretty Beagle of grey Cullor, Yt hath a head like a swyne, eares, Feet, and Taille like a Ratt, she carryes her young ones vnder her belly in a piece of her own Skynn, like as in a bagge, which she can open and shutt, to let them out or take them in as she pleaseth, and doth therein lodge, carry, and succle her young, and eates in tast like a Pig; (124)

and that of Smith:

> An Opassom hath a head like a Swine, & a taill like a *Rat*, and is of the bignes of a Cat. Vnder her belly shee hath a bagge, wherein shee lodgeth, carieth, and sucketh her young. (12)

4. MS. Ash. 802: 175v.

5. In *A Voyage to Virginia in 1609*, ed. Louis B. Wright (Charlottesville: University Press of Virginia, 1964), 82.

6. MS. Ash. 802: 171r.

7. MS. Ash. 226: 310r.

8. Louis Adrian Montrose, "'Shaping Fantasies': Figurations of Gender and Power in Elizabethan Culture," *Representations* 2 (1983), 61–94. This dream is recorded in MS. Ash. 226: 44r.

9. MS. Ash. 226: 44v (February 1597), 310r (January 1598).

10. MS. Ash. 411: 8v.

11. MS. Ash. 236: 223v.

12. MS. Ash. 1490: 106v. These were the membranous seeds with wings of ash trees; "they are called in English ashe keyes because they hang in bunches after the maner of keyes" (*OED*).

13. Forman does not include them in any of the medical recipes I have examined. Lady Grace Mildmay, however, calls for "ash keys 1 great handful" in a remedy for flatus hypochondia (abdominal gas); this remedy is also labeled "an approved course for the melancholy." Linda Pollock, *With Faith and Physick: The Life of a Tudor Gentlewoman, Lady Grace Mildmay, 1552–1620* (New York: St. Martin's, 1995), 121.

14. MS. Ash. 384: 156v.

15. MS. Ash. 208: 252r–252v.

16. MS. Ash. 1472: 807v.

17. MS. Ash. 219: 23r.

18. MS. Ash. 219: 31r.

19. MS. Ash. 219: 202r.

20. MS. Ash. 236: 215r.

21. MS. Ash. 411: 22r (February 9), 25v (February 12), 30r (February 20 and 21), 31v (February 25).

22. MS. Ash. 411: 32r (February 26), 50v (March 18).

23. MS. Ash. 411: 49v. The words in brackets are conjectural.

24. MS. Ash. 411: 50r.

25. In his recent study of the culture and court of King James, Curtis Perry remarks on the aftereffects of the Overbury affair: "The enormous attention focused on the scandal from start to finish helped make the corruption of the court notorious. Generally speaking, these events contributed to a change in English attitudes toward James, as responses to him and his court became more clearly polarized." *The Making of Jacobean Culture: James I and the Renegotiation of Elizabethan Literary Practice* (Cambridge: Cambridge University Press, 1997), 3.

26. Several accounts of the Overbury murder and the trials which followed have been written in the twentieth century: among them are William McElwee, *The Murder of Sir Thomas Overbury* (London: Faber and Faber, 1952); Beatrice White, *Cast of Ravens* (London: John Murray, 1965); Edward LeComte, *The Notorious Lady Essex* (London: Robert Hale, 1969); and David Lindley, *The Trials of Frances Howard: Fact and Fiction at the Court of King James* (London: Routledge, 1993).

27. Howell, comp., *State Trials*, 11: cols. 931–32.

28. Howell, comp., *State Trials*, 11: col. 932.

29. Howell, comp., *State Trials*, 11: col. 931.

30. Howell, comp., *State Trials*, 11, col. 932.

31. Howell, comp., *State Trials*, 11, col. 933.

32. Howell, comp., *State Trials*, 11: col. 935. For various descriptions and interpretations of this "note," see chapter 1, note 68.

33. In a recent study of Frances Howard's reputation, David Lindley points out in detail how much of her character as a scheming murderess and sexually voracious adulteress is formed by misogynist stereotypes that reshape even the events of her early years, see *The Trials of Frances Howard*. I argue that Forman's reputation has been similarly reshaped by the trial testimony and its subsequent retellings.

34. Howell, comp., *State Trials*, 11: col. 935; my emphasis.

35. Stuart Clark's argument that the deep religious belief of the period required a demonic "other" to complete it has explanatory power in this instance: "religious polemic demanded that the demonic be required more and more to complete the knowledge of things godly—required, that is, by the demands of a logic that related God and the devil as hierarchical opposites." Clark goes on to describe the devil's association with magic. *Thinking with Demons: The Idea of Witchcraft in Early Modern Europe* (Oxford: Clarendon Press, 1997), 142–143.

36. Reprinted in Alfred S. Reid, ed., *Sir Thomas Overbury's Vision (1616) and Other English Sources of Nathaniel Hawthorne's "The Scarlet Letter"* (Gainesville, Fla.: Scholars Facsimiles and Reprints), 193.

37. Reid, ed., *Sir Thomas Overbury's Vision*, 200.

38. Wing (W2886) attributes the pamphlet to Arthur Wilson (1595–1652).

39. Reid, ed., *Sir Thomas Overbury's Vision*, 59.

40. Reid, ed., *Sir Thomas Overbury's Vision*, 59.

41. Reid, ed., *Sir Thomas Overbury's Vision*, 60.

42. "The Court and Character of King James," in *Secret History of the Court of James the First*, 2 vols. (Edinburgh: James Ballantyne, 1811), 1: 417–418.

43. "Aulicus Coquinariae," in *Secret History*, 2: 224–226.

44. Alfred S. Reid argues in the introduction to the facsimile of *Sir Thomas Overbury's Vision* that the Overbury trials provide the primary source for Hawthorne's novel. In Reid's scheme, not only is association with Forman used to make Chillingsworth sinister, but Forman is the inspiration for the "Black Man," seen by various of the novel's characters (vi).

45. [Moysey], *Forman: A Tale*, 1: viii.

46. [Moysey], *Forman*, 1: 103.

47. [Moysey], *Forman*, 2: 184.

48. [Moysey], *Forman*, 3: 290.

49. It is not without irony that the latest entry in the field of Forman-fashioners acknowledges her debt to the "Forman" of yet another printed text, that written by A. L. Rowse in 1974. Judith Cook has published three "thrillers" about "Dr. Simon Forman— Elizabethan doctor and solver of mysteries" (cover copy on all three volumes). Beginning in 1591 with Forman established in a house on the Bankside, the series of three tales has progressed through late summer of 1593 (with eighteen years to go until Forman's death in 1611, this could be a lengthy series). Forman is portrayed as a dashing, generous, romantic adventurer in Cook's novels. He combines doctoring and sleuthing while completely denying involvement in necromancy. See *The Death of a Lady's Maid* (1997), *Murder at the Rose* (1998), and *Blood on the Borders* (1999), all published by Headline Book Publishing, London.

❦ BIBLIOGRAPHY ❦

I. ARCHIVAL SOURCES

Ashmole, Elias. Ashmole MS. 1790. Bodleian Library, Oxford University, Oxford.

Forman, Simon. Ashmole MSS. 174; 195; 205; 206; 208; 219; 226; 227; 234; 236; 240; 244; 338; 354; 355; 363; 384; 389; 390; 392; 403; 411; 802; 1403; 1429; 1430; 1436; 1453; 1457; 1472; 1488; 1490; 1491; 1494; 1495; 1763. Bodleian Library, Oxford University, Oxford.

———. MS. 16. King's College Library, Cambridge University, Cambridge.

———. Sloane MSS. 2550; 3822. British Library, London.

Napier, Richard. Ashmole MSS. 174; 204; 227; 338. Bodleian Library, Oxford University, Oxford.

II. PRINTED SOURCES

Anderson, Anthony. *An Approved Medicine Against the Deserved Plague.* London, 1593.

Ariès, Phillipe. *Centuries of Childhood: A Social History of Family Life.* Trans. Robert Baldick. London: Jonathan Cape, 1962.

Ashmole, Elias. *Theatrum chemicum Britannicum.* London, 1652.

Bamborough, J. B. "Robert Burton's Astrological Notebook." *Review of English Studies* n.s. 32 (1981): 267–85.

Barrough, Philip. *The Method of Physick, Conteining the Causes, Signes, and Cures of Inward Diseases in Mans Bodie from the Head to the Foote.* London, 1590.

Beier, Lucinda McCray. "In Sickness and in Health: A Seventeenth-Century Family's Experience." In *Patients and Practitioners: Lay Perceptions of Medicine in Pre-Industrial Society.* Ed. Roy Porter, 101–28. Cambridge: Cambridge University Press, 1985.

———. *Sufferers and Healers: The Experience of Illness in Seventeenth-Century England.* London: Routledge & Kegan Paul, 1987.

Black, William. H., comp. *A Descriptive, Analytical and Critical Catalogue of the Manuscripts Bequeathed . . . by Elias Ashmole.* Oxford, 1845.

Boorde, Andrew. *The Breviary of Helthe.* London, 1547.

Burke, Peter. "Representations of the Self from Petrarch to Descartes." In *Rewriting the Self: Histories from the Renaissance to the Present.* Ed. Roy Porter, 17–28. London: Routledge, 1997.

Burton, Robert. *The Anatomy of Melancholy.* Ed. Holbrook Jackson. 3 vols. New York: Dutton, 1932.

———. *Philosophaster.* Ed. and trans. Connie McQuillen. Binghamton, N.Y.: Medieval & Renaissance Texts & Studies, 1993.

Calder, I. R. F. "John Dee Studied as an English Neoplatonist." Ph.D. diss., University of London, 1952.

Carlson, David. "The Writings and Manuscript Collections of the Elizabethan Alchemist, Antiquary, and Herald, Francis Thynne." *Huntington Library Quarterly* 52 (1989): 203–72.

Cerasano, C. P. "Philip Henslowe, Simon Forman, and the Theatrical Community of the 1590s." *Shakespeare Quarterly* 44 (1993): 145–58.

Clark, George. *A History of the Royal College of Physicians of London.* Vol. 1. Oxford: Clarendon Press, 1964.

Clark, Stuart. "The Gendering of Witchcraft in French Demonology: Misogyny or Polarity." *French History* 5 (1991): 426–37.

———. *Thinking with Demons: The Idea of Witchcraft in Early Modern Europe.* Oxford: Clarendon Press, 1997.

Cook, Harold J. *The Decline of the Old Medical Regime in Stuart London.* Ithaca: Cornell University Press, 1986.

———. "Good Advice and Little Medicine: The Professional Authority of Early Modern English Physicians." *Journal of British Studies* 33 (1994): 1–31.

———. "Institutional Structures and Personal Belief in the London College of Physicians." In *Religio Medici: Medicine and Religion in Seventeenth-Century England.* Ed. Ole Peter Grell and Andrew Cunningham, 91–114. Aldershot: Scolar Press, 1996.

Cook, Judith. *Blood on the Borders.* London: Headline, 1999.

———. *Death of a Lady's Maid.* London: Headline, 1997.

———. *Murder at the Rose.* London: Headline, 1998.

Cressy, David. "A Drudgery of Schoolmasters: The Teaching Profession in Elizabethan and Stuart England." In *The Professions in Early Modern England.* Ed. Wilfred Prest, 129–53. London: Croom Helm, 1987.

Debus, Allen G. *The English Paracelsians.* New York: Franklin Watts, 1965.

Dee, John. *The Private Diary of Dr. John Dee.* Ed. James Orchard Halliwell. 1842. Reprint, New York: Johnson Reprint Corporation, 1968.

———. *A True and Faithful Relation of What Passed for Many Yeers between Dr. John Dee and Some Spirits.* Ed. Meric Casaubon. London, 1659.

Delany, Paul. *British Autobiography in the Seventeenth Century.* London: Routledge & Kegan Paul, 1969.

Donne, John. *The Anniversaries.* Ed. Frank Manley. Baltimore: Johns Hopkins University Press, 1963.

Eccles, Audrey. *Obstetrics and Gynaecology in Tudor and Stuart England.* Kent, Ohio: Kent State University Press, 1982.

Edmond, Mary. "Simon Forman's Vade-Mecum." *The Book Collector* 26 (1977): 44–60.

Elton, G. R. "Reform and the 'Commonwealth-Men' of Edward VI's Reign." In *The English Commonwealth, 1547–1640: Essays in Politics and Society.* Ed. Peter Clark, Alan G. R. Smith, and Nicholas Tyacke, 23–38. New York: Barnes & Noble, 1979.

Ficino, Marsilio. *Three Books on Life.* Ed. and trans. Carol V. Kaske and John Clark. Binghamton, N.Y.: Medieval & Renaissance Texts & Studies S7, 1989.

Forman, Simon. *The Autobiography and Personal Diary of Dr. Simon Forman*. Ed. James Orchard Halliwell. London, 1849.

———. *The Groundes of Longitude* . . . . London, 1591. Reprinted in *The English Experience: Books Printed in England before 1640*. Amsterdam: Theatrum Orbis Terrarum, 1979.

Geoffrey of Monmouth. *Histories of the Kings of Britain*. London: Dent, 1904.

Goodall, Charles. *The Royal College of Physicians of London*. . . . *And an Historical Account of the College's Proceedings against Empiricks and Unlicensed Practisers*. London, 1684.

Greenblatt, Stephen J. *Renaissance Self-Fashioning: From More to Shakespeare*. Chicago: University of Chicago Press, 1980.

Greene, Robert. *Friar Bacon and Friar Bungay*. Ed. Daniel Seltzer. Lincoln: University of Nebraska Press, 1963.

Harkness, Deborah E. "Managing an Experimental Household: The Dees of Mortlake and the Practice of Natural Philosophy." *Isis* 88 (1997): 247–62.

Hawthorne, Nathaniel. *The Scarlet Letter*. In *Novels*. New York: Library of America, 1983.

Henry, John. "Doctors and Healers: Popular Culture and the Medical Profession." In *Science, Culture and Popular Belief in Renaissance Europe*. Ed. Stephen Pumfrey, Paolo L. Rossi, and Maurice Slawinski, 191–221. Manchester: Manchester University Press, 1991.

Henslowe, Philip. *Henslowe's Diary*. Ed. R. A. Foakes and R. T. Rickert. Cambridge: Cambridge University Press, 1961.

Herring, Frances. *Rules for Pestilentiall Contagion*. London, 1625. Reprinted in *The English Experience: Books Printed in England before 1640*. Amsterdam: Theatrum Orbis Terrarum, 1979.

Hoeniger, F. David. *Medicine and Shakespeare in the English Renaissance*. Newark, Del.: University of Delaware Press, 1992.

Holmes, Clive. "Women: Witnesses and Witches." *Past and Present* 140 (1993): 45–78.

Hood, Thomas. *The Use of Both the Globes, Celestiall and Terrestrial*. London, 1592.

———. *The Use of Two Mathematicall Instrumentes, the Crosse Staffe . . . and the Jacob's Staffe*. London, 1590.

Howell, Thomas Bayly, comp. *Cobbett's Complete Collection of State Trials and Proceedings for High Treason and Other Crimes and Misdemeanors from the Earliest Period to the Present Time*. 34 vols. London: R. Bagshaw, 1809–26.

Johnston, Stephen. "Mathematical Practitioners and Instruments in Elizabethan England." *Annals of Science* 48 (1991): 319–44.

Jones, Peter Murray. "Reading Medicine in Tudor Cambridge." In *The History of Medical Education in Britain*. Ed. Vivian Nutton and Roy Porter, 153–83. Amsterdam: Rodopi Press, 1995.

Jones, Whitney R. D. *The Tudor Commonwealth 1529–1559*. London: Athlone Press, 1970.

Jonson, Ben. *Ben Jonson*. 11 vols. Ed. C. H. Herford and Percy and Evelyn Simpson. Oxford: Clarendon Press, 1925–52.

Joseph, Harriet. *Shakespeare's Son-in-Law: John Hall, Man and Physician*. Hamden, Conn.: Archon, 1964.

Josten, C. H. *Elias Ashmole (1617–1692)*. 5 vols. Oxford: Clarendon Press, 1966.

Kassel[l], Lauren. "How to Read Simon Forman's Casebooks: Medicine, Astrology, and Gender in Elizabethan London." *Social History of Medicine* 12 (1999): 3–18.

Kiessling, Nicolas K. *The Library of Robert Burton.* Oxford: Oxford Bibliographical Society, 1988.

Lane, Joan. *John Hall and His Patients: The Medical Practice of Shakespeare's Son-in-Law.* Stratford-upon-Avon: Shakespeare Birthplace Trust, 1996.

Laqueur, Thomas. *Making Sex: Body and Gender from the Greeks to Freud.* Cambridge: Harvard University Press, 1990.

Larner, Christina. *Witchcraft and Religion: The Politics of Popular Belief.* Oxford: Basil Blackwell, 1985.

LeComte, Edward. *The Notorious Lady Essex.* London: Robert Hale, 1969.

LeFanu, W. R. "A North-Riding Doctor in 1609." *Medical History* 5 (1961): 178–88.

LePan, Don. *The Birth of Expectation.* Vol. 1 of *The Cognitive Revolution in Western Culture.* London: Macmillan Press, 1989—.

Lilly, William. *Mr. William Lilly's History of His Life and Times from the Year 1602 to 1681.* London, 1715.

Lindley, David. *The Trials of Frances Howard: Fact and Fiction at the Court of King James.* London: Routledge, 1993.

Love, Harold. *Scribal Publication in Seventeenth-Century England.* Oxford: Clarendon Press, 1993.

MacCaffrey, Wallace T. *Elizabeth I: War and Politics, 1588–1603.* Princeton: Princeton University Press, 1992.

MacDonald, Michael. "The Career of Astrological Medicine in England." In *Religio Medici: Medicine and Religion in Seventeenth-Century England.* Ed. Ole Peter Grell and Andrew Cunningham, 62–90. Aldershot: Scolar Press, 1996.

———. *Mystical Bedlam: Madness, Anxiety, and Healing in Seventeenth-Century England.* Cambridge Monographs on the History of Medicine. Cambridge: Cambridge University Press, 1981.

Marcus, Leah S. *Puzzling Shakespeare: Local Reading and Its Discontents.* Berkeley: University of California Press, 1988.

Marotti, Arthur F. *John Donne, Coterie Poet.* Madison: University of Wisconsin Press, 1986.

McElwee, William. *The Murder of Sir Thomas Overbury.* London: Faber and Faber, 1952.

Merlin or the Early History of King Arthur. Ed. Henry B. Wheatley. 1899. Reprint, 2 vols. New York: Greenwood Press, 1969.

Montrose, Louis Adrian. "'Shaping Fantasies': Figurations of Gender and Power in Elizabethan Culture." *Representations* 2 (1983): 61–94.

[Moysey, Abel]. *Forman: A Tale.* 3 vols. London: Ogle, Duncan, and Co., 1819.

Munday, Antony. *John a Kent and John a Cumber.* Malone Society Reprints. Oxford: Oxford University Press, 1923.

Mustain, James K. "A Rural Medical Practitioner in Fifteenth-Century England." *Bulletin of the History of Medicine* 46 (1972): 469–76.

Niccols, Richard. "Sir Thomas Overbury's Vision." In Niccols, Richard. *Sir Thomas Overbury's Vision (1616) and Other English Sources of Nathaniel Hawthorne's "The Scarlet Letter."* Ed. Alfred S. Reid. Gainesville, Fla.: Scholars Facsimiles and Reprints, 1957.

Nichols, John. *The Progresses and Public Processions of Queen Elizabeth.* Vol. 1. London, 1832.

Nungezer, Edwin. *Dictionary of Actors and of Other Persons Associated with the Public Representation of Plays in England before 1642.* Cornell Studies in English, vol. 13.

New Haven: Yale University Press, 1929.

Osborn, James M. *TheBeginnings of Autobiography in England: A Paper Delivered at the Fifth Clark Library Seminar, 8 August 1959*. Los Angeles: William Andrews Clark Library, University of California, 1959.

Osborne, Francis. "Osborne's Traditional Memoirs." In *Secret History of the Court of James the First*. 2 vols. Edinburgh: James Ballantyne, 1811, 1:123–297.

Pelling, Margaret. "Compromised by Gender: The Role of the Male Medical Practitioner in Early Modern England." In Scott, Sir Walter. *The Task of Healing: Medicine, Religion and Gender in England and the Netherlands 1450–1800*. Ed. Hilary Marland and Margaret Pelling. Rotterdam: Erasmus Publishing, 1996, 101–133.

———. "Knowledge Common and Acquired: The Education of Unlicensed Medical Practitioners in Early Modern London." In *The History of Medical Education in Britain*. Ed. Vivian Nutton and Roy Porter, 250–79. Amsterdam: Rodopi Press, 1995.

Pelling, Margaret, and Charles Webster. "Medical Practitioners." In *Health, Medicine, and Mortality in the Sixteenth Century*. Ed. Charles Webster, 165–235. Cambridge: Cambridge University Press, 1979.

Perry, Curtis. *The Making of Jacobean Culture: James I and the Renegotiation of Elizabethan Literary Practice*. Cambridge: Cambridge University Press, 1997.

Phayer, Thomas. *The Regiment of Life Wherunto Is Added a Treatyse of the Pestilence with the Booke of Children*. London, 1543.

Pollock, Linda. *With Faith and Physick: The Life of a Tudor Gentlewoman, Lady Grace Mildmay, 1552–1620*. New York: St. Martin's, 1995.

Rappaport, Steve. *Worlds within Worlds: Structures of Life in Sixteenth-Century London*. Cambridge Studies in Population, Economy, and Society in Past Time, 7. Cambridge: Cambridge University Press, 1989.

Rowse, A. L. *Simon Forman: Sex and Society in Shakespeare's Age*. London: Weidenfeld and Nicolson, 1974.

Rowland, Beryl, ed. and trans. *Medieval Woman's Guide to Health: The First English Gynecological Handbook*. Kent, Ohio: Kent State University Press, 1981.

Ruderman, David B. *Kabbalah, Magic, and Science: The Cultural Universe of a Sixteenth-Century Jewish Physician*. Cambridge: Harvard University Press, 1988.

Sanderson, William. "Aulicus Coquinariae." In Scott, Sir Walter. *Secret History of the Court of James the First*. 2 vols. Edinburgh: James Ballantyne, 1811, 2:91–298.

Sangwine, Eric. "The Private Libraries of Tudor Doctors." *Journal of the History of Medicine and Allied Sciences* 33 (1978): 167–84.

Sawyer, Ronald C. "Patients, Healers, and Diseases in the Southeast Midlands, 1597–1634." Ph.D. diss., University of Wisconsin, 1986.

———. " 'Strangely Handled in all her lyms': Witchcraft and Healing in Jacobean England." *Journal of Social History* 22 (1989): 461–85.

Schaffer, Simon. "Self-Evidence." *Critical Inquiry* 18 (1992): 327–62.

Scot, Reginald. *The Discoverie of Witchcraft*. London, 1584.

Sharpe, James. *Instruments of Darkness: Witchcraft in Early Modern England*. Philadelphia: University of Pennsylvania Press, 1997.

Sherman, William. *John Dee: The Politics of Reading and Writing in the English Renaissance*. Amherst: University of Massachusetts Press, 1995.

Sidney, Philip. "A Defense of Poetry." In *Miscellaneous Prose of Sir Philip Sidney*. Ed. Katherine Duncan-Jones and Jan van Dorsten. Oxford: Clarendon Press, 1973.

Siraisi, Nancy G. "Girolamo Cardano and the Art of Medical Narrative." *Journal of the History of Ideas* 52 (1991), 581–602.

———. *Medieval and Early Renaissance Medicine: An Introduction to Knowledge and Practice.* Chicago: University of Chicago Press, 1990.

———. *Taddeo Alderotti and His Pupils: Two Generations of Italian Medical Learning.* Princeton: Princeton University Press, 1981.

Smith, John. *A Map of Virginia with a Description of the Country.* 1612. Amsterdam: Theatrum Orbis Terrarum, 1973.

Smith, Steven R. "Communication: The London Apprentices as Seventeenth-Century Adolescents." *Past and Present* 61 (1973): 141–61.

Speak, Gill. "An Odd Kind of Melancholy: Reflections on the Glass Delusion in Europe (1440–1680)." *History of Psychiatry* 1 (1990): 191–206.

Stallybrass, Peter. "Patriarchal Territories: The Body Enclosed." In *Rewriting the Renaissance: The Discourses of Sexual Difference in Early Modern Europe.* Ed. Margaret Ferguson, Maureen Quilligan, and Nancy Vickers, 123–42. Chicago: University of Chicago Press, 1986.

Stephens, Walter. *Giants in Those Days.* Lincoln: University of Nebraska Press, 1989.

Stone, Lawrence. *The Crisis of the Aristocracy, 1558–1641.* Oxford: Clarendon Press, 1965.

Sparks, H. F. D., ed. *The Apocryphal Old Testament.* Oxford: Clarendon Press, 1984.

Stow, John. *A Survey of London Written in the Year 1598.* London: Chatto & Windus, 1876.

Strachey, William. *The Historie of Travell into Virginia Britania 1612.* Ed. Louis B. Wright and Virginia Freund. The Hakluyt Society, n.s. 103. London, 1953.

———. "A True Reportory of the Wreck and Redemption of Sir Thomas Gates, Knight." In *A Voyage to Virginia in 1609.* Ed. Louis B. Wright. Charlottesville: University Press of Virginia, 1964.

Strype, John. *The Life and Acts of John Whitgift.* 2 vols. Oxford: Clarendon Press, 1822.

Talbert, Ernest William. "The Notebook of a Fifteenth-Century Practicing Physician." *Tennessee Studies in English Literature* 21 (1942): 5–20.

Taylor, E. G. R. *The Mathematical Practitioners of Tudor and Stuart England.* Cambridge: University Press, 1954.

Thirsk, Joan. *Economic Policy and Projects: The Development of a Consumer Society in Early Modern England.* Oxford: Clarendon Press, 1978.

Thomas, Keith. *Religion and the Decline of Magic: Studies in Popular Beliefs in Sixteenth- and Seventeenth-Century England.* London: Weidenfeld and Nicolson, 1971.

Thorndike, Lynn. *A History of Magic and Experimental Science.* 8 vols. New York: Macmillan Co., 1923–58.

Traister, Barbara. "New Evidence about Burton's Melancholy?" *Renaissance Quarterly* 29 (1976): 66–70.

———. " 'Matrix and the Pain Thereof': A Sixteenth-Century Gynaecological Essay." *Medical History* 35 (1991): 436–451.

Webster, Charles. "Alchemical and Paracelsian Medicine." In *Health, Medicine, and Mortality in the Sixteenth Century.* Ed. Charles Webster, 301–34. Cambridge: Cambridge University Press, 1979.

Weintraub, Karl J. "Autobiography and Historical Consciousness." *Critical Inquiry* 1 (1975): 821–48.

Weldon, Anthony. "The Court and Character of King James." In *Secret History of the Court of James the First.* 2 vols. Edinburgh: James Ballantyne, 1811, 1: 299–482 and 2: 1–12.

White, Beatrice. *Cast of Ravens*. London: John Murray, 1965.

Whythorne, Thomas. *The Autobiography of Thomas Whythorne*. Ed. James M. Osborne. London: Oxford University Press, 1962.

Willis, Deborah. *Malevolent Nurture: Witch-Hunting and Maternal Power in Early Modern England*. Ithaca: Cornell University Press, 1995.

Wilson, Arthur. "Five Years of King James." In Niccols, Richard. *Sir Thomas Overbury's Vision (1616) and Other English Sources of Nathaniel Hawthorne's "The Scarlet Letter."* Ed. Alfred S. Reid. Gainseville, Fla.: Scholars Facsimiles and Reprints, 1957.

Woudhuysen, H. R. *Sir Philip Sidney and the Circulation of Manuscripts, 1558–1640*. Oxford: Clarendon Press, 1996.

Wright, Peter W. G. "A Study in the Legitimisation of Knowledge: The 'Success' of Medicine and the 'Failure' of Astrology." In *On the Margins of Science: The Social Construction of Rejected Knowledge*. Ed. Roy Wallis. Sociological Review Monograph 27, 85–101. Keele: University of Keele, 1979.

Yates, Frances A. *The Art of Memory*. London: Routledge & Kegan Paul, 1966.

———. *Giordano Bruno and the Hermetic Tradition*. London: Routledge & Kegan Paul, 1964.

———. *Theatre of the World*. Chicago: University of Chicago Press, 1969.

✽ INDEX ✽